**Projections 15**
in association with
The European Film Academy

in memory of Ingmar Bergman (1918–2007),
founding president of the European Film Academy
(Picture: EFA/Holger-Andre.de)

# Projections 15
## European Cinema

*Edited by* PETER COWIE *and* PASCAL EDELMANN

*From the great names of auteur cinema
to independent producers, multi-language actors
and the new avant-garde*

Projections *in association with* The European Film Academy

*faber and faber*

First published in 2007
by Faber and Faber Limited
3 Queen Square London WC1N 3AU

Photoset by RefineCatch Limited, Bungay, Suffolk
Printed in England by TJ International, Padstow, Cornwall

The right of European Film Academy e.V. to be identified as author of this work has been asserted in accordance with Section 77 of the Copyright, Designs and Patents Act 1988

The views and opinions of individuals expressed herein do not necessarily state or reflect those of the European Film Academy e.V.

*This book is sold subject to the condition that it shall not, by way of trade or otherwise, be lent, resold, hired out or otherwise circulated without the publisher's prior consent in any form of binding or cover other than that in which it is published and without a similar condition including this condition being imposed on the subsequent purchaser*

A CIP record for this book
is available from the British Library

ISBN 978-0-571-23529-2

10 9 8 7 6 5 4 3 2 1

# Contents

# Acknowledgements

Thanks to all those who contributed to the realisation of this book. We would also like to thank the following people who have helped us and whose names do not feature elsewhere in the book:

Pierre-Yves Bazin
Alla Beliak
Dagmar Boguslawski
Alessandra Bracaglia
Beniamino Brogi
Guillaume Cailleau
Ann Cattrall
Françoise Cowie
Jaume Cuspinera
Virginie Devesa
Walter Donohue
Lotta Edoff
Sohela Emami
Attila Galambos

Aurélie Garault
Sofia Georgikakou
Mihai Gligor
Gerlinde Gruber
Amélia Guyader
Pilar de Heras
Danielle Heynickx
Søren Høy
Amy Jackson
Agnes Johansen
Galina Kalinina
Manuela Kay
Pati Keilwerth
Zsuzsanna Kohegyi

Nicolai Korsgaard
Andreja Kralj
Laurencina Lam
Silke Lehmann
Purni Morell
Jacob Neiiendam
Marie Nöregard
Armelle Oberlin
Geert-Jan Orie
Karin Padgham
Csaba Zoltán Papp
Bárbara Peiró
Vítor Manuel Pinheiro
Ainara Porrón
Gaëlle Puccio
Dani Rosenberg
Manuela Rossing
Christine Sabrou
Caroline Schreiber
Irena Strzalkowska
Robin Spätling
Bettina Westhausen
Gabe Wortman

Eva Yates
Nadja Zvirbulis
Sabria

and the EFA Board :

Brenda Blethyn
Adriana Chiesa di Palma
Pierre-Henri Deleau
Mike Downey
Ulrich Felsberg
Per Holst
Stephan Hutter
Cedomir Kolar
Stefan Laudyn
Yves Marmion
Nikita Mikhalkov
Antonio Perez Perez
Nik Powell
Domenico Procacci
Volker Schlöndorff
Assumpta Serna
István Szabó
Els Vandevorst

# A Note on the Editors

**Peter Cowie** (born in 1939) has been writing about European film-makers since the early 1960s, with books on Ingmar Bergman and on the national cinemas of Finland, Iceland, Norway, Sweden, and the Netherlands to his credit. Founding Editor of the annual 'International Film Guide' (1963–2002), he has served on the board of the European Film College, and is a special consultant to the Berlinale. Cowie was for many years International Publishing Director of Variety Inc.

**Pascal Edelmann** (born in 1970) grew up in different international meditation and yoga communities in Switzerland, Austria, France and Germany. He worked as PR representative and tour co-ordinator for an international education programme in the Netherlands, Switzerland, Germany, Austria and Hungary and studied communications, English and Jewish studies at the Freie Universität Berlin. During his studies he worked as tour guide, translator and production manager for theatre, and eventually settled as a freelance journalist and translator. He acted as press officer for the first Berlinale Talent Campus and started working as press officer for the European Film Academy in 2003.

## Foreword

by Derek Malcolm

Paul Schrader, the American writer and director, who has had a good many run-ins with Hollywood, once ticked me off for inveighing against Tinseltown and its attempt to smother the European cinema. He said that so many European directors, writers, actors and technicians had worked in Hollywood over the years that you could easily claim that Europe was alive and well, and living in Los Angeles.

There's some truth in that remark. Even those film-makers who never made it to Hollywood often wish they had. Fassbinder always wanted to make an American film, and I'm pretty sure that Almodóvar would accept a reasonable offer. And I'll always remember having lunch with a gruff Luis Buñuel towards the end of his career and asking him if he had any regrets. 'Yes,' he said, 'I never made a film in Hollywood.'

Very few of Europe's film-makers regard themselves as somehow apart from the mainstream and locked up for ever in their own small countries. They would like to make internationally regarded movies, seen by the world and not just their home audiences. And sometimes, without going to Hollywood, they succeed.

The effect on many of them when they do is profound. And not always beneficial. We often get Euro-puddings, or international co-productions, which seem to belong nowhere and get nowhere at the box-office. Aping the Americans from well outside Hollywood is not something Europeans are good at, though there are some exceptions. We forget that Hollywood's strength, apart from its financial clout, star system and ability to entertain ordinary film-goers, lies in the fascination for the most powerful country in the world that seems to hypnotise European audiences.

Europe cannot possibly defeat this by attempting to make carbon copies of American films. We have a harder task. And that is to keep making the kind of films Hollywood would either never finance or would be incapable of making. That way is unlikely to attract mass audiences.

But it is likely, if the films are made well enough, to attract large local audiences and all those in other countries, across Europe and the world, who want to see something other than the fare handed to them week after week by the major Hollywood companies.

This is not to say that they don't want to see Hollywood films. But it is becoming clear that, almost everywhere, there is a substantial minority of film-goers open to European films of quality because they feel they offer something different.

A case in point, as far as my own country is concerned, was the considerable success of Michael Haneke's *Caché* (*Hidden*), a difficult film, much praised by the critics, that drew to the cinema a large number of those who were curious about it. And Stephen Frears's *The Queen*, whose distributors envisaged a short cinema run in the UK prior to a television showing, suddenly became an international success on the back of its reviews.

Yet for every success there are a dozen failures. Even the excellent *L'Enfant*, awarded the Golden Palm at Cannes, gathered much less than its due across Europe and the world. And it is rare that a European film can make its mark outside its own country even when bought and enthusiastically sold by its distributors.

Depressing as this often is, we should, however, remember that Hollywood has plenty of failures too and that far more American films do badly at the box office as do well. Making films is an expensive and tricky business, wherever you produce them, and you need a lot of luck to manufacture a success.

The only way to do it is to keep the faith, to make films that you think are relevant and to make them as well as possible within the constraints of your budget. It can be done – Mike Leigh and Ken Loach in Britain have done it. But it will never be, and never was, easy. You only have to look at the list of what are now considered great films but were financial failures to understand that.

When you look at the past and measure it against the present in Europe, there is a sense that the golden age for European films has passed. Where are the Bergmans, Fellinis, Fassbinders, Truffauts and Tarkovskys of today? And even if they existed, would they really be financed and distributed so eagerly today? Sandip Ray, the film-making son of the great Satyajit Ray, once told me that if his father was starting out now, he would have to make his films for television and DVD. It doesn't get easier to foster the outstanding talents. It often gets more difficult.

Yet European film obstinately survives, and there are clear signs that audiences from the countries in which they are made are increasing rather than fading away. That survival, perhaps surprising during times when everything has to be like everything else to be noticed, and when you can go to any European capital and see substantially the same American films, has to be built upon slowly but surely.

One of the ways to do so is to understand that the European cinema cannot exist by simply appealing to the seventeen to twenty-five age group that Hollywood finds so essential. There is an older audience out there which used to go regularly to the cinema but now seldom does. Catch even a small percentage of those people and the outlook would be much changed.

In my own country, an exhibitor once told me that if those over thirty went to the cinema once a month rather than three or four times a year, the outlook for quality films would be totally different.

At the moment, European films suffer from the fact that, because of the necessity of subtitles, they are almost invariably thought of as 'art films', even when they are patently not geared in that direction.

If that is the case, we have to make sure that there are enough smaller screens in Europe to accommodate them successfully. In Britain, we have found that audiences attracted to quality films from Europe do not want to see them in multiplexes where audiences frequently eat, drink and talk during screenings. They tend to wait until their local art-house shows the film they want to see, if it ever does.

I often feel that all the European subsidies put into the production of film might be better spent in helping the smaller cinemas to flourish.

The answer as to whether the European cinema will survive as an entity (if it really is an entity at all) is to encourage audiences of a wider age group to visit cinemas that have a coherent programme of quality films and to make sure that budgets are low enough to sustain minority interest.

Sometimes, of course, a European film will break through all the barriers put in front of it. There will always be exceptions to the rule. And it is to be hoped that its lucky directors do not immediately fly off to Hollywood on the promise of bigger salaries and a chance to reach much wider audiences.

Some of them will, and good luck to them. But it is really in the hands of those brave souls that remain to sustain European cinema. It has something to say, and does so in what is often a unique way. It will never die, even if its regular visits to hospital might sometimes suggest its time is almost up.

**Derek Malcolm** (born in 1932) is a British film critic and historian who has worked as chief film critic of the *Guardian* for 35 years and is now chief film critic for the London Evening Standard. He was president of the international federation of film critics, FIPRESCI, for which he now serves as honorary president.

## Introduction
## A Family Affair: Uniting the Talents of Europe
## by Peter Cowie

Just as jazz enjoyed its heyday during the 1920s, so European cinema reached what many would term its apogee in the period 1958–1968. A revolution occurred that dismissed the hidebound, politically moribund cinema of the old guard in France, Germany, Britain, Sweden, Spain, and Eastern Europe. Italian neo-realism had shown the way towards a method of film-making that was ideologically committed and marked by a desire to shoot on location.

The work of such giants as Ingmar Bergman, Federico Fellini, Michelangelo Antonioni, Andrzej Wajda, François Truffaut, and Jean-Luc Godard endowed the brand 'European Cinema' throughout the world as something at once entertaining and artistically challenging. Art-houses in Europe and the United States flourished on this diet of films from the new breed of *auteurs*. The 'next wave' strengthened the image of European cinema as financially viable in its own right, with directors like Bernardo Bertolucci, Rainer Werner Fassbinder, Wim Wenders, Volker Schlöndorff, István Szabó, and Krzysztof Zanussi pursuing a distinctive vision, against the grain of Hollywood movie-making.

Krzysztof Kieślowski receives the award
for Best Film for *A Short Film About
Killing* at the inaugural European Film
Awards in 1988
(Picture: EFA/Holger-Andre.de)

Yet within a comparatively short time, 'European cinema' would lose its gloss, and be regarded in ambivalent terms by critics and distributors alike. So, in 1988, the European Film Academy was launched, in the hope that bringing together talent from across the continent would reinvigorate the cinema both culturally and commercially.

Many of the greatest names traditionally attached to the term 'European cinema' have passed away since the Academy was established: Federico Fellini, Krzysztof Kieślowski, Louis Malle, Maurice Pialat, Gillo Pontecorvo, Karel Reisz, Claude Sautet and, most recently, Ingmar Bergman and Michelangelo Antonioni. Others have slipped away, mourned but somehow forgotten all too quickly: Bill Douglas, for instance, André Delvaux, or Derek Jarman. Ingmar Bergman, one of the original founding members of the EFA and its first president, and probably the greatest film-maker produced by Europe, finally withdrew from the fray with *Saraband* in 2003.

Nikita Mikhalkov presents Curt Bois with a bag full of caviar at the European Film Awards 1988 (Picture: EFA/Holger-Andre.de)

The European Film Awards were presented for the first time in 1988, at a time when Mikhail Gorbachev had initiated the perestroika (economic restructuring) programme in the Soviet Union, and the collapse of the Berlin Wall would occur the following year, none of which could of course have been foreseen at the time.

So the 1988 ceremony was still marked by the feelings of a family gathering whose members were living so close and yet so far from each other. The film-makers coming from East and West embraced each other with love, with curiosity and with what Wim Wenders later described as 'cinematic brotherhood'. During the ceremony, broadcast live by Eurovision (West) and Intervision (East), some unforgettable moments occurred. Soviet director Sergei Paradjanov suddenly jumped on stage to present Fellini's wife and actress Giulietta Masina with an amulet and Nikita Mikhalkov surprised German actor Curt Bois during his acceptance speech with a bag full of Russian caviar.

Only a few months later a prestigious group of film-makers including Bernardo Bertolucci, Claude Chabrol, Stephen Frears,

Krzysztof Kieślowski, Jiří Menzel, István Szabó and Wim Wenders came together again in Berlin to found the European Cinema Society which was later renamed the European Film Academy. While dining in a Berlin restaurant after the founding meeting they wrote a letter of solidarity to the then-interned Václav Havel which they all signed and which was sent the following day to Havel's prison in Prague.

Marcello Mastroianni, recipient of the Lifetime Achievement Award, and Giulietta Masina at the European Film Awards 1988 (Picture: EFA/Holger-Andre.de)

By the early 1990s, younger idols had come to replace the old masters like Bergman, Fellini, and Fassbinder. Now the names on everyone's lips were Pedro Almodóvar, Emir Kusturica, Krzysztof Kieślowski, Mike Leigh, Chen Kaige (Chinese), Peter Greenaway, Wong Kar-wai (Hong Kong), Zhang Yimou (Chinese), and Aki Kaurismäki. Comets flashed across the European skies – Léos Carax, Kenneth Branagh, Terence Davies, Peter Cattaneo, Gaspar Noé – but not all fulfilled their immense promise, or recovered the first fine careless rapture of their breakthrough films.

Cinema, to be honest, has proved much livelier in territories such as Turkey, and Iran, than it has in the traditional strongholds of Western

Pedro and Agustin Almodóvar
receive the European Film
Award for Best Young Film
1988 for *Women on the Verge
of a Nervous Breakdown*
(Picture: EFA/Holger-Andre.de)

or Eastern Europe. During the first decade of the EFA's existence, the awareness of Asian cinema increased to dramatic effect. Japan no longer ruled the roost. Instead, Hong Kong, Taiwan, South Korea, and eventually mainland China began to assert themselves as sources of some of the most inventive and technically immaculate films of the time.

Although leading festivals have tended to drop the habit of referring to films by their nationality, it is intriguing to discover that the top European Film Awards have been attributed to a wide range of countries. While a director like Gianni Amelio has won the Best Film prize on three occasions, no single nation has predominated. Italy, France, Germany, Spain – the 'big four' in industrial terms – have enjoyed their fair share of statuettes, but the UK has won three times, while Denmark, Greece, Poland, and Russia have each prevailed once.

There have been aberrations, of course. But at least no single winner of the European Film of the Year statuette has abandoned the continent and sought fame and fortune in Hollywood, as happened to earlier generations (Alan Parker, or Hugh Hudson, for example, or even Michelangelo Antonioni for *Zabriskie Point*). On the other hand, talented Europeans have ventured into other regions of the world, with often excellent results – Wim Wenders and *Buena Vista Social Club* (Cuba), Hans Petter Moland and *The Beautiful Country*, or Lasse Hallström and *What's Eating Gilbert Grape?* and *Chocolat*.

The EFA has shown itself prescient over the years in recognising Michael Haneke's early film, *Benny's Video* (1993, FIPRESCI Award), and in charting the progress of such auteurs as Pedro Almodóvar, Jean-Pierre Jeunet, and Lars von Trier. In 2006, Florian Henckel von Donnersmarck came from left field to seize the European Film of the Year statuette with *The Lives of Others,* as had Fatih Akin in 2004 with *Head-On.*

## What is Europe?

The Academy's concept of Europe has always been more idealistic and wide-ranging than political reality might dictate. Poland, long before joining the EU, had triumphed with Kieslowski's *A Short Film About Killing*, and Russia, still beyond the political pale, won European Film for Nikita Mikhalkov's *Urga* in 1993. Films from Iceland, Israel, Romania, and Turkey have been nominated for the European Film Awards. Israeli and Palestinian film-makers are fully acknowledged by the European Film Academy. They can become members and their films are eligible for the European Film Awards.

Eastern Europe, once the prime source of creative cinema on the continent, has suffered during the past eighteen years following the demise of the Soviet Union. The censorship of politics has, to quote Krzysztof Zanussi, been replaced by the censorship of money. Film-makers in former Communist countries now find themselves judged on box-office returns, while little resources are available to promote their work. Institutions like Film Polski, Hungarofilm, Romania Film, and DEFA no longer represent their nation's film-makers at festivals and markets. Household names like Andrzej Wajda, Krzysztof Kieślowski, Miklós Jancsó, and Jiří Menzel have not been replaced by a fresh generation of charismatic auteurs.

The integration of Poland, Hungary, the Czech Republic, and the Baltic Republics into the European Union should, on paper, improve conditions for quality film-making in those countries. At present, however, the most promising young directors are emerging from the strife-torn region of the Balkans, as witnessed by the success of Danis Tanović's *No Man's Land* (2001), or Jasmila Žbanić's *Grbavica, Land of My Dreams* (2006). Both these films, made with neither stars nor large budgets, succeeded in achieving distribution throughout Europe and further afield. *No Man's Land* won a European Film Award and the Oscar for Best Foreign Film, and *Grbavica* earned the Golden Bear at the Berlinale and was nominated for the European Film Awards.

Any truly European enterprise must face the language dilemma: is English the easiest way out? What about French or Spanish? Even Russian, which half the population of Eastern Europe learned at school and should be able to speak, isn't helpful. Every year, this is reflected in the awards ceremony. It seems that there is no easy solution. The event is criticised either for its lack of diversity and the pre-dominance of English, or for its babel of various languages. There may now be more than thirty tongues officially accepted at European Union meetings, but the authenticity of experience and the intensity of feeling in many of the best European movies transcend these linguistic barriers. Dubbing has been normal practice in the four principal markets of Germany, France, Spain, and Italy, while subtitling for 'foreign films' is preferred in Britain, Scandinavia, Benelux, and central Europe. As Ken Loach comments in an interview in this book, nothing is more frustrating than to find that your carefully constructed dialogue track has been replaced by a kind of standardised dubbing.

Successful films in Europe have often travelled better outside the continent than they have across national borders, perhaps due to long-standing rivalries, prejudices, or the issue of language already mentioned. Lasse Hallström's *My Life as a Dog* attracted huge audiences in its native Sweden and in the United States, but failed utterly in neighbouring Finland. A triumph in France may go unnoticed in Britain, and a majority of Italian films do not even reach cinemas in other European countries.

In these circumstances, the traditional hierarchy in European cinema has seen its dominance wane. France, Italy, Spain, Germany, and the UK have long constituted the engine-room of the continent's art as well as its industry. For decades, their productions were assured of 'seeding' at the major festivals. Of the big five nations, only Germany has significantly improved its reputation for film-making.

Scandinavia has seen a shift in the balance of power. Denmark, for long in the shadow of Ingmar Bergman's Sweden, has taken a dominant role, notably due to the Dogma movement, which Lars von Trier, Thomas Vinterberg and others introduced as a means of returning to the basics of film-making. Dogma films had to be shot in a traditional format, on location, without extraneous effects, visual or musical, and without even the director receiving a credit. It all smacked of what Godard and Truffaut had done forty years earlier, but in the mid–1990s it came like a shot in the arm to a Nordic cinema in danger of wasting away in self-contemplation and imitations of daily life. Danish cinema may have moved on from Dogma, but it is thriving as never before. Norway, too, has improved out of all recognition as a film-making nation. Aki Kaurismäki has succeeded Rauni Mollberg as the flag-bearer of Finnish cinema.

The Dutch have enjoyed a certain prestige in the United States, with three Academy Awards for Best Foreign Film since 1987, but have not enjoyed much reward at the European Film Awards. The uncompromising vision of the brothers Jean-Pierre and Luc Dardenne has helped Belgium to revive the tradition of André Delvaux and Henri Storck. Ireland, thanks principally to Neil Jordan, has also featured among the nominees at the European Film Awards. And the indefatigable Manoel de Oliveira, supported by João Cesar Monteiro, has taken Portuguese film-making well out of the shadow of its big Iberian neighbour.

## Preoccupations

The predominant issues in European cinema have changed since the 1960s and 1970s. 'Committed cinema' of the kind represented so forcefully by Lindsay Anderson and Francesco Rosi, has but a single true surviving champion: Ken Loach, who has won EFA prizes for *Riff-Raff* and *Land and Freedom*, as well as the Palme d'Or at Cannes for *The Wind That Shakes the Barley*. Mike Leigh has broadened his range during the past few years, and the spectre of war looms larger than it ever did even in the 1940s – contemporary conflicts such as those in Afghanistan (*The Road to Guantanamo*), Iraq (*Flandres*) and the former Yugoslavia (*No Man's Land*), and the Second World War, which continues to exert its fascination in films as disparate as *Downfall* and *Life is Beautiful*. If a spiritual dimension continues to haunt the European cinema, its greatest proponent – Krzysztof Kieślowski – is dead, and the field is left to *auteurs* like Wim Wenders, István Szabó, and the octogenarians Alain Resnais and Eric Rohmer.

During the past two decades, Hollywood has strengthened its hold over the world movie audience by producing entertainment loud and clear. Urban thrillers, historical adventures, science-fiction epics, and gross-out comedies have been presented with much-improved sound and imagery, swamping the European opposition. Against this tide, Europe has been obliged to develop its own brand of thoughtful cinema. The agit-prop of the 1960s may have been abandoned, along with much of the navel-gazing that Bergman's imitators rendered fashionable. Instead, small-scale human stories have come to the fore.

They may seem innocuous at first glance, like Peter Cattaneo's hilarious portrayal of male camaraderie in northern England, *The Full Monty* (1997), which beneath the banter seethes with indignation at the unemployment in a once-mighty steel town such as Sheffield. Or like *Good Bye Lenin!*, for example, when only after the film has ended does one realise that Wolfgang Becker and his screenwriter Bernd Lichtenberg are questioning the fundamental concept of German reunification. Or like Michael Haneke's *Caché*, which calls into question the invasive power of technology – the fact that we are all under observation and that secrets, good or bad, can no longer be hidden (a theme also running like an ominous bass line through the EFA's 2006 winner, *The Lives of Others*). Or like *The Vanishing* (*Spoorloos*, 1988), a masterpiece of the macabre directed by the Dutchman George Sluizer. The remake, directed by Sluizer himself for Fox some five years later, illustrated the crucial difference in subtlety between European cinema at its best and Hollywood's thriller genre.

Problems of immigration and assimilation colour the contemporary European cinema at every turn. In *Gegen die Wand* (*Head-On*), Fatih Akin turns his unblinking gaze on a scabrous neighbourhood in prosperous Hamburg, charting the fate of a German Turk who's fallen prey to alcohol and cocaine in the wake of his wife's death. This and many other films do more than just hint at the deracination of so many migrants, and even first-generation immigrants in moments of crisis reach out for a traditional culture that is no longer readily to hand. The same applies to the young Italian in Gianni Amelio's *Lamerica* (1994), who finds himself literally and figuratively lost in a post-Communist Albania. Bille August's forceful study of Danish pastoral life in the late nineteenth century, *Pelle the Conqueror* (1988), touches on the same issue, as Max von Sydow's Lasse and his son Pelle emigrate from Sweden and then struggle to scrape a living in neighbouring Denmark, coping with humiliation at every turn. Another, more recent Swedish production, *Zozo*, directed in 2005 by Josef Fares, tackles the issue of racial prejudice in the land of blondes and virgin forests, as a young Lebanese orphan flees Beirut to settle in the Swedish countryside with his grandparents.

More than ever before in its history, European cinema reflects the struggle of individuals to cope with conflicting cultures. Indigenous films are often less interesting today than those made by immigrants, such as Josef Fares or Reza Parsa in Sweden, Gurinder Chadha in Britain, Samir Jamal-Aldin in Switzerland, Khalid Hussain and Ulrik Imtiaz Rolfsen in Norway. The influx of other cultures has enriched the native soil of German and Scandinavian cinema, for example, just as it did the French cinema in the 1960s.

In many European countries, control of drug-trafficking has been seized by immigrant groups, at first desperate for survival and then finding in their power an intoxicating prosperity of sorts. Over the past twenty years, many excellent films have analysed this trend. The *Pusher* trilogy (1996–2005), directed by the Dane Nicolas Winding Refn, matches the slickest Hollywood thrillers in terms of pace and violence, and made stars of Mads Mikkelsen and Zlatko Buric. In Norway, Erik Poppe's *Schpaaa* (1998), Aksel Hennie's *Uno* (2004), and Ulrik Imtiaz Rolfsen's *Izzat* (2005) all confront the harsh turf-wars involving Balkan and Pakistani immigrants.

## Compassion and Tolerance

One of the greatest living Europeans, Theo Angelopoulos, won the European Film of the Year award in 1989 for *Landscape in the Mist*, which follows two children in their futile quest for a mythical father-figure, presumably living in Germany. Beneath the classical, art-house aestheticism of Angelopoulos's technique lies a kind of forlorn tenderness, and indeed tenderness is a quality that emerges from numerous European films of the 1990s and 2000s. It characterises the vision of Pedro Almodóvar, in films like *All About My Mother* (1999), with the young writer searching for his true father, or *Talk to Her* (2002), with the vulnerable, compassionate men devoting their every thought and gesture to the stricken women they adore. Compassion becomes the *leitmotiv* of Jean-Pierre Jeunet's *Le fabuleux destin d'Amélie Poulain* (2001), with Audrey Tautou as the waitress who, like some contemporary Candide, sets out across Paris to bring happiness to others. Tenderness may even lurk beneath the coarse-cut texture of Lars von Trier's *Breaking the Waves* (1996), with its bleak Scottish community and a woman trying, in her own repressed way, to remain 'faithful' to her lover.

Memories of childhood have also inspired some of the best European films in recent memory, whether it be John Boorman's quasi-autobiographical account of a young boy in London during the Blitz, *Hope and Glory* (1987), or Terence Davies's evocation of a Liverpool during the Second World War, *Distant Voices, Still Lives* (1988), which blends the tone of a daytime soap with the austere dignity of a Carl Theodore Dreyer. Most poignant of all, Louis Malle's *Au revoir les enfants*, which won the award for Best Script at the inaugural European Film Awards of 1988, and revealed (as had Malle's earlier *Lacombe Lucien*) a repugnant moment during the occupation of France.

Films about children have always been persuasive in European cinema, notably those from the Nordic region, where portions of the official production funding are earmarked for such work. In Norway, for example, Torun Lian's *Only Clouds Move the Stars* (1998) deals with a world in which truth resides in childhood, and adult life marks an incapacity to deal with tragedy. Berit Nesheim's *Frida – Straight from the Heart* (1991) reaches within the mind and emotions of a young teenager who yearns for reconciliation between her divorced parents. In Sweden, Lukas Moodysson's debut, *Fucking Åmal* (1999), dissected the humdrum provincial existence of a group of youngsters, and the stirrings of lesbian love between two teenagers. In the UK, Stephen Daldry proved with *Billy Elliot* (2000) that a young boy's story could make compelling, and witty, cinema of the most inspiring kind.

In European cinema's finest hour (1958–1968), the Second World War remained too close for comfort, too close for film-makers to see it in perspective. By the 1990s, film-makers could take greater artistic risks in dealing with the Holocaust. Roberto Benigni's *La vita è bella* (*Life is Beautiful*) won the EFA's award for European Film 1998, and established Benigni's reputation beyond his native Italy as a satirist with a romantic eye. Benigni – who also won the prize for European Actor for his role as Guido – beguiles the spectator in the first half of his film by tracing his Tuscan hero's courtship of a girl from a nearby town, and then leaping forward to the occupation of Italy by Nazi forces and Guido's despatch to the camps where, by some miraculous *legerdemain*, he convinces his young son that his grim destiny is nothing but a game.

If a sizeable minority found *Life is Beautiful* too frivolous in its treatment of the Holocaust, none could accuse Roman Polanski's *The Pianist* of anything but candour. Nominated in four categories, and winner of the EFA's cinematography statuette in 2002, *The Pianist* managed both to show the ghastly cruelties of the Warsaw ghetto, and to locate some source of hope in the fleeting relationship between the 'pianist' and a German officer in the ruins of the city. Perhaps only after the lapse of half a century could Polanski see the demon of Nazism in such a wise yet unblinking light.

## The Business Realities

The year after the European Film Awards, then called Felix, were inaugurated, so too was Eurimages, an initiative of the Council of

Europe aimed at bolstering co-productions within Europe. Since then, Eurimages has supported some 900 co-productions involving Europe and neighbouring countries.

But the funding situation became so dire that in 1990, Dieter Kosslick, then head of the European Film Development Organisation (EFDO), declared: 'If people don't sit up and take notice within the next year or so, European film will cease to exist.'

Politicians had indeed taken notice of such comments and, starting in 1991, the MEDIA Programme in Brussels set aside some €200 million to promote the development of the European audiovisual industry – stimulating production, distribution, and exports both within and beyond Europe itself. This legislation was pursued, in somewhat mutated form, in the MEDIA II, and MEDIA Plus pro-grammes, with the MEDIA 2007 legislation assigning more than €1 billion to the whole range of pre- and post-production activities in a vastly enlarged European Union. *Über*-bureaucrats like Holde Lhoest at the MEDIA programme and Nicolas Steil at Euro Aim may have been mocked in some quarters in the early 1990s, but with hindsight their achievement looks impressive.

Indeed, would European cinema have survived without the funding and nurturing of bodies such as Eurimages, or MEDIA 'quangos' like Euro Aim, EFDO, the European Script Fund, CARTOON, EAVE, Europa Cinemas, European Film Promotion, AGICOA and so on? Certainly. But one doubts if 700 films each year would be emerging from the various studios and independent production companies across the continent without such subsidy systems.

## Stars and Players

In recent years, the European Film Promotion initiative, 'Shooting Stars', has sought to dispel the myth that there are no European stars, only players. The exceptions only underline the rule. Jeanne Moreau *is* a star, as is Gérard Depardieu, and as was Marcello Mastroianni. But the concept of a star whose name above the title can 'open' a picture across the world remains unique to Hollywood. Beloved figures such as Roberto Benigni in Italy, or Daniel Brühl in Germany muster the young and the faithful without having the global appeal of a Jim

Carrey or Tom Cruise. However, the 'Shooting Stars' programme has honoured many successful actors in their early years, among them Rachel Weisz (*The Constant Gardener*), Ludivine Sagnier (*Swimming Pool*), Franka Potente and Moritz Bleibtreu (*Run Lola Run*), and certainly not least Daniel Craig, the new James Bond.

## Euro-puddings, and Courageous Producers

Co-productions existed long before the 'Euro-pudding' fervour of the 1980s and 1990s. They had enjoyed their heyday during the 1960s, when almost every Italian or Spanish film of note was made in tandem with partners in France or Germany. As far back as the silent period, there were co-productions in all but name, and Pabst's 'French' version of *Die Dreigroschenoper* in 1931 was in effect the equivalent of a modern co-production. But during the past fifteen years, co-productions have become the norm rather than the exception. Bodies such as the Filmstiftung NRW and Channel Four Films invested in scores of European films over the past two decades. Until the turn of the millennium, Canal Plus in France was a rich source of funding, not just for French productions but also for films from numerous European countries. Auteurs like István Szabó, Peter Greenaway, and Bernardo Bertolucci attracted financial support from different parts of Europe for films that nonetheless reflected their own national culture. Indeed, Greenaway's film about Rembrandt, *Nightwatching* (2007), attracted financing from Canada, France, Germany, Poland, the Netherlands, and the UK.

The eagerness to embrace English as a kind of Esperanto that would enable European films to crack the world market can be traced back to the 1960s, when pioneers like Pim de la Parra and Wim Verstappen in the Netherlands shot low-budget films in a heavily accented English. During the 1980s and 1990s the trend gathered pace, often with horrible results. With the best intentions, a director from one country would be hired to make a film in another territory, with a 'motley crew' and actors from all quarters of the continent. As Irène Jacob says in her interview in this book, 'You have to be careful that a film retains its identity.'

Producers burned their fingers badly on numerous occasions. The German Rainer Kölmel, the Yugoslavian-born Cédomir Kolar, and the French producer Humbert Balsan can be described as enterprising, courageous, and, some would say, foolhardy. Balsan specialised in supporting film-makers from Africa and the Middle East, and did so at the eventual cost of his own life (he had also served with passionate commitment the cause of the European Film Academy, as its chairman from 2003–2005). Jeremy Thomas, based in London, but a citizen of the world where his role of producer is concerned, has survived through the decades, having recognised the gifts of Bertolucci, Cronenberg, Linklater, Roeg, Wenders and many others.

The German producer Bernd Eichinger persisted with expensive, star-driven pictures that could prove disastrous (*Smilla's Sense of Snow, The House of the Spirits*), successful (*The Name of the Rose*), or victorious on almost every count (*Der bewegte Mann, Perfume: The Story of a Murderer*). *Perfume* represents an approach to cross-border European cinema that, given the right material and the right director, can work. Based on the best-selling novel by Patrick Süskind, directed by Tom Tykwer (*Run Lola Run*), and admirably acted by an international cast in English, *Perfume* earned over $100 million at the box-office.

## The Future

The advent of digital equipment has enabled film-makers to become even more peripatetic than before. Michael Winterbottom and Danis Tanović are just two examples of directors who have taken their cameras into locations where the paraphernalia of traditional equipment would attract too much attention. The post-production stage, however, still stands in the path of the digital revolution. Until cinemas have been converted to digital projection, films will still have to circulate in cumbersome cans of 35mm celluloid.

Within another two decades, will European cinema be viewed primarily on iPhones or YouTube? Paradoxically, the migration of much low-budget European cinema to the Internet may solve the perennial problem of distribution in North America. It may also ensure that a new generation of film-goers will become interested in European cinema – and appreciate its diverse qualities.

Will wall-mounted flat-screen installations, already forecast in 1965 by François Truffaut in *Fahrenheit 451*, be as common as saunas are in Finnish homes? If so, film-makers will have to adjust the very essence of their endeavours, acknowledging an audience of one or a handful of people, while movie theatres may be reserved for spectacular Hollywood presentations, packed with special effects in 3-D. The shared experience may be replaced by individual involvement. The long shot and the detailed composition within the frame may once again – as it was when television first held sway – fall into disuse.

On the other hand, none of this may happen. A prominent British publisher proclaimed in the early 1990s that the traditional book would be dead within ten years. As yet, that particular patient remains in reasonably good health. The hope for the future of European cinema is that film-makers will reject the easy formula, and continue to espouse the issues of the day, remaining always one beat ahead of their audience.

**Peter Cowie** (born in 1939) has been writing about European film-makers since the early 1960s, with books on Ingmar Bergman and on the national cinemas of Finland, Iceland, Norway, Sweden and the Netherlands to his credit. Founding editor of the annual *International Film Guide* (1963–2002), he has served on the board of the European Film College, and is a special consultant to the Berlinale. Cowie was for many years international publishing director of Variety Inc.

# 1   Ingmar's Dream

The European Film Academy

A conversation with
István Szabó

*In a then still-divided Europe and Berlin, the European Film Awards
were presented for the first time on 27 November 1988. Originally
planned by Berlin's senator for culture as a one-off project for the
conclusion of the programme of the European Capital of Culture year
in Berlin, a group of renowned European film-makers such as Ingmar
Bergman, Federico Fellini, Wim Wenders and István Szabó made the
initiative their personal matter. They took the European Film Awards
into their own hands and soon founded the European Film Academy.
On 1 December 2007, when the European Film Awards are presented
for the twentieth time, the academy will unite 1,800 film-makers from
across Europe. From the first days, and throughout all these years, the
Hungarian director István Szabó has been a committed companion of
the European Film Academy.*

**How was the idea for the European Film Academy born?**
István Szabó: Volker Hassemer, then Berlin's senator for culture, had
the idea of founding a European club for film-makers – he is the father

of the European Film Academy. I can well remember how, based on Ingmar Bergman's directions, I was to write up an appeal he wanted to send to select film-makers. We formulated this letter and with a pounding heart I waited to find out whether Ingmar would accept it. Ingmar accepted the letter as it was and I was happy as a child in kindergarten.

**That was this famous appeal to European directors?**
Yes, it was then signed by a total of fourteen film-makers – Federico Fellini was one of them, Theo Angelopoulos, Richard Attenborough, Bernardo Bertolucci, Claude Chabrol, Claude Goretta, Dušan Makavejev, Jiří Menzel, Manoel de Oliveira, Eric Rohmer, Wim Wenders. It was a great experience to meet with the history of European film and to simply shake hands, listen, discuss.

**And then the first European Film Awards were held and the night before you all sat here in Berlin in the Atlantik-Suite of the Kempinski hotel. Joining you were people like Mikis Theodorakis, Ben Kingsley and Isabelle Huppert. Bernardo Bertolucci was lying on the bed and Wim Wenders sat on the floor – it was a small, relaxed and at the same time enormously impressive summit of European film in a hotel room.**
. . . and it was then that Ingmar suggested to enlarge this group a little and to found an academy.

**And during the awards ceremony on the next day, you went on stage and announced it.**
Yes, we really wanted to do something for European film. At the time, European film wasn't just alive, it had great strength and there were so many great artists, people who thought and worked in completely different ways. And we really had a big audience, a film by Ingmar Bergman or Federico Fellini was a world success! And world success meant that people were standing in long queues to get tickets for these films.

**Nevertheless European cinema was going through a serious crisis, which was also the reason for you to say we need to do something to**

strengthen European cinema and to position it against the overriding power of Hollywood.

Yes, but it's important to emphasise that from the very beginning we never wanted to fight *against* American film. What we wanted was to offer something alternatively, alongside American film, to position ourselves in world cinema. We wanted to show the audience that European cinema is valuable and lively and that it means a great diversity, which we have to preserve.

**In your appeal you also mentioned the power of cinema and the great responsibility of film-makers, a responsibility which comes along with the use of this powerful tool.**

That was very, very important to us and we had long discussions about it: What does this responsibility mean? There were many examples of abuse. Photographed images always show a part of reality and it is easy for spectators to confuse reality and truth. Of course reality is always a part of the truth but sometimes it has nothing to do with the entire truth. And the fact is that you can lie unbelievably well using reality. This responsibility was important to us – to have an awareness as film-makers that there are certain things you simply mustn't do because the audience cannot see behind them. That's why film-makers have to know: Careful with the camera! There really are people who are willing to use the camera as a weapon, and even to kill others with the camera.

Ingmar Bergman at the founding assembly of the European Film Academy in 1989
(Picture: gerhardkassner.de)

How do you see the European Film Academy today? Was it possible
to keep this spirit of the early days? A lot has changed in the past
twenty years: Europe is no longer divided, great political and
economic changes took place, the power of the media is very different,
much stronger than before, often the rules of the market determine
what happens – not least in the film business . . .

Ingmar Bergman wanted to found an academy for artists – for directors, cinematographers, screenwriters, actors – people you can share
your problems with. It's not that other people wouldn't be able to
understand these problems but when you share these problems of an
almost philosophical nature with your colleagues, this responsibility
that we talked about is truly passed on at first-hand. Basically we
thought it would be a small club with people who are honest with
each other and who aren't there primarily to do business. This club,
and later the Academy, was to have no more than ninety-nine members, only select film-makers who were experienced and proud of their
profession. They were to come together once a year, in a small restaurant or in any other place where we'd have the time to talk about
films and in the end have an open vote. The result was to be given to a
few select journalists who would write about it and tempt the audience to see these films. That was Ingmar Bergman's dream, and had it
come true and stayed real until today, that would have been
wonderful.

Bernardo Bertolucci, Stephen
Frears, Claude Chabrol and
Hanna Schygulla at an EFA
meeting in 1989
(Picture: EFA/Kristina Eriksson)

**Is it possible that this dream was based on the idea of a better world? Experience has taught us that such a club gets very little support.**

You see, there are two possibilities. Either you organise a show, you sell a product, and then you need money. Or you accept that you won't get any money and come together privately. You get to spend a weekend with Ingmar Bergman, Theo Angelopoulos, Bernardo Bertolucci, Jiří Menzel and Claude Chabrol, and you can talk about anything: about life and about art, about old and new films, and about the nicest films we have watched together over the weekend – this year I would for example want to talk about Stephen Frears's *The Queen*. And when everybody is ready, we find out which film wins the majority. Everybody pays for his or her coffee, and for the travel. That's it! That's all! There is no big show and the prizes don't look as pretty. Maybe the certificate is just a page torn out of an exercise book, but signed by Ingmar Bergman and Manoel de Oliveira and Bernardo Bertolucci etc.

**That sounds like a small, very distinguished, but really private enterprise . . .**

Well, of course you can also run a big European Film Academy with big plans, supported by the EU and other financiers. They aren't easy to find and you have to give something in return.

These are simply two different paths – Ingmar didn't want it small, but he wanted it intense. And valuable. But we went with the times and have decided to go in a different direction. I wanted to stay and support everything I can. However, deep in my heart I still carry Ingmar's dream. I am convinced that our European films are valuable and that we need to do something for them. Films are after all the most beautiful way to learn something about others, to get to know people. And if you understand that people all over the world share similar problems, that everywhere people are born and die, and have two ears and a nose, it becomes more and more difficult to accept the concept of an enemy.

**Do you think that the new technologies influence how we tell stories today? Or even distract from an honest way of storytelling?**
It is completely irrelevant whether you write with a feather, a pencil or a ballpoint pen, on a typewriter or a computer. There are relations between the words and they tell something about people. The moving images have, however, discovered something that the other arts didn't discover – and couldn't discover: the living face that shows human emotions, emotions that come into being in front of our eyes, or that change, that show how love turns into jealousy. Only this strange art of the moving image can show this, the intimate view of a close-up. And it is completely irrelevant what technique is employed to show your face. Your smile, the way you now smile at me, how this smile comes into being and what's behind it, what I can see in your eyes – it doesn't matter whether that's recorded digitally or with an old-fashioned camera. What matters is the relation between your eyes and your mouth and this fantastic shape we call *the face*.

**These fantastic close-ups like Ingmar Bergman did of Liv Ullmann for example, do you still see them in contemporary cinema?**
You know, two weeks ago I watched Frears's film *The Queen*, where five minutes before the ending there is a conversation between Queen Elizabeth and Tony Blair in the corridor at Buckingham Palace. And Stephen shows a close-up of Helen Mirren, when she thinks about the kind of life she has had. I haven't seen something so beautiful in years! It's a long scene and you can see in her face and in her eyes how fragile and how responsible and humane the person behind this mask of duty is. It takes a long time, a minute or a minute and a half. And I really was afraid that it would be cut any moment, that I wouldn't be able to look at Helen Mirren's face any longer.

**Let's talk about actors for a bit who are such an important vehicle for a film. You once said that actors convey a certain feeling of a certain time and through this they become stars, protagonists of an era, human reflections of the zeitgeist.**
It is not by coincidence that at a particular time the European audience went mad over Gérard Philipe. After Gérard Philipe came someone

with a harder face, a boxer, a fighter, but at the same time he was as light and humorous as Gérard Philipe – Jean-Paul Belmondo. And after a while a colder face became very important for the European audience, Alain Delon. And after Alain Delon the audience projected their feelings – probably because they felt more protected through someone who regards the world with a cynical view – on to an older man who represented a certain cynicism: Michel Piccoli. The times for the older, fine and loyal man, carried by tradition and humanistic attitude like Michel Simon in *L'Atalante* by Jean Vigo for example or Jean Gabin in *La Grande illusion* by Jean Renoir, those times are over. The audience now wants someone who can protect them and they look for him in actors who embody a muscular energy and a strong cynicism.

**In your film *Meeting Venus* you lent your name to various characters: Stephen Taylor, Etienne Tailleur, Stefano Sarto, Stefan Schneider – all of which are literal translations of István Szabó. Would your films be different if their director had not been called István Szabó, but instead Stephen Taylor, Etienne Tailleur, Stefano Sarto or Stefan Schneider?**
Sure, my films are Central European films, meaning that they are influenced by everything that has happened in Central Europe during the twentieth century. But, more than anything, my films are also films from Budapest because Hungarian politics and history have so deeply influenced and directed me that to this day I have been unable to free myself of them. Even more to the point, my films have strongly been influenced by two, probably even three people – so strongly that I can hardly express it: One of them is Adolf Hitler, the second is Josef Stalin and the third János Kádár, the leader of the Hungarian Communist Party after 1956. Whatever happened to me in my life has been influenced by politics, also my family. Everything that happened to me was a fight for survival and to find a way to free myself from all that happened to the people in my country or in my city. That's why all my films deal with such problems, I can only tell stories of people who have been broken by ideologically motivated politics, who have been murdered – even if they're still physically alive. I think that it is my task to tell the stories we experienced.

**In a way, all European films are very much marked nationally or locally and tell stories out of a personal experience.**
Every script is a struggle because we know much more than we are, in the end, able to tell. That's why you have to follow your aim very carefully and strictly and forget everything that doesn't belong to it a hundred per cent. One of the greatest difficulties is to stay focused – and I almost never manage because I always want to tell more – not to chat, but to tell only and exclusively the important things. The very worst of my experiences I can share with three or four people because I was, thank God, never alone. With many, also bad, experiences, I was together with hundreds, even thousands of people. And during some of them I was even with millions of Hungarians or central Europeans because the Czechs, the Slovaks, the Serbs, the Croats, the Poles, even a part of the Austrians and the Germans have experienced something similar. We have to try to tell these stories because things are repeated. And for that we need artists who can tell these stories in a way so that people understand them.

**If you were to publish this appeal to European film-makers again today, which of the younger film-makers would you like to take on board?**
Well, the man who loves people, who tries to bring people close to other people, this man whom I can love, that's Pedro Almodóvar. I would like to invite him for dinner one day and talk with him until midnight and learn a little from him, from where these beautiful emotions stem that make him love the people so much.

**And as a final question, if you owned a cinema for one day, which films would you screen for your audience?**
*Ivan the Terrible* by Sergei Eisenstein, *Ladri di biciclette* (*Bicycle Thieves*) by Vittorio De Sica, *Wild Strawberries* by Ingmar Bergman, *Ashes and Diamonds* by Andrzej Wajda, *8½* by Federico Fellini, *Les Quatre cents coups* (*The 400 Blows*) by François Truffaut and to close the programme: *The Red and the White* by Miklós Jancsó.

Interviewed by Marion Döring in Berlin on 6 February 2007.
Translated from German by Pascal Edelmann.

**István Szabó** (born in Budapest in 1938) is and has been an internationally highly regarded director for decades. Four of his films were
nominated by the American Film Academy for the Oscar (*Confidence,
Mephisto, Colonel Redl, Hanussen*). In 1981, *Mephisto* won the Oscar
for Best Foreign Language Film. *Colonel Redl* was decorated with the
BAFTA award for Best Foreign Language Film (1986). In 1992, he
won the European Film Award as European Scriptwriter for *Dear
Emma, Sweet Böbe* and shared the same prize together with Israel
Horovitz for *Sunshine* in 1999. He made *Taking Sides* in 2002 and, in
2004, shot *Being Julia* with Jeremy Irons and Annette Bening. István
Szabó has been a founding member of the EFA and member of the
Board since the Academy's very beginning.

**Marion Döring** (born in 1953 in Hannoversch Münden) studied
French and Portuguese at the University of Mainz from 1972 to 1975.
From 1976 to 1979 she worked as editor for the daily newspapers
*Fuldaer Zeitung* and *Hessisch/Niedersächsische Allgemeine*. Moving
to Berlin, she worked as a freelance journalist between 1980 and 1985;
from 1985 to 1988 as press attaché of the '750 Years Anniversary
Berlin 1987' and 'Berlin – European Capital of Culture 1988'. She has
been connected to the history of the European Film Academy since its
very beginnings in 1988: first as PR manager of the European Film
Awards, later as project manager for the Academy's activities and publications, and since 1996 as the Academy's director. Starting in 2004,
she also acts as producer for the European Film Awards and since
2006 as managing director of EFA Productions gGmbH, the company
producing the Awards together with the European Film Academy.

## 2 Dreamland Europe

*The lights go down, the curtains open (and if you're lucky there is no sound of popcorn or crunching crisps around you) – going to the cinema is a magic experience. You witness a story, you step into fiction, for an hour or more you are no longer in the world as it is outside. When you emerge, you take something with you, a little treasure. It might be the image of a woman standing in the Trevi fountain, it might be the discovery of hearing people's thoughts in a library or the tiny wrinkles beneath the eyes in a close-up, the wrinkles that do a little jump before the face turns into a smile and starts to laugh. But whatever it is, cinema enchants us, it surprises, disturbs and fascinates people all over the world.*

*European cinema tells our stories, the stories we didn't know about our neighbours, the stories we didn't know about ourselves, and the stories that unite us, stories we share. And if the only thing that truly unites Europe is a curiosity in finding out more, that is a good thing to be united by, and one to cherish. A book about European cinema can only be incomplete, and rather than attempting to give a concise picture of what European cinema is, this chapter offers a glimpse of some of the ideas, experiences, trends, and philosophies that motivate film-makers and transform stories into films.*

# What's So European About Us?

by Wim Wenders

The other night I watched the Oscars again.
Yes. It's some kind of an addiction, I know.
Once a year, in February,
I spend hours and hours in front of the TV,
usually from midnight until dawn,
(depending on where I am,
mostly in some hotel room somewhere on the planet
far away from the one called Hollywood)
sometimes rooting for a friend, some actor or some movie,
sometimes just staring in a state of stupor and fascination
at the endless display of self-involvement and vanity,
ready to admire anybody who breaks out of that mould
to speak up modestly, honestly or bravely.
(The fact is also: all of us who make movies in whatever capacity
can't help identifying with walking that carpet
or standing up there on that stage, at least once!)
This is pretty powerful branding,
and don't tell me you can escape it.

Anyway, as I followed the last ceremony,
half dozing away, half waiting for the decisions I was interested in,
(is there justice on Earth, will Scorsese finally win his Oscar?)
walking around during the endless commercial breaks
or opening the window and looking out into the night to keep me
　　awake,
I started to pay attention to a phenomenon
that struck me that night, in spite of my fatigue.
(I was pre-conditioned, I guess,
knowing I had to write a short text about European cinema,
and I had already missed my deadline . . .)

The thing was: Every now and then in some montage
either from the history of cinema
or from the history of the Oscar ceremony itself,
brief flashes from European films popped up.
There was a short Fellini excerpt,
a sudden appearance of an Ingmar Bergman shot,
yes, here I caught a piece of Truffaut's *Nuit américaine*,
a couple of seconds from *Nuovo cinema Paradiso*,
*Tin Drum* for a brief moment,
and, hey, that was Benigni in *La vita è bella* . . .

Also, as a few European films were present among the nominations,
their clips allowed additional glimpses into present-day European
　　production.

So, first subconsciously, then paying more attention,
the question formed in the back of my mind:
What was it about these instants of European films
that instantly caught my attention each time?
What was so special about them?
Was I just 'nostalgic',
or was there something about these European images
that distinguished them from the rest of the visual bombardment?
Or to put it bluntly:

What was specific about that European imagery?
Was it just my imagination
or did these films have something in common
that set them apart from their American counterparts?

Well, I don't think my late-night thoughts
could be considered 'conclusive' in any way.
But I did come up with a few tentative answers.
They are what they are, take them or leave them.
And keep in mind that all generalisations
are contradicted by their exceptions.
(Luckily, in the field of cinema,
it is not the rules that rule . . .)
So here's what I made out of my scribbled notes and sleepy efforts
to pinpoint a very subjective perception.

Each time any of these 'European' images popped up,
I couldn't help feeling that they were more deeply 'rooted',
    somehow.
That was the little word on my notepad: 'Rooted!'
Easy to say. Rooted in what?
(And wasn't it just my own European sensitivity
that gave me that very idea?)
What were those 'roots'? (If there were any . . .)

Wim Wenders and Juliette
Binoche at the European Film
Awards 1997 in Berlin
(Picture: dpa / Volkmer
Hoffmann)

When a story is told in 'moving pictures'
it can obey all sorts of rules and patterns.
It can be story-driven.
It can be character-driven.
It can be motivated by a sense of place and local colour.
It can come out of one man's (or woman's) vision.
It can follow a formula.
It can be totally original and not owe anything
to any story told previously.
It can be outrageously fictional,
based on facts or 'real stories' (that contradiction in terms),
or even be utterly grounded in reality.
It can stem from dreams and nightmares
as well as from novels, newspaper articles
or actual experiences.
It can be funny, tragic, dramatic, poetic, epic . . .
And it can belong to any combination of these categories.
(And you might add a few more to the list.)

But whatever was the initial impetus driving that film
you can sense a trace of it in every shot, I think,
and even in a short excerpt.

Anyway, in my dazed perception that night,
in those quick peeks at European films,
I felt that there was more of the presence of 'a person'
behind each shot, however brief it was.
I seemed to recognise a more individual voice.
There definitely was a stronger bond between each image
and the soul or the place it was stemming from.

Their 'Europeanness', if you want,
was lying in a somehow more individual point of view behind them
as well as in an enhanced 'local colour', a local touch,
a dedication to a specific place.
Being wholeheartedly Italian, Swedish, French,

Spanish, Russian, German or whatever
*that* appeared to me that night
as a liberty, a luxury and a privilege
these films could only afford to take
in the context and under the protection of 'European Cinema'.
Our national cinemas would long have vanished
in the maelstrom of global entertainment.
(Annie Hall would say 'globalisised' . . .)
Maelstrom? Mainstream?
In my late-night vocabulary I mixed up the words.
The excerpts of American cinema on the other hand
impressed with their efficiency, their panache
and their in-built confidence.
The priority of 'story' and 'plot' over 'character' and 'place'
(again, the exceptions always confirm the rules)
seemed deeply encrusted into the texture of each American image.

European films seemed definitely more concerned
        with (and rooted in) '*content*'
(which is that great contemporary word
        to define what things are all about)
while a more pronounced sense of '*style*'
        and heightened production value
easily marked 'American products'.
I don't use this term condescendingly.
After all, the industrial aspect behind American cinema is no secret.
If anything, European cinema could benefit
from a bit more of an industrial purpose.
We're just so much more abashed about
our art also being an industry.

Overall, in the course of the night,
dreamily following those thoughts,
I kept thinking how much these two notions of cinema
were complementing each other
and, in fact, needed each other.

In the past, European influences
have often brought out the best in American cinema.
And European film-makers learned a lot from Hollywood in return.
Like myself:
Everything I know about the grammar and the vocabulary of cinema
I have studied in American movies.

When this year's Oscar ceremony came to a satisfying end
(Scorsese not only got 'his' award, finally,
he got a second one on top, as you all know by now)
so that I could turn off the TV with a big sigh of relief,
I decided to refuse to talk any more
about 'European' and 'American' imagery.
(I still had to finish this text here, though,
forgive me for this last inconsistency . . .)
We should be happy about the differences
and continue making the most of it!
Like our 'European Film Awards'!
For so long it seemed that they could only exist as a copy of the Oscars.
But then we made it clear (and proved it, too)
that we just could not cultivate that sense of competition
that drives the American Academy Awards.
Our European Film Academy
is driven by an astonishing sense of family and solidarity instead.

So watching the Oscars is totally okay!
It is not even a 'guilty pleasure', as somebody insinuated the other day.
It is a strange delight, period.
This year, it came with the added pleasure
of realising, deep in my heart,
how much I cherished that difference . . .

**Wim Wenders** worked as a film critic for various German publications,
and was a founding member of Filmverlag der Autoren. In 1976 he set
up his own production company, Road Movies, and in 2002 Reverse
Angle. Often hailed as one of the most important German directors on

the international scene, Wenders has received various international awards, including the Golden Lion (*The State of Things*, 1982), the Palme d'Or and BAFTA (*Paris, Texas*, 1984), as well as a European Film Award (*Wings of Desire*, 1988) and a Silver Bear (*The Million Dollar Hotel*, 2000). His latest productions include *Land of Plenty* and *Don't Come Knocking*. Wim Wenders became president of the European Film Academy in 1996.

Manoel de Oliveira (right) and Michel Piccoli on the set of *Je rentre à la maison* (Picture: Canal Plus/Cinetext Bildarchiv)

## The Land of Dreams
## by Manoel de Oliveira

Europe is the land of film and film is the land of dreams – to understand this is a *poetic* act.

To craft the planning and then the shooting of a film is not easy. But if asked, one would say that it is just as difficult, after having presented a film, to explain all that the director managed to express in those happy moments. And it is even worse when it is expressed in a strange way, as with surrealism or 'super-rationalism' – for want of a better definition that explains the rationalisation of the poetic, the mysterious where reason can only acknowledge since it's up against the unknown.

Notwithstanding, it is these characteristics, those of the realm of the unknown, that are the richest of all expressions – a mystery encompassing poetry, and poetry encompassing mystery. And is this not the strongest feature of European film?

Film began with the Lumière brothers and continued with Méliès and Max Linder and the great masters that followed them, raising it to the category of Art, thus earning the title 'the Seventh Art', and with this classification it spread and penetrated the world and particularly some eastern countries. The expressions, being poetic, are to some degree mysterious, since they stem from the subconscious or feelings beyond the bounds of reason, as well as deep revelations of hidden feelings that overlay reason. That is why such riches, so obvious in film, are difficult if not impossible to define or explain. Nevertheless, this is a condition that is typical of the Arts. They thus become a conveyor belt, characteristic of the purest and most intimate meaning in its many forms, whose expression becomes the loftiest way of bringing to people a deeper knowledge of the human condition and of human nature.

That is how the Greeks thought at the height of the classical age. During this period, democratic governments paid playwrights to write tragedies, paid the actors to play in them and even the public to go to see them.

Nowadays, the aim is to attract the public in the most vulgar and increasingly mediocre fashion, in ways that are increasingly stereotyped and sophisticated in terms of technique – as if technique belonged to the realm of expression and not to that of science. We believe that expression is the very essence of art and not techniques that belong to science – although art can use technique to enhance its expression. This highly sophisticated and bombastic path used by certain films is no longer expression, they go beyond the limits, and merely appear as circus effects. Once, in Tokyo, I watched a performance of Kabuki theatre and at one moment there was a play of fans between the women, and the audience applauded. I asked the interpreter who was with me whether they applauded because it was part of the Kabuki ritual. She said no and added: the audience sometimes likes these artifices, but critics hate them because they believe that the real Kabuki is something serious and that this is not Kabuki but circus. Quite honestly, true art belongs to expression and not to technique, whilst technique is on the side of science. It can help expression but is not expression.

With the advent of sound and colour, film became – of all artistic expression – that which most approximated the imitation of real life. Thus, as a synthesis of all the arts and perhaps as a result of its unparalleled power of persuasion, an indiscriminate search for audiences arose, with a single aim – profit – dragging it towards artistic and ethical decadence, which has generally meant the overriding use of violence for its own sake, sex for its own sake and revenge – which is the worst of human sentiments, and the most ancient. The most used and effective recipe is that of the executioner who humiliates and mistreats his victim, until the public steps into the shoes of that victim and then develops its own desire to see itself avenged. This revenge, obviously, is suited to the audience's taste and they leave the cinema with the idea that they are living in the best possible world. Here we see the disparagement of artistic merit as it falls into a discredited mediocrity that plays to people's taste and to profit in this virtual world of capitalist-socialism.

Turning to the alleged characteristics of European film, we now move into very complex terrain:

Characterising European film, which encompasses the different countries that make it up and which now form the European Union, globalising different languages and idiosyncrasies, is an easy thing – when it comes to currency, unified in the Euro. But while the globalisation of a theoretical point of view may seem easy, in practice it often proves difficult to realise. Similarly, it is difficult to define or characterise European film.

I would mention as equally difficult the shift from *silent film* to *talking film*. Linguistic difficulties did not arise in silent film since the subtitles with the dialogue were neutral and in the language of the country where the film was shown. The difficulties arose with the coming of sound and the language differences between the countries that formed Europe and that, at the same time, gave each country and the continent its identity. Fernando Pessoa once said 'My country is my language.' One can have a single currency – it does not alter one's identity. But the same is not true of the languages or the idiosyncrasies of each nation that Europe comprises.

It is true that the techniques are common ones and because of a cultural *métissage* there are films that are spoken in different languages according to the nationality of the characters, although that would be possible only in certain films. And let us not forget the affirmation of the personality of each director as they introduce themselves with films that are outside the normal mould. Are we all to film in English, which is now the universal language, thus destroying the idiosyncrasies of each people or nation? The problem of the European Union is not in the area of the economy, or currency or mathematics but precisely in the characteristics specific to each nation's people, its geographical situation which hampers and hinders globalisation. It is true that the modern world is embarked on the route of artificiality, in some way changing the natural course of nature which we are part of and that, unbelievably, we treat so badly.

On the other hand, we have commercially driven cinema, where what matters are the box-office takings, and not the artistic quality of the films. In bygone days, the small *art-house cinemas* existed thanks to the fact that a more specialised public would come in good numbers. However, the big commercial companies, given this unexpected success, organised the production of false films as *films d'auteur* and invaded the small cinemas, trying to deceive audiences.

But the specialised film-goer realised the fraud and stopped going to this kind of cinema. The result was a disaster. Without enough people going to see these films, the commercial movies have returned to reclaim their usual audience. And with this fraud 'the honest man has to pay for the sinner' and the *art-house cinema* venues disappeared.

In this way Hollywood became the film Mecca and not Paris – its homeland – with the advantage that US films were spoken in the universalised English language. Attracted by the idea of profit, Europe attempts frequently and wrongly to imitate this model, with less developed techniques and in the language of each country, which hampers the globalisation process.

I know there are a thousand reasons that may justify these films whose costs run into tens or hundreds of millions and whose advertising costs are just as high: they are advertised world-wide, and appear on the front pages of all the newspapers and magazines. This is something that does not happen with European films world-wide, not even in Europe itself. Generally speaking, they are mentioned in the entertainment section or, more rarely, in the culture section.

In some ways, this reflects the current political games being played out in the European Union.

Thank goodness for the most important European festivals – festivals that started in Europe and are now starting to be conquered by the United States.

I certainly don't wish to offend or, even less, to hurt anyone with this statement. We live in a democracy and we have our free will. That is, are we *really* free?

Manoel de Oliveira
Porto, 2 February 2007
Translated from Portuguese by Cinescript.

Born almost one hundred years ago in 1908, **Manoel de Oliveira** started working in film at the time of silent films. He started making documentaries in the 1930s (e.g. *Douro, Faina Fluvial*), finally gained international recognition in the 1960s and among the more than forty films he has by now directed are *A Divina Comédia* (1991) for which he received the Grand Special Jury Prize in Venice, *Viagem ao Princípio do Mundo* (1997), winner of the FIPRESCI prizes in Cannes and at the European Film Awards 1997, *La Lettre* (1999) which won the Jury Prize in Cannes, and *Um Filme Falado* (2003) with Catherine Deneuve and John Malkovich.

Ingmar Bergman on the set for
*Persona*
(Picture: Bo A. Vibenius © AB
Svensk Filmindustri)

## How Bergman Can Change Your Life

by Gunnar Bergdahl

Almost ten years ago I met a South African man in his fifties, Warren Snowball, for lunch. He had looked me up at the cultural festival in Grahamstown, South Africa's biggest annual cultural event, where I found myself introducing a programme of Swedish films. The somewhat conservative Mr Snowball wanted to recount a film experience that had come to determine his life. I have often thought about that lunch and Mr Snowball's story about how a few hours in a cinema can change a man's life. It was, of course, a film by Ingmar Bergman.

Today, Ingmar Bergman has withdrawn. He has left film and television behind him, he has even left the Royal Dramatic Theatre, and all the actors he loved so passionately working with. He has abandoned Stockholm, his structured creativity, and now lives on Fårö. 'Full time Fårö old fart,' as the almost eighty-nine-year-old Bergman puts it. For company he has his cinema in the old barn that once served as his small film studio, and in his house at the beach he has music and books. Also, the black notebooks, the sharpened pencils, the desk and lit working lamp, the view over the shifting sea, walks along the beach and dreams and memories. This is what he said when I interviewed him a few years ago, on the occasion of Swedish Radio Theatre's 75th anniversary:

'It's definitely over now. I did 49 radio plays, 126 theatre plays, and if you put my cinema and television films together there are more than 60. I now read books and look at films in my cinema. There are 15,000 tourists to Fårö every summer. Thank God I live on the side of the island where few people venture. I have also sold a bit of my land to a man that keeps young bulls. And there is a gate with a sign, "Beware – young bulls". It is extraordinary how off-putting it seems to be. I have a beach of flat stones flanked by a cold sea current so the water is never more than 13 degrees.'

Bergman's film reign stretches over sixty incredible years. From his time as a 'script slave' at Svensk Filmindustri – that's how he himself calls his apprenticeship during the Second World War – to his farewell with *Saraband* in December 2003. When the young Bergman entered into Swedish film – he came from student theatre – it was another age. It was then possible for an opinionated debutant to get more than one chance without the instant and immediate judgement of the box-office. He made a name for himself with the screenplay of *Torment* in 1944. To the young Bergman's frustration, the film was directed, however, by the great Alf Sjöberg. But four films followed which Bergman has described as directing experiences more than memorable works – films that mirrored their time and the contemporary trends. Looking back I am most fond of the little neo-realistic and seldom screened *Port of Call* from 1948. But his big artistic breakthrough came with *Prison* a year later. From then on, the 'script slave' transformed himself into one of film's most daring pioneers.

What is it that makes Bergman great? Perhaps it is his ability, in film after film, to weave in so many other forms of cultural expression. As in no other film-maker, music, theatre, literature and art live side by side. And not as fleeting punctuations or façades. But rather as the heartbeats of traditions, breaths of the magnificence that man has accomplished, a rhythm from the past that takes place here and now in the cinema when our senses open to a new story of the difficult art of living as a human being. With insights on death's inexorability and the hope of reconciliation conjoined in a solid alloy between the past and the future. Briefly, a secretive ability to touch our hearts.

As few artists of the cinema, Bergman has a great love of the distinctive nature of film, its combination of circus and profundity. He loves the sawdust and the rubbish it enhances. He has often talked of film as a 'whore's business' where commercial and artistic interests literally form two sides of the same coin. But in his case it is prostitution according to conditions that he himself has laid down. This is how he has played a decisive role in Swedish and international film. Not as a monolith in his own artistic universe, but as a guide on a communal journey. He was the hub – as director and producer – in the 1960s of what we describe today as the golden decade of Swedish film. As much an inspiration for those who, like Bo Widerberg or Mai Zetterling, turned against his films as for those, like Jan Troell or Kjell Grede, who were encouraged and took strength from them.

From that perspective it is absolutely logical that Ingmar Bergman became the European Film Academy's first president. A greater freedom for film could only be achieved in coordination with reality. Just as he had, through the years, created his highly personal films, not as expressions facing away from reality in a cultural enclave, but as an organic part of an expanding art form.

An explanation of Bergman's influence on the development of film is his own insatiable love and curiosity for film and its expression. Every afternoon at three, the projectors roll in his cinema on Fårö. Films from young film-makers are blended with the classics in a living relationship and with a specific affection for films from the silent era. It is, in truth, inspirational. I remember one of the occasions I had the opportunity to interview him. We spoke about film, of course, and two cameras were there – it was to be a television interview and later it became the film *The Voice of Bergman* – and I asked him if he ever grew tired of seeing films. He guffawed with his generous laugh and said: 'Oh no . . . film is an expanding universe. The more you see, the more you find.'

His own films are proof of this simple theory. Because there is a fantastic breadth in Bergman's pioneering border crossings through the 'kingdom of cinematography'. As no other film director in the world, he has given himself the liberty to test expressions and renew genres. There are many examples. In François Truffaut's *The 400 Blows*, one of the French New Wave's first great masterpieces, you can notice the young Jean-Pierre Léaud and his friend transfixed before a poster outside a cinema where they are showing Bergman's *Summer with Monika* from 1952. It is no coincidence. With that film, Bergman left the claustrophobic world of the studio and he lets Harriet Andersson, in a magical finale, turn her gaze directly into the camera, at us. Bergman both destroys and strengthens the film's illusion in that single moment. He gave young, future directors in Paris the founding impulses to a new film language as they sat in the *cinémathèque* and wondered what a then relatively unknown Swedish film director had invented. The young Wim Wenders is often said to have created a whole new film genre, the road movies, in the 1970s with films like *Alice in the Cities* and *Kings of the Road*. But already in 1957, when Wenders was still attending school in Düsseldorf, *Wild Strawberries*, the most extraordinary road movie ever, had its premiere.

*Smultronstället* (Wild Strawberries)
(Picture: Louis Huch © 1957 AB Svensk Filmindustri)

Not to mention the hunt for fleeting light with Sven Nykvist (their collaboration started in earnest with *The Virgin Spring* in 1959) which achieved its fullest expression with *Winter Light* in 1962, still a reference point for directors and cinematographers the world over. In the mid–1970s, the newly launched Swedish Family Guidance Council suddenly got very busy. Thousands of Swedes turned to them to question their lives and relationships. The reason was a pioneering drama, the very first 'soap', called *Scenes from a Marriage* which had the Swedish population glued to their televisions in 1973. One of the many Bergman examples which illustrate that it is really no problem – as many other film-makers continually claim – to migrate between film and television and still carry one's sense of imagery and ambition into the smaller format.

Bergman's inventive toying with his own childhood experience of silent film in cinemas around Stockholm, in *Prison (Fängelse)* for instance, is still an important inspiration for film-within-a-film experiments today. *Prison*, that introverted film, opens in a light, happy moment as the young couple hide in an attic and look at an old silent film farce – a scene that points straight to Alexander's magical box theatre in Bergman's masterful farewell to feature films, *Fanny and Alexander* in 1982. Or for that matter, to the nightmare sequences that launch *Sawdust and Tinsel* (1953) and *Wild Strawberries*. They are also small silent films, greetings to an ever-present film history. Bergman's films continually turn on their own axle, observing themselves – and us – with renewed intensity.

Above all, Bergman's singular most important contribution to the development of film is the possibilities of the close-up. He has expressed it himself: 'The close-up, man's naked, open face is cinematography's greatest conquest.' And how he has sought to support this statement! His fascination for this distinctive character of film, of the small shifts and movements in a person's face when they talk or are silent in *Persona* (1966) or *A Passion* (1969) and with film titles such as *Cries and Whispers* (1972) and *Face to Face* (1975), became his artistic credo.

Ingmar Bergman is loved today. Even in Sweden. But the road to the Swedish people's heart has been long. The trends of the time have never steered Bergman. His no-compromise genre renewals far removed from political correctness are one of the most important reasons for his greatness. He was 'wrong' already in the literary 1940s, his existential depictions were referred to as excrement by the Swedish cultural establishment in the 1950s and the cultural left of the 1960s attacked both his bourgeois background and his artistic expression.

Not to mention the Swedish state's revenge on its existential critic – the fabricated tax scandal that led to his German exile for much of the 1970s.

As a seventeen-year-old Vietnam activist, I handed out flyers at the opening night of *Shame* in Stockholm in 1968 and protested against this 'groundless comment on the Vietnam war'. Ten years later I happened to see the film again on television. Privately, a lot had happened to me, I had wandered through my own war zone and the people's struggle had been won in Vietnam. But at what price? Suddenly, this film was a portrayal of relevant questions. How do we reconcile knowledge of the burning world with our own lives? This film – which perhaps doesn't figure as one of Bergman's best – became a decisive experience which changed my view on things.

*Fanny and Alexander*
(Picture: Arne Carlsson ©
1982 Svenska Filminstitutet)

It was only with *Fanny and Alexander* in 1982, whose full-length version (five hours long) is shown on Swedish television every Christmas, that Bergman became loved in Sweden. It was only then that he received the broad population's recognition, only then that he was welcome into the Swedish 'Folkhemmet' (literally the 'People's Home', a Swedish societal concept that was introduced post war by the Social Democrats). I am a child of this 'Folkhemmet' myself, being born in the early 1950s, fed with safety and enclosed in a Swedish secured reservation isolated from the rest of the world.

My very first Bergman film was *The Seventh Seal* which I saw in a basement film studio at school. It was the mid 1960s and those of us who were there tried to be somewhat exclusive and different teenagers. Even then, in the midst of the Swedish 'Folkhemmet', Bergman's films were foreign, 'cultural'. The 'Folkhemmet's' founding idea was the safe, broad road, built on collaboration, on community. In the 'Folkhemmet' everything was to be in conformity – and better. Omnipresent *angst* was something 'un-Swedish'. In the mirror of the 'Folkhemmet', we Swedes were always healthier, wealthier, happier and wiser than all the others. The opposite was the case in Bergman's film mirror.

For my own part, when I look back, his films hit me as if in sleep. Because the image of the happy Swedish 'Folkhemmet' was constructed, in large part, on suppression. You can't say that about Bergman's films. On the contrary, they were about the consequences of suppression. Not even love could work as a romantic route to traditional escapism. The world and contemporary events were present like 'demons' in his films. Of course, you could say that his environments and characters are 'old fashioned' – if you choose not to want to see any further than the superficial props. Professors, teachers, clowns, circus directors, move in landscapes from the Middle Ages as in *The Virgin Spring*, or in dream-like, timeless environments as in *The Silence* from 1963. The spirit of timelessness is even woven into his later films like *Saraband*. Often in his work, old toys and playthings make an appearance and large clocks strike heavily in silent corridors. But the questions his characters ask themselves and each other!

In Sweden, in which the 1980s were stamped by the assassination of Olof Palme, in which the 1990s were darkened by the *Estonia* ferry disaster, and the first years of this century were marked by the image of a young woman foreign minister dying on a stretcher in a department store on a normal Swedish weekday, and where this whole period has seen a shift of the nation from an illusory utopia to a European country among many others, Bergman's films are more contemporary than ever. They often burn like welding blowtorches, just like the arc of light that opens *Persona* – an extraordinary dream journey in images, a sequence that is still more virtually challenging than any art video from this decade.

Bergman's films are almost always about ties to the past, often to the child within us. A blatant contact with imagination's interpretation of life that we so easily lose as drifting memory fragments of half-forgotten dreams. Consider *The Silence* with its opening sequence of the boy who wakes in a train carriage and looks straight into the camera, into us, into our silence before the world. A strange country, terrifying, *angst*-ridden with death ever-present and life as an incomprehensible undertaking. And the same boy returns in *Persona* – it is my absolute favourite film if the truth will out – where Bergman lets him almost stroke the double-exposed images. Pure magic and nothing else!

Of course there is a theatrical aspect to some of Bergman's films. For better and worse. Not everything is masterful. When a French film critic wrote in 1978 that 'Bergman has with *Autumn Sonata* made a Bergman film', Bergman himself thought that it was a precise and telling formulation. He saw the consequences and realised once more the need to tread new paths. And this led to the astonishing *From the Life of the Marionettes* and the more powerful and conclusive *Fanny and Alexander*.

But it was nevertheless *Autumn Sonata* that Warren Snowball in Grahamstown saw and that inexorably entered into his life. During that lunch in Grahamstown, which so often returns to me, as we sat and looked out over the land from the restaurant at the cultural centre with the shanty town down below in the valley, he told me about the late 1970s. He was then newly married and he and his wife had recently graduated with PhDs at Grahamstown University where they also ran a small cinema. They had a child, a son who was severely brain-damaged. Their friends advised them to put him into an institution and get on with their lives.

'One evening,' continued Mr Snowball, 'we screened an Ingmar Bergman film at the cinema. Blenda was at home with Roger and I took the projector and 16mm copy home with me to show her the film without telling her what I thought of it myself. I went home, woke her up, and in the middle of the night we watched *Autumn Sonata* together. When the film ended, we looked at each other and said, 'No institution.' We sold everything we had and went to the States where the best care for Roger was to be found. Ten years later, Roger had died and my wife had succumbed to cancer. I had no more money and I travelled back alone. Everything had been in vain. But I don't regret a second. I am so grateful to that film!'

This is what Warren Snowball told me. It sounds like a Bergman-esque film tale, but it is real.

Not only is film an expanding universe, every individual is as well. Bergman's films have allowed many people to grow through coming to this realisation.

Bergman is now a soon-to-be ninety-year-old man with death, chess-playing or not, approaching. When I filmed the interview film *Ingmar Bergman: Intermezzo* in 2002, we met on an autumn day at the Royal Dramatic Theatre in Stockholm. He had just started work on *Ghosts*, Henrik Ibsen's play that he himself had newly translated from the Norwegian over the summer on Fårö, during which time he had also 'delivered' the screenplay of *Saraband*.

I asked him if one thought more of death as one got older.

'Think of what?' asked Bergman (if I was unclear or if his hearing failed him we'll leave unsaid).

'DEATH,' I said.

'Oh, death,' said Bergman and laughed. 'I have thought about death every day since I was a child. But now that it is a physically evident reality, it is a lot less frightening. The fear has fallen away,' he said and fell silent.

Just as the silence was about to be definite, he suddenly continued: 'No, I don't have time for this any more!'

He looked at his watch, got up and walked out with vigorous steps to work on what would be his last theatre production. Beyond Ibsen's play I can catch a glimpse of the stone beach on Fårö. A pearl necklace of film stretches out to the horizon. Like the rays of a distant lighthouse. An old man looks out over the sea whilst the winter darkness of the hour of the wolf deepens. Ingmar Bergman leaves behind a feeling that we all can and should use our short moment on earth.

Translated from Swedish by Alexander Keiller.

Born in 1951, **Gunnar Bergdahl** is a film critic, director, and publisher who started the Swedish film magazine *Filmkonst* in 1989. He was the director of the Gothenburg Film Festival from 1994 to 2002 and a member of the board of the Swedish Film Institute from 1999 to 2003. His filmography includes works like *The Voice of Bergman* (1997), *The Voice of Ljudmila* (2001), *Ingmar Bergman: Intermezzo* (2002), *The Voice of Silence* (2003) and *Ljudmila & Anatolij* (2006).

Theo Angelopoulos at the
EFA press conference 1989
(Picture: gerhardkassner.de)

# The Poetic Power of Theo Angelopoulos
by Michel Ciment

Among the most salient characteristics and admirable aspects of Theo
Angelopoulos's cinematographic career and output, one should single
out his determination to impose a coherent body of work – twelve
films so far in thirty-seven years – marked with an individual style,
without making the usual compromise that goes with the film-making
process. This is all the more striking since he worked within a very
small industry – that of Greece – with almost no tradition of great film
artists and based mostly on cheap comedies and lurid melodramas. To
accomplish this feat, one needs courage and steadfastness, as well as
a strong belief in one's own star, qualities that were not lacking in
Angelopoulos and which provoked sometimes hostile reactions in his
own country. But it was his early international recognition and co-
productions with foreign countries such as Italy, France and Germany
that allowed him his creative freedom. Indeed, the director's capacity to
integrate foreign actors, for instance, into his world view, is quite remarkable, as witness his work with Omero Antonutti, Julio Brogi, Marcello Mastroianni, Jeanne Moreau, Harvey Keitel, Maïa Morgenstern,
Erland Josephson, Bruno Ganz, and Isabelle Renauld.

His emergence on the world scene in the 70s coincided with the decline of the new waves that had appeared a decade before in many countries – France, Brazil, Great Britain, Czechoslovakia, etc. – and he was, with Fassbinder, Wenders and a very few others, one of the rare new major figures in European cinema, though his style owed very little to the aesthetic revolution that had recently shaken the cinema world – hand-held camera, realism, improvisation, autobiographical elements. His highly composed *mise en scène* with its complex camera movements, long takes and depth of field, his investigation of the past through metaphoric devices, his use of off space and sound are more akin to directors like Antonioni, Mizoguchi, Welles or Murnau than to Godard and Cassavetes. In many ways, Angelopoulos is a modernist with a deep sense of tradition, and his epic cinema with its historical issues, its distancing process to make the audience think, and its theatrical stylisation relate him to Brecht and the Greek tragedies.

Angelopoulos was born on 27 April 1936, in an upper middle-class family and, in a sense, he would later react against this background. After a few years of studying law, while publishing verse and short stories, his discovery of *A bout de souffle* in a Greek cinema in 1960 prompted him to go to Paris after his military service where he briefly studied at the Sorbonne before entering IDHEC, the famous film school from which he was expelled after doing a provocative 360° pan shot. Before returning to Greece at the end of 1963, he worked with Jean Rouch at the Musée de l'Homme and at night as an usher at the Cinémathèque française where he acquired the essentials of his film culture. Back in Athens, he wrote a weekly film column for the left-wing paper *Dimokratiki Allaghi* (*Democratic Change*) from 1964 to 1967 when it was closed down by the colonels who had taken power. Meanwhile, in 1965, he had started a partly documentary feature, *The Forminx Story*, about a pop group in the wake of Richard Lester's *A Hard Day's Night*, but abandoned the shooting after a conflict with the producer. In 1968, he directed a 28-minute short film, *I Ekpombi* (*The Broadcast*), a cinema *vérité* exercise in the manner of Jean Rouch, based on street interviews about people's fantasies of their ideal mate. It was his first collaboration with Giorgios Arvanitis, the great cameraman who contributed so creatively to all his films, except the latest one, *The Weeping Meadow*.

In his first feature, *Anapastassi (Reconstruction*, 1970), Angelopoulos immediately found his style and the film became the matrix of his future work. Shot in twenty-seven days in a half-deserted village, with a crew of five and a cast of villagers, it was inspired by a newspaper article about a man murdered by his wife and her lover. The film is indebted to the realistic tradition of Italian cinema – the Visconti of *Ossessione* as well as the Rosi of *Salvatore Giuliano* – but it already has a unique flavour. The actual crime is never shown, the enquiry is interrupted by flashbacks about the circumstances preceding the murder, and the drama recalls Greek myths like the killing of Agamemnon by his wife Clytemnestra and her lover Aegisthus after his return from the Trojan War. Like T. S. Eliot's poetry and James Joyce's *Ulysses*, Angelopoulos's films will be regularly suffused with indirect and subtle references to classical myths and literature. The setting of *Reconstruction*, Northern Greece, would become a constant background to his stories with its rain and its clouds, its cold colours and bleak vistas, so far away from the tourist image of sunny Greece. The director has marked his territory but his landscape is as much a landscape of the mind as the one of his native country.

*Landscape in the Mist* (Picture: Theo Angelopoulos Film Productions)

During the 1970s Angelopoulos directed a tetralogy of political and historical films which established his international status. *Days*

*of '36* (*Imeres tou 36*, 1972) was presented at the Berlinale's Forum, *The Travelling Players* (*O Thiassos*, 1975), turned down by the Cannes selection committee, was a landmark event at the Directors' Fortnight, *The Hunters* (*I Kynighi*, 1977) was his first participation in the Cannes competition, while *Alexander the Great* (*O Megalexandros*, 1980) won the Venice Golden Lion for experimental cinema. These four films span several decades of Greek history. *Days of '36* is about the year (besides being the director's birth date) when the government was toppled by the dictator Metaxas; *The Travelling Players* is a four-hour journey, from the fall of Metaxas in 1939 to the election of Papagos in 1952; *The Hunters* takes place on New Year's Eve 1977 when a party of bourgeois hunters discover the body of a partisan from the 1947 civil war whom they decide to bury again; *Alexander the Great* portrays a charismatic leader who wants to establish a utopian socialist community on the eve of the twentieth century. Those films, unmistakably bearing the mark of their creator, nevertheless offer a great variety of aesthetic approaches. *Days of '36* mostly takes place in a prison where a former police inspector is charged with the murder of a trade unionist. It is almost a silent film, a work about what is not said, and reflecting the conditions in which the director was working – unable to speak up during the dictatorship of the Greek colonels. *The Travelling Players* is devoted to a group of actors, simple people caught in the turmoil of history, from the German occupation to the civil war, and performing from town to town a pastoral melodrama, *Golfo the Shepherdess*. Using all the means at his disposal, from ballet to music, from references to the myth of the Atrides to the parallel between theatre and life, Angelopoulos creates some stunning spatial and temporal effects, such as his favourite device of timeshifts within a single take that starts for instance with a character walking along a railway track in a soldier's uniform ready for the war in 1940, and ending in a jeep during the Papagos election campaign in 1952. *The Hunters* is an almost Buñuelian study of the phantoms and the fantasies of the ruling class, a nightmarish vision of the bourgeoisie with strong psychoanalytical overtones. *Alexander the Great* is a 210-minute coda about the corruption of power, with a central Stalin figure who pretends to liberate

the people in order to enslave them. Angelopoulos, the Marxist committed artist, thus closes his tetralogy by questioning ideologies and
revealing his political disenchantment.

In the 1980s, politics moves to the background and the films are
more devoted to individual portrayals, as witness the trilogy as defined
by the director himself of *Voyage to Cythera* (*Taxidi sta kithira*,
1984, Best Script at Cannes), or the silence of history, *The Beekeeper*
(*O Melissokomos*, 1986), or the silence of love, *Landscape in the Mist*
(*Topio stin omichli*, 1988, Silver Lion in Venice and European Film of
the Year 1989), or the silence of God. *Voyage to Cythera* is a turning
point and a last comment on the disillusionment of politics. The old
Spyros, after thirty years of exile due to the civil war, comes back to
Greece to be kept off shore and rejected a second time by the collective
desire of a selfish society that has decided to turn the page of history.
The image of the father is also present in *The Beekeeper* also named
Spyros (like the director's father), and in *Landscape in the Mist* where
two children travel through Greece and cross the border in search of a
lost father, an echo perhaps of Angelopoulos's harrowing experience
as a young boy when he looked with his mother for the corpse of his
father, supposedly killed during the civil war, before he reappeared in
their life.

A third phase is illustrated by another trilogy – *The Suspended Step
of the Stork* (*To Météoro vima tou pélorgou*, 1991), *Ulysses' Gaze* (*To
Vlemma tou odyssea*, 1995, Grand Prize in Cannes and Felix of the
Critics 1995) and *Eternity and a Day* (*Mia Eoniotita ke mia mera*,
1998, Palme d'Or in Cannes), witnesses a return of the political themes
combined with individual portrayals. It is a new world marked by the
wars in Bosnia and Kosovo, the first conflict in Iraq, refugees from
Albania and elsewhere who cross borders, are grouped in camps and
haunt the Mediterranean. More than ever Angelopoulos's characters
are on their way, shifting from place to place in an endless journey. In
*The Suspended Step of the Stork*, a reporter, Alexander, investigates a
brilliant political leader who has disappeared ten years before, after
writing a book called *End of the Century Melancholia*. In *Ulysses'
Gaze* a Greek film director, A (for Angelopoulos or Alexander?),
comes back from his exile in America, in search of three missing reels

from an early silent film by the Manaki brothers. From Florina, in the North of Greece, to Sarajevo, he travels through Albania, Bulgaria, Romania, Serbia and Bosnia in a Grail-like quest. In *Eternity and a Day*, another Alexander (again obviously a substitute for Angelopoulos), a writer this time, undertakes a personal trip before entering the hospital and appears in a flashback as he is today, reminiscent of Bergman's *Wild Strawberries*. He saves an Albanian orphan from the police and then from a gang of hoodlums who sell children to rich Westerners. He also lives with a souvenir of his dead wife who appears in sunny sequences on the seaside, an almost unique occurrence in the cinema of Angelopoulos. In these last two films, the director has never been more personal, identifying with the artists who are the protagonists of his tales, sharing with them the same sense of exile, melancholia and disenchantment.

With the coming of the new century, Angelopoulos has undertaken a new trilogy, more premeditated than ever before. Its first part, *The Weeping Meadow* (*To Livadi Pou Dakrisi*, 2004, European Film Academy Critics Award 2004 – Prix FIPRESCI), inaugurates a vast fresco which deals with the Greek Diaspora throughout the twentieth century. As usual, the director alludes to the situations and locations of his earlier films, and, after a period where Homer's *Odyssey* seemed the main reference, goes back to his earlier interest in Greek tragedy. *The Weeping Meadow* covers thirty years between the flight from Odessa in 1919 of the Greek aristocratic families after the Soviet revolution and the end of the Greek civil war in 1949.

A group of musicians is a substitute for the travelling players of the earlier film, and the film adopts a more choral structure after the introspective dimension of those of the nineties. Never has the cosmic sense of Angelopoulos been more evident with its extraordinary images of a flooded village and a funeral ceremony performed in barges. His latest opus exhibits once more the fusion of all the elements that make cinema a synthesis of all the arts, from the score of Eleni Karaindrou (the magnificent composer who has worked with him since *Voyage to Cythera*) to the poetic contributions of Tonino Guerra (his screenwriter since the early 1980s) and the images created this time by cinematographer Andreas Sinanos but which bear the inimitable stamp of the director.

From Kurosawa to Wenders and Bergman fellow film-makers have acknowledged Angelopoulos's exceptional mastery of the medium and his artistic capacity to fulfil his high ambitions. In a time when cinema seems less and less daring, the sensory experience and the food for thought offered by his films is a comfort for those who still believe in the power of the image.

Paris, February 2007

Born in Paris in 1938, **Michel Ciment** is a renowned film critic, editor of the magazine *Positif*, university lecturer and radio journalist (France-Inter) and producer (France-Culture). He wrote one of the best-known volumes on Stanley Kubrick, along with fifteen other books on influential figures in cinema like Joseph Losey, Elia Kazan, John Boorman, Francesco Rosi, Fritz Lang – and Theo Angelopoulos. He is also an honorary president of the international federation of film critics FIPRESCI.

*La Notte*
(Picture: Cinetext Bildarchiv)

## Cinema as a Way of Life
## Notes from a conversation with Jeanne Moreau

*Jeanne Moreau is the European actress par excellence. The length and abiding vigour of her career, allied to her creative alliances with such brilliant directors as Antonioni, Losey, Malle, Truffaut, and Welles, has given her a pre-eminence that none of her contemporaries can match. Turning eighty in 2008, she exults in her profession. (Her awards include Best Actress at the Cannes Film Festival 1960, the Lion d'Or at the Venice Film Festival 1992, Fellowship of BAFTA in London 1996, European Film Academy Lifetime Achievement Award in 1997, Special Tribute at the Academy of Motion Picture Arts and Sciences in Los Angeles 1998, and the Festival Trophy at Cannes in 2003.)*

'It's a calling,' she emphasises. 'I never leave the set. Being a director as well as an actor, I'm interested in everything that's going on. When I read a new script, not only am I concerned with what I have to do, but with all the other performers.'

**You are half-French, half-English. Do you find that this blend of cultures has helped you in your career – perhaps to think of Europe in a wider context?**

Jeanne Moreau: I think so, in many ways. I find in myself a touch of Irish blood. I can be very shy, very introverted, but when I start speaking in public, I love it.

I didn't look forward to the life of an average woman: marriage, raising a family and so forth . . . I loved studying. I had to pass an exam each year, I never failed. So now, when I receive an award or a tribute in a festival, there's a little girl inside me that says 'You see, I was good!' Then I think of my father's antagonism; he despised actresses and women artists.

My mother was born in Oldham, Lancashire. My grandfather and grandmother moved to the south, and when I spent time with them in the summer, we used to live on the yacht my grandfather had bought to teach sailing. We were in small harbours on the south coast – Hove, Southwick and Littlehampton. My sister lives in Brighton now, and I still have family on the Isle of Man. My grandma was born in Ireland, in the same county where Nora, James Joyce's wife, was born and raised.

I started films and theatre at the same time. I made a lot of films before I worked with Louis Malle, and then became famous in internationally successful movies. Before – in the 1950s – physically I didn't meet the usual standards of beauty, it was the period of Martine Carol, Françoise Arnoul, Dany Robin – blonde girls, big eyes and 'tits'.

*While still young, she became a highly regarded stage actress at the Comédie Française and the Théâtre National Populaire, but found herself confined to supporting roles in gangster films like* Touchez pas au grisbi, *with Jean Gabin.*

*Her talent attracted attention, nonetheless. In 1953, Michelangelo Antonioni wanted to sign her for* I Vinti, *but the Comédie Française refused to release her. Also in the early 1950s Orson Welles wanted her to act in his stage production,* The Unthinking Lobster, *at the Théâtre Edouard VII in Paris. But once again, her contract held her fast.*

One evening Maurice Bessy, a French journalist, came to my dressing room and said that Orson was in town and wanted to meet me. I was then playing Bianca in *Othello*. Orson sat opposite me at the table, and years later he reminded me that when he'd dropped me in the street outside my apartment, I had been too shy to say anything and that he was 'dying' to kiss me.

*Moreau would go on to take parts in four of Orson Welles's films:* The Trial, Chimes at Midnight *(Falstaff),* The Immortal Story, *and* The Deep, *which was shot in Yugoslavia and remains unreleased to this day.*

I persuaded him to meet Romy Schneider, whom he took for *The Trial*. During that time, Orson was staying at the Hotel Meurice in Paris, and from his balcony he could see the two huge clocks of the Gare d'Orsay across the Seine. We used to peer through the barred gates of the old, abandoned railway station at night, and he finally chose it as the location for *The Trial*.

When I started appearing in films, it did not automatically bring money and fame. At least it didn't for me. In fact I am *born* on the stage of a theatre. All the time I wanted to prove to my father that I was right to have chosen that craft. My decision provoked a real break between him and myself. My mother had gone back to England, and my father literally threw me out of the house.

My meeting with Louis [Malle] was like a rebirth for me. Miles Davis agreed to do the music after seeing the scene of my walking along the Champs-Elysées at night in *Lift to the Scaffold* (*Ascenseur pour l'échafaud*).

**What is a European film? How does it differ, at its best, from the typical American studio production?**
It implies a very special approach towards people and emotions that can bring the best and the worst in films. There was a very important book that everyone who's involved in cinema knows, a book about the *cinéma d'auteur* by André Bazin, the godfather of François Truffaut. That theory inspired some great directors, and some

*Ascenseur pour l'échafaud*
(Picture: Cinetext Bildarchiv)

disastrous ones, because not everyone can write his own script, and direct his own script.

What came with the New Wave was that powerful energy, that aggressive antagonism and the lack of money. The crew was very reduced. Hierarchy as such didn't exist. Prior to that, you couldn't imagine someone playing the main part, the *star*, without a car, a driver, a personal assistant, dresser, make-up, hairdresser ... When I made *Ascenseur*, I did my make-up, my own hair, the costumes were my clothes, there was no driver, and nobody was following me around. I used to do the make-up in a café at a quiet table out of sight, usually near the toilets, surrounded with the smell of urine and detergent! An assistant would close his eyes, holding a big coat while I undressed and changed.

### Can you recall some personal memories from the European Film Awards?

What makes the European Film Awards so special is the friendly atmosphere of the event. At my first ceremony (Ingmar Bergman was not coming any longer) it was Wim Wenders who presented the evening. I liked the fact that people came from all over the world for this event. In 1997, we gave awards to *The Full Monty*, Juliette Binoche for *The English Patient*, Bruno Dumont's *La Vie de Jésus*, Manoel de Oliveira ... In 2002, in Rome, the winner of the European Film and European Director prizes was a man who has become a close friend, Pedro Almodóvar. And in 2003, it was *Good Bye Lenin!*, and Charlotte Rampling for *Swimming Pool*. The European Film Awards are less sophisticated than Cannes. This year [2006], when Pedro won his statuette for the European Director's prize for *Volver*, everybody went to hug him, it was wonderful. Nothing is more provocative than cinema. It shows the life of the world. It gives us the knowledge of other people, of other cultures. For me, my life feeds my art, and my art feeds my life. The cinema is a way of life more than a career.

Interviewed by Peter Cowie in Paris, 19 December 2006.

**Jeanne Moreau** (born 1928, in Paris, France) has made some 130 films over a span of more than 59 years. She had already made twenty screen appearances when she was chosen by Louis Malle to appear as the femme fatale in *Lift to the Scaffold* (*Ascenseur pour l'échafaud*, 1958). In the years that followed, she became the emblematic star of numerous New Wave films, from *Jules et Jim, La Mariée était en noir* (Truffaut) to *Une Femme est une femme* (Godard), from *Les Liaisons dangereuses* (Vadim) to *La Baie des anges* (Demy). She worked with some of the greatest directors, including Welles, Losey, Antonioni, Jacques Demy, Tony Richardson, Martin Ritt, Fassbinder and Buñuel, as well as several times with Malle (*Les Amants, Le Feu follet, Viva Maria!*). In 1975 she made her debut as a director with *Lumière*, and in 1979 also directed *L'Adolescente*. She portrayed Marguerite Duras in *Cet amour-là* directed by Josée Dayan. In 2005 she appeared in *Time to Leave* (*Le Temps qui reste*, by François Ozon). In recent years she has made frequent appearances in important television series. She has been president of the jury at Cannes, Tokyo, New Delhi, Berlin, Ghent, and San Sebastian. Jeanne Moreau has also served ten years as chairperson of Equinoxe, a European initiative for scriptwriting, and is an honorary member of the board of the European Film Academy. She directs a cinema school in Angers once a year during summer.

Vittorio Storaro

# The Meaning of Light

An interview with
Vittorio Storaro

*Vittorio Storaro has been working in film for more than forty years.
As a true philosopher of light, he has studied all forms of artistic
expression to develop his own system of giving a story visual expression – a system that has helped him to create the imagery of films such
as* Apocalypse Now, The Last Emperor, Reds, Goya en Burdeos, *and*
Flamenco, *to name just a few.*

**How did you first know that you wanted to work in cinematography?**
Vittaro Storaro: Well, honestly, I am the realisation of the dream of my
father. He was a film projectionist who worked for many years with
a big company in Italy, Lux Film. And, without a doubt, screening
these movies, he dreamed of being a part of the images. So, he pushed
me to study photography and cinematography. It was a bit like in
*Cinema Paradiso*, I was a little kid and sometimes I went with him to
watch the films they were screening. And, of course, I was enchanted –
particularly with the Charlie Chaplin movies.

When I was fourteen, they let me start at the photography school
and from then on, step by step, I went into this magic world and

finally, when I was eighteen, I took the entrance examination to the cinema school, the Centro Sperimentale di Cinematografia. And then I realised that this had become my dream, that failing that examination would mean abandoning my journey. I wouldn't have known what to do if I hadn't passed this test and at that time only three people were accepted every year! But I was lucky, I passed.

**How did your education continue?**
The two years at the film school were wonderful because we were really able to study what we love. It was great, particularly in the second year, to talk with a director about the vision, the story, starting to do it without the pressure of a production, without the responsibility you would normally have. But I soon realised that unless I started to really get into film production, I wouldn't be in balance with myself, because in school you only learn theory. So I asked my father to help me and to talk to some producers he knew.

And so I stepped into the film production, without being paid, of course, in the summer between those two years and also after I finished my second year. I continued to really get to know the set. And very soon I was able to understand what was going on because I had studied nine years of photography and cinematography. The cinematographers I met at the time were surprised about how young I was and how knowledgeable I was. So, at the age of just twenty-one, I became the youngest camera operator in Italy.

Soon I realised that some kind of composition and rhythm was very important, so even had I been offered a job as a cinematographer right away I would have said no. I needed to learn the concept, the *mise en scène* of the camera first. I was young and eager to find out exactly how I could tell a story through the camera.

**When did you get to do your first film as cinematographer?**
In 1968, when I was only twenty-eight, there was a moment during filming when I didn't feel any emotion operating the camera and a friend of mine told me 'Vittorio, this is the time for you to move on, to really start expressing yourself completely in light.' A very good Italian director, Franco Rossi, asked to see the short film I was doing with

some friends and then he offered me to photograph my first film, *Giovinezza, Giovinezza*. It was like a dream because he gave me the freedom to express myself. At the same time he was directing me like everyone else. But he was a father figure for me. And I remember, at the end of that picture, that this emotion, like first love, was coming to an end, that in a few days the shooting would be over, and there was no way I could feel that kind of vibration again. I could probably do another hundred movies, bigger or smaller, wonderful or mediocre, but in no way could it be the same. And I cried. But at the same time I realised that that was the right way, to go step by step, with every movie, to open a new door and get to know new things. And I liked that.

Then one day I went into a church with my fiancée, who is now my wife, and I saw a painting. I didn't know the painter then but that painting really touched me very strongly. Later I found out that it was a painting by Caravaggio, *The Calling of Saint Matthew*. The beam of light on top of the painting that divides the divine from the humans, light and darkness, is represented in such an unbelievable way that I thought I need to understand the reason, the meaning of light. When I arrived in the film industry I had been educated as a cinematographer. Film school normally educates you mainly in technology, you are not really taught about all the other arts – no music, philosophy, painting, architecture, theatre. So I started to go deeper, trying to know more.

Cinema is almost like the last of the muses, it nourishes itself from all the other arts, from literature, painting, music, philosophy, and so on. So I started to learn, to read, to listen, to watch, to do everything to understand the meaning of what I was doing, not just using the techno-logical knowledge from school. Up to this point I had been working only through emotion, but I didn't know exactly what light or shadow, and later on, one colour or another could really mean – they are really characters; light tells a story through colour exactly like words in literature or notes in music, they are telling the emotion of a story. From that moment on, I never stopped being a student. So, I was working professionally but at the same time I kept searching. I wrote three books, a trilogy, *Writing with Light*, where I put together all the knowledge it was possible to get from all these philosophers, painters and scientists. And so I was professional but at the same time I was an amateur because with every movie I was doing I tried to put on screen what I had learned from Plato and Aristotle, from Mozart and Dostoyevsky – any emotion that I have through any form of art. I'm still searching, and I love that.

**So, with all your experience, if you look back today, is there any single working experience that has most influenced you?**
Many people ask me this but it is very hard to answer because actually, as a writer, a cinematographer, or a musician, throughout our lives we usually do one single project. If we're writing many articles, doing many films, composing many songs, each one is a little step in our lives, representing one specific moment; but we are really doing just one single piece of work, the film of our life. In other words, we're trying to answer our own questions, we're trying to understand the meaning of our lives. Every single movie, good or bad, represents one specific step. You cannot take a single page out of a book and say this is the best page, you cannot take one note out of a symphony and say this is the best note. And it is the same with cinema. Cinema, in contrast to photography or painting, is movement; it needs rhythm, it needs time to go from a beginning through a journey to an end.

Maybe I can name some [film] titles which were crucial junctures for me and if you look at these you can see the development in my creative life. But any intermediate point between one crossing point and another is also very important. For example, there is no doubt that *Giovinezza Giovinezza* was a milestone in my life and maybe the next one is *The Conformist*. But I could have never done *The Conformist* without having done the other two or three movies that I did in between because they gave me maturity, the chance to prove what I had learned from that first experience. *The Conformist* was the opening of a new door, the chance to discover the vibration, the emotion of the colour blue.

After *The Conformist* I went on doing several other projects to express character and emotion through this colour – until *Last Tango in Paris*. It was in the same city, Paris, but with another story and I discovered the colour orange to express the emotions of that character.

And after that, *1900*, which was about finding a balance between different periods of life: it's the story of two characters, a peasant and a landlord, and we follow their story in four different moments – childhood, growing up, adulthood, old age, like the four seasons in nature.

And after that came *Apocalypse Now* – it was like a zoom on every experience and research I had made in light. I could have never made that film the way I did without the experiences I had had before because I put every philosophical concept into it. When I spoke with Francis Ford Coppola about how we could solve the problem of symbolic characters like Kurtz, of course I spoke about philosophy. He represents the dark side of civilisation, so he has to be represented like the unconscious part of ourselves. The shadow, the world of darkness, does not exist, it only exists because of light – light is the element that creates shadows. The world of darkness belongs to the world of civility, so only from the blackness that represents the unconscious can it evolve, step by step, like a puzzle, showing us the face of horror – the horror of any war. It was a philosophical concept, we didn't just come up with that idea by chance. When I decided to put very violent colour into nature – the smoke colour that is used for helicopters to signal if they're supposed to land or fly away – I put an artificial colour on top of the natural colour, an artificial energy, with my light, on top of the natural energy, because the concept of Joseph Conrad was that – one culture gets on top of another, in an act of violence. And I had to show that concept in visual terms.

All those studies, all this research, have helped me to express myself through the elements I have. Like a musician has notes, I have light, shadow, and colour. And that's what I've tried to do since the beginning. After *Apocalypse Now* I felt that I needed to stop because I had arrived at a point where there was no way to continue unless I found out more about the concept of light. So I stopped working for one year and went back to being a student, reading books, and tried to find out what light consists of. And I discovered colours. It was a wonderful joy – I discovered the symbolic value, the meaning, the philosophy, the physiology of colour. Every colour changes our metabolism, our blood pressure, and only through this discovery was I able to do *La Luna* with Bertolucci.

I recognised the physiology of colour, that each colour changes our body, our attitude. And this enabled me to do *The Last Emperor*, the story of the life of a single man, from beginning to end. How can I represent his life? Through the metaphor of light! So, if life contains several different moments, sentiments, and emotions, then light contains several different colours and maybe I could make a connection and visually tell the journey of his life.

**Listening to you one gets the impression that cinematographers should be educated in philosophy . . .**
Absolutely. In fact, more than ten years ago I put together with a friend of mine a university of images called 'an academy of images' following the concept that a student should be educated in all different kinds of art. You don't have to be an actor to be a cinematographer, you don't have to be a poet, a philosopher or a painter, but you need to at least know *something*. For example, in *Ladyhawke* I was lighting a Romanesque church. Why is there a certain kind of architecture in a certain period, in this case the Middle Ages? What is the difference between Romanesque and Gothic? In order to use light properly, you need to know the fear of the end of world, the fear of God, that dominated people so much at the time and the liberation through Gothic architecture – the windows become very high, there is more light inside, there is hope for the future. Those kinds of little elements are essential.

How is it possible that I studied nine years of photography, two years in the Italian film school, and nobody ever told me about a painter called Caravaggio? I discovered that by chance, by myself. Nobody told me that there was a musician called Mozart. Nobody told me about Faulkner, Dostoyevsky or Chekhov. I think it's essential for being a cinematographer.

**You are very committed to getting more recognition of the cinematographer as part of the creative crew. Maybe you could talk a little bit about that?**
In Italy, as in all of Europe, the law recognises script, music, and director. But those elements don't make a movie, a movie is the

language of images. Without the image, you can write the music, but then you have only the audio, not the video. If you're a writer, you can do literature, you can do theatre – but it's not a movie. Only through cinematography does it become a film. In my opinion the balance between images, music and words constitutes a good movie. That's why we cinematographers are fighting in Europe to get recognition as a co-author of the movie. The Italian film law now finally recognises us as an author of film photography. But we have to get recognition world-wide. I mean, I honestly don't think that the Bertolucci movies that I did would be the same had somebody else done them. They could be better. Or worse, whatever – but they wouldn't be the same.

**From your perspective, do you think there is a distinctly European look in cinema?**
Well, I've only worked with a few American directors like Francis Ford Coppola and Warren Beatty. And they were searching for a visual aspect that would support the story in a specific movie. That's exactly what we do in Europe. Without any doubt, the film industry, particularly the American film industry, can be like a factory, where you do movies that are all very similar to each other, with the same target, the same format. In general, the European attitude is to try to give each movie a specific look. That's the difference between the majority of European cinema and the majority of American cinema. For us it's normal to find a specific idea in every movie. Maybe they don't search so much for a unique look, they try to follow a look that has already been established, that's safe. Maybe we are more experimental, risking more.

**What does a project need today to get your interest?**
I just finished shooting *Caravaggio* and at the same time I'm working with Carlos Saura on a project called *Io, Don Giovanni*, the story about the making of the opera *Don Giovanni*.

So, as you can see, I'm interested in historical projects, epic projects, or stories of visionary people, that give me the chance to be visionary myself. It's great when you have the chance to study, to do research, to get to know that period, that character, that kind of expression.

What is great is if you work and at the same time you are experiencing pleasure. For me, there is no difference between my personal and my professional life. Sometimes I get asked 'Aren't you tired?' I'm not tired when I do something that I love. It is as if I'm always working and at the same time I'm always on a holiday.

**If you owned a cinema for one day, what films would you screen?**
*2001: A Space Odyssey.* I saw it when I was doing my first film in 1968. I came back home from the town where we were shooting because my wife was pregnant with our second son and on Sunday we went to see this movie. I was mesmerised. I don't know how many times I saw that movie.

Telephone interview by Pascal Edelmann on 8 February 2007.

Starting as Italy's youngest camera operator in 1960, **Vittorio Storaro** has long established himself as a true master of photography. In 1970 he did *The Conformist* with Bernardo Bertolucci – the beginning of a collaboration that would continue to include films such as *Last Tango in Paris* (1972), *1900* (1976), *The Last Emperor* (1987) for which he received a David di Donatello for Best Cinematography and an Oscar, and *Little Buddha* (1993). In 1979 he collaborated with Francis Ford Coppola on *Apocalypse Now* which won him his first Oscar. He has also repeatedly worked with Carlos Saura, e.g. on *Flamenco* (1995), *Tango* (1998) and *Goya en Burdeos* for which he received the European Film Academy's European Cinematographer 2000 Award.

# 3 A Greater Europe

*Although Europe hasn't geographically changed, it feels different today than it did when the first European Film Awards were presented in 1988. The old continent is no longer divided, the collapse of Communism and the fall of the Iron Curtain has made it much easier to cross borders, both for individuals and for films. Still, the continent watched, somewhat helplessly, but nevertheless for the most part passively, as Yugoslavia disintegrated and war once again became a European reality. The enlargement of the European Union has put some countries back where they belong, at the heart of Europe.*

*The radical changes that have led to today's situation have left behind images of unionists chained to a dockyard gate, joyous people partying on the Berlin Wall, discoveries of mass graves, and many others. And behind every one of these images lie personal experiences, experiences of film-makers or experiences film-makers have turned into films, or both. How have these experiences influenced European cinema? What does the new situation mean for films and their makers?*

# A Voice From Central Europe

## An interview with Agnieszka Holland

*Agnieszka Holland is a wandering Pole, an established film-maker who has directed in the United States, Canada, France, Germany, Slovakia, Britain and elsewhere, as well as in her native country. Her 2006 release,* Copying Beethoven, *for example, was made with funding from Hungary, Germany, and the UK, and distributed in the United States by MGM. We asked her how she felt about Poland now belonging to the European Union. After all, Kieślowski, when accepting the maiden European Film Award for* A Short Film about Killing *in 1988, uttered the rhetorical question: 'I hope Poland is part of Europe.'*

**Do Polish film-makers nowadays feel a part of Europe, in fact?**
Agnieszka Holland: Well, I think there is a kind of paradox. In a certain way, the Polish film-maker felt much more a part of Europe during the time when we were set apart from Europe than he does now. It's a complex issue, and one that I don't fully understand myself.

It has something to do with the fact that in the European Union, the more united countries are economically and politically, the less interest there is in the movies of neighbouring nations. If, for example, you look at the box-office figures during the 1960s and 1970s, you would find that in Germany you could see a lot of French and Italian movies, in Sweden you would see all the new European films, and so on. By the same token, in Russia, in Poland, in Hungary, in Bulgaria in Czechoslovakia during the same period, European films were at the top of the list.

I think there is always this complex that we are in some way an inferior Europe – that Central Europe is different from Eastern Europe and Western Europe. It's a concept we Poles share with the Czechs and the Hungarians. Central Europe is in some way the real and most important one, which was abandoned by the West as a consequence of several political and historical processes. But in terms of the culture, in terms of our Christian tradition, we are indeed Europe. So in one way we have this superiority complex, and in another we have the *inferiority* complex that we are somehow politically immature, poorer, having been oppressed by various totalitarian regimes during the twentieth century. We are not rich enough, not active enough to compete. This conflict between the complexes provides fertile ground for xenophobic and nationalistic tendencies.

**Presumably the system under Communism was more favourable for the film-makers in the sense that they could get backing for their work more easily?**
Yes, but the difference was also that there was great interest from western festivals like Cannes, Berlin, and Venice, and from TV stations abroad, to show our work. Audiences were more appreciative too. Of course it was because Poland had been oppressed, but also because we lived in the shadow of this huge, mysterious Russian entity, which somehow made our film statements attractive and interesting. People were curious about our cinema, our opinions, and our stylistic devices where film-making was concerned. And at the very moment when we acceded to the family of 'normal' European countries, with their

democracy, and their 'normal' political and economic problems, we became aware of our inadequacy, our struggle with identity, with our guilt, with our past – but all these issues were not so interesting to people abroad.

In some way, this lack of interest created a similar lassitude inside Poland itself. When I watch the work of today's Polish film-makers, I find them much more provincial in their interests, and in their knowledge of what's happening in the cinema around the world, than in the time when they had been practically cut off by the Iron Curtain.

**Your compatriot Krzysztof Zanussi once remarked that since the fall of Communism, the censorship of politics has been replaced by the censorship of money . . .**
Sure, and box-office became the yardstick – not just in Poland, but even in France, in Britain, in Germany . . . Twenty-five years ago it was possible to make a film that did not make a lot of money at the box-office, but that was artistically interesting and challenging – and it was considered successful. Once it was just trade papers like *Variety* and the *Hollywood Reporter* that published box-office statistics, but now regular newspapers around the world publish these figures. So today people go to a movie because they have read that it's successful money-wise. Everything is in flux with the process of globalisation, the Internet and so on, and I'm sure that something good will come out of all this – but for the moment it's killing invention and curiosity, and it's difficult to remain independent.

**Is the traditional training system still in place in Poland – attending film school, making shorts, followed by a medium-length film for television, and only then a feature film for the cinema?**
The film school is still considered as the best port of entry into the profession in Poland. But everything is shakier, and many film-makers are coming from writing and other spheres. Some are independent amateurs, who bring family money to the table, and some of these are breaking into the mainstream. But the mainstream is very weak! The biggest problem facing Polish cinema is that the budgetary and

financing system has become even weaker in our time than during the Communist era.

The establishment of the Polish Film Institute [in 2005] offers some hope, but the Institute is not financing projects one hundred per cent, any more than the CNC does in France; and the money for a film must stem from various sources. And that's difficult, because the only institution rich enough – and to some extent, obligated – to give substantial funds to film-making, is public television. And because public television already contributes via the taxation system to the budget of the Polish Film Institute, it's reluctant to give much more to individual film projects. Private TV stations are not really interested, and when they do provide some small amount of funding, it's for the most commercial films, mediocre romantic comedies that look as though they were made before the Second World War! During the 1990s, private investors enjoyed some initial success with big historical epics drawn from Polish literature, but then the genre started to flag, and so the banks behind these investors decided to withdraw from the movie scene. Co-productions are difficult, and there is not much interest on the part of other countries in Europe.

### Are producers reaching out to neighbouring countries?

Well, they try, but most former Communist countries are as impoverished as we are, and Western countries are not really interested in Polish cinema. Of course you can raise some small sums, and if you succeed in getting co-production money from three countries, you can apply to Eurimages and funds of that kind. But it involves a bureaucratic process that's complicated and not always very logical, economically or artistically. It takes for ever, it demands some skill, and it's a difficult process. What often happens is that producers will apply to the Polish Film Institute for fifty per cent of the budget. They will be accorded this half of the budget based on promises from other sources. Then those other sources will commit some ten per cent, and so the producer will wind up doing his movie for sixty per cent of the original budget.

This means that such films are not very well made, they don't have the luxury of experimentation, and remain on the technical level of an average TV movie. So they need great scripts, and great passion, in order to break through. And right now I don't sense this great passion in Polish cinema. A further point is that because most of the funds available for movie-making in Poland are state funds, their distribution depends very much on the political and ideological situation in the country – which at the moment is disastrous! At least by the final stages of the Communist era, the people in charge of distributing cultural subsidies felt some kind of guilt towards artists and the intellectuals, so they attempted to be friendly, to show that they were not so bad after all. Today, it is the opposite. They are arrogant, they have nothing to do with culture, and despise all artists and intellectuals. They are nationalistic, they are xenophobic, they are homophobic, and they are right-wing, as well as Catholic in the extreme. They are opposed to minorities, to diversity in all its form, indeed to modern thinking as such. I am really afraid of the return of some kind of political censorship. For example, I know a Polish film-maker who wrote a script about an event that occurred in a village called Jedwabne during the Second World War, when Polish peasants killed every Jew in their midst in circumstances of exceptional cruelty. The massacre only became public about five years ago. This project enables us to confront very important questions concerning Poland's past and Poland's identity. The screenplay was rejected on the grounds that it was 'anti-Polish,' because it shows some darker, guilty aspect of our history. The ruling party in Poland recently supported a law decreeing that anybody who accuses the Polish nation of any kind of Nazi or Communist crime can go to prison for three years. So this inhibits any kind of historical truth. It's similar to the Turkish law against those who speak about the Armenian holocaust. An important Turkish-Armenian journalist [Hrant Dink] has just been killed by a fanatic influenced by this kind of legislation and official propaganda.

**When you yourself are making films in different countries, do you feel a citizen of the world, or do you still regard yourself as Polish?**
Of course, my Polishness is my *self* – it's my point of view, it's my experience, it's my sensitivity, my sense of humour. But I haven't tackled a Polish subject during the past ten years or more. I would like

to make a film in Poland, but I really worry about the situation, and fear that Polish democracy could be at stake. It's a great pity, because finally we've achieved something with a generation of Poles worth fighting for, and now a group of hateful individuals try to re-write history. The major problem in Poland is a fundamental disillusionment with politics and with the state of democracy (only about forty-five per cent of Poles voted in the last elections). So along with my sister and my daughter, I developed the idea of creating a drama series for Polish TV, showing the workings of Polish politics not idealistically but realistically – and demonstrating that politicians *can* be great people. But public television has turned us down, even though we've been through about fourteen versions of the script, and even though it's quite attractive from a technical and narrative point of view.

**Two of your recent projects, *The True Story of Janosik and Uhorcik*, and *Catherine and Peter* are both set in Eastern Europe.**
Yes, three years ago we shot half of *The True Story of Janosik and Uhorcik* in Slovakia, and then ran out of funds. The Poles were supposed to participate, but so far we've had promises and no money. The idea was to make it a Slovak-Czech-Polish co-production, because it's based on the true story of a very popular eighteenth-century bandit, somewhat akin to Robin Hood but more complex. *Catherine and Peter* is a Russian story, but as we have not found sufficient money inside Russia to shoot it in that language, it will be made in English.

**In the two decades since the European Film Academy was founded, you have worked in a remarkable number of countries. Where would you say that the 'system' is most favourable to your kind of cinema?**
Technically speaking, it was France, although now it's a little less inviting. But France remains a place where film-makers coming from different nations can find financing and the production wherewithal to do their movies. Once the film is released, of course, it's much more difficult for a foreign film-maker's film to feel 'French'. I also found financing in Germany, although with the reunification of West and East Germany, many German films have been made on very important

topics and have done well with local audiences. So I feel that Germany is somewhat less eager to support the work of directors coming from outside the country than it once was. The whole situation cannot be compared with 1982, when I left Poland and found that a young film-maker was welcomed in many countries.

Telephone interview by Peter Cowie on 13 October 2006.

**Agnieszka Holland** (born 1948 in Warsaw), began her career with shorts during the early 1970s, when she could also be glimpsed acting in Zanussi's masterpiece *Illumination*. In 1977, she made her feature debut, co-directing *Screen Tests* with Jerzy Domaradzki. The follow-ing year she co-wrote Wajda's *Rough Treatment*. She continued to contribute to Wajda's screenplays, notably on *Danton, The Possessed*, and *Korczak*. Subsequently, she would collaborate on the scripts of her friend Kieślowski's great trilogy, *Three Colours*. As a director she quickly established her reputation with *Angry Harvest* (1985, nominated for an Academy Award for Best Foreign Film), *Europa Europa* (1990, which won her a Golden Globe and a nomination for Best Adapted Screenplay at the Academy Awards), *The Secret Garden* (1992), and *Total Eclipse* (1995). She always has two or three projects in hand, and has directed several productions for television. Agnieszka Holland joined the European Film Academy in 1997.

Marco Hofschneider in
*Europa Europa* (Picture:
CCC Film)

*The Perfect Circle*
(Picture: Argus Film/Cinetext)

## Filming to Survive

### An interview with Ademir Kenović

*Ademir Kenović began his career as a director one year after the first European Film Awards were held, with the feature film* Kaduz *(1989). By the late 1990s, he was well known in Europe for his compelling study of a war-torn Sarajevo in* The Perfect Circle *(1997).*

Ademir Kenović at the EFA
Conference 1989
(Picture: gerhardkassner.de)

**In 1994, while the war was still raging, you visited Berlin to accept the documentary award for *MGM Sarajevo* . . .**

Ademir Kenović: When we won the European Film Award we kept screening the film for the members of the Academy and others present in Berlin, in order to remind them that although we were happy to be there to receive a prize, we needed the international community to do something about the ghastly things that were occurring in Sarajevo. Nobody reacted for another two years, but we tried anyway. *MGM Sarajevo*, of course, was a documentary not so much about war as about a state of mind. Looking back, I am shocked to see how graphic and outrageous it looks, and how devastated our minds were at that point.

**Your film *The Perfect Circle* swept the festival circuit in 1998, and shocked people with its images from a war-torn Sarajevo. Were you able to raise the money from other countries, or did you have to rely on sources of funding in Bosnia itself?**

It was a co-production between Hungary, the Netherlands, France, and Bosnia. The CNC in Paris supported us, as did Canal Plus and ARD Degeto. We even got some funding from Jadran Film in Croatia, as well as from Bosnian television. Eurimages also came on board. One should not forget that in that period Sarajevo may well have been the most expensive place in the world! There was no infrastructure, no equipment, everything had to be brought into the country.

**How had the film originated?**

After a couple of months of living in Sarajevo, in those extreme circumstances, I realised that the situation should be documented on film. So we started making movies every day. In the autumn of 1992 I began writing *The Perfect Circle*, but we did not start shooting until February 1996, because it was unrealistic to do so earlier in view of the war situation.

The greatest pressure on me as a director was to be objective, and not show a one-sided view of the situation. So I travelled abroad as much as I could and met with the international media.

We had three different plans for each day's filming. One was a schedule known to everyone, and this we published because we didn't want people shooting at us. Of course we did not use those locations. The second schedule included places where we thought our small unit *would* be able to film. And the third schedule was a fall-back plan, if we were unable to shoot in the locations we hoped to use. Unfortunately, although the war was almost over, sporadic violence still occurred, and once a tram was hit, and some people killed, right next to the place where we were filming.

I remember that we had a dog called Nina appearing in the film, who was supposed to be hit by a mortar shell. So we attached a pair of wheels to her hind legs, so the dog was running just with her front legs and the back ones were stiff. But it took about two months for the dog wrangler to train her how to run like that! One of the main actors had bet me that she would never be able to do so, and so I won a bottle of whisky!

**Can you talk about the Sarajevo Group of Authors (SAGA)? Many Bosnian film-makers belonging to this loose association started by making documentaries during the war, didn't they?**
I initiated this at the beginning of the war. I just called my friends – fellow film-makers, my students (many of whom, like Pjer Žalica, Srdjan Vuletić, Danis Tanović and Jasmila Žbanić became successful directors), and told them that from now on we would be creating films just like Charlie Chaplin – one movie a day! Sarajevo seemed like a concentration camp surrounded with people shooting at the prisoners. All you could do was to try to survive by working at whatever you knew how to do – which was filming, filming neighbours, kids, hospitals, graveyards . . .

**How has the Sarajevo Film Festival helped to stimulate production locally?**
The event was launched during the war, and we managed to bring in the first films on VHS, U-matic, or Beta, any format we could lay our hands on, and brought them in boxes on war planes. Then we projected them as best we could on walls or makeshift screens. It

continued after the war because although our film community is small, everyone lived, and continues to live, very intensely.

Firstly, the Sarajevo Festival screens productions from this entire region of Central or Eastern Europe and the Balkans, an area of some 140 million people. So it became a meeting place where people could see these films once a year. The organisers realised that there was also a business element involved, so they forged strong links with the Rotterdam Festival's Cine-Link programme, enabling producers and film-makers to get together on feature-length projects with the potential for theatrical distribution, created by film-makers from Albania, Bosnia and Herzegovina, Bulgaria, Croatia, Hungary, Macedonia, Romania, Slovenia, and Serbia and Montenegro.

The third element in the festival is a survey of world cinema. And the fourth element is a strong support for our local Bosnian cinema. All this is shown in an atmosphere that makes visitors want to come again and again to the festival.

Telephone interview by Peter Cowie on 20 September 2006.

**Ademir Kenović** made his debut with *A Little Bit of Soul*, which he shot for TV in 1986, and which opened the Directors' Fortnight in Cannes in 1991. In 1994 he and his team won the Felix for European Documentary of the Year at the European Film Awards for *MGM Sarajevo*. In 1997 he directed *The Perfect Circle*, and then *Secret Passage* (2004) with John Turturro, a powerful film set in 1492 at a time when Spain was forcing Jews to convert to the Catholic faith. He has also served as producer on numerous feature films.

*No Man's Land*
(Picture: Noé Productions/
Cinetext)

## The Idealist

An interview with Danis Tanović

*Danis Tanović exploded on to the international scene with* No Man's
Land *(2002), which travelled like wildfire from festival to festival,
and gained recognition as one of the finest war films of modern time.
Tanović, a Bosnian then in his early thirties, has gone on to make films
in France and India.*

**Your entire early career was marked by the shadow of war. Was the
conflict in any way the trigger for your wanting to make movies?**
Danis Tanović: I was studying film and theatre at the Sarajevo Art
Academy before the war broke out. It was a multi-discipline programme in direction. So I was at the same time studying theatre,
feature film-making, radio and TV. The idea was that directing is the
same job, whatever the medium.

I would consider myself a disciple of Dušan Makavejev. Makavejev's
cinema is interesting, and provocative, from an intellectual and an
emotional point of view. I'd like, at the end of my career, to be like
Dušan is today – still exciting, still courageous.

**Did the war bring film people together in a very positive way, for example – pushing them to make documentaries and fiction films dealing with the folly of war?**
I must say that I personally had no interest in documentary film-making prior to the outbreak of the war. Then, very soon after the Serbian army had started shelling Sarajevo on 6 April 1992, I went to the local police station and volunteered, basically. But after a couple of weeks I realised that although I was in so-called 'special forces', I was not that special – so I just took my camera and started filming. At one juncture, I remember realising how stupid I felt when even considering making feature-length movies. I still loved watching them, but I much preferred being on the spot with a camera, observing real life rather than worrying about character development or production design. What I saw was so much more interesting, overwhelming, and more true.

If you lived through war in the way that I did, the only thing you are going to care about in the final analysis is not nationality or sides, it's the humanity that exists in all of us. In spite of the conflict, and everything I saw, which made me cynical at first, I do remain an idealist. I would not have had four children had I not thought that way.

Now I have the chance to travel a lot and to go to different parts of the world. I am just about to shoot a film in India, and I am more and more convinced that people are the same everywhere. Take Pakistan. It's pretty much the same country as India, and then someone just decided to divide it. All these different political systems, all these different religions – I believe that most people want the same thing: they want to be able to work, to feed their children, to have a warm house, to be able to travel . . . But today we live in a world where the most important issue is the economy, always growing, growing – why do we want the economy to grow?

**In your youth, were you aware of the keen difference between the six republics of the former Yugoslavia?**
Don't misunderstand me, but I'm rather nostalgic for the former Yugoslavia, which in microcosm was the idea for the larger Europe. I think that Europe's biggest failure was to allow what happened in my

country. Yugoslavia could still be in existence today, in the form of a federation, as a part of Europe. Don't forget that it was the most developed of all Eastern European countries – a kind of bridge between West and East. I am Bosnian, and I can't *divide* people, and today, even after this war, my best friends are orthodox Catholics, Jews, and Muslims, mixed. People in Serbia felt Serbian, and people in Croatia felt Croatian, but in Bosnia we felt ourselves to be Yugoslav more than anything. I now consider myself as European, as much at home in Berlin as in London, in Barcelona as in Dubrovnik.

**Do you think that living close to war, and to conflict between nations, makes European cinema distinctive from Hollywood cinema?**
Yes, I agree. I am a member of both the American Academy of Motion Pictures, and of the European Film Academy, and so I'm surrounded by DVDs. And when you watch the DVDs from the United States, frankly, they are all about money and form. But the European films, from so many countries, and often made on small budgets, are filled with so many good ideas, so many opinions. We have so many interesting film-makers who nobody knows. And if they do rise and are recognised, they are snatched up by Hollywood.

**When you were growing up in the 1980s, which European film-makers exerted an impact on you?**
Well, from a very young age I was always impressed by Italian neo-realism. Just last night I watched De Sica's *Bicycle Thieves* again, and when I look at how he treated his subject, I find it overwhelming. It still carries so much emotion. I also remember seeing *La Strada* for the first time, when I was about nineteen, and after that final scene on the beach we just sat there for about ten minutes, in virtual shock. I was also a big fan of Bertolucci's early work, and even today I can sit and watch *1900* for three and a half hours without moving!

**How easy was it to get financial backing from other countries for your first feature film? Could *No Man's Land* ever have been made without help from Western European producers/production funds?**
No, I don't think so. But all the credit for that goes to Cédomir Kolar,

who then became my partner, and we have a company together. We are always in financial difficulties, and if you saw our accounts, you'd be amazed (*laughs*)! So even though *No Man's Land* made money, two weeks after it won the Academy Award for Best Foreign Film, Noé Productions had to close – not because of my picture but because they had another movie which did not work. So one moves from film to film, and when you enjoy success with one particular title, you have a little bit of credit, and if you have a failure, you have very little or no credit at all. More and more, it is the TV companies that are deciding who will make movies.

**Can you describe the conditions under which you made *No Man's Land*? You were close to some real military skirmishes, I believe.**
At the time we were shooting the film, the Slovenian army was involved in military exercises. There is an ongoing dispute between Slovenia and Croatia about the territory where we were filming, but we were never shot at! The shoot was hellish, because it rained all the time, with bad outbreaks of thunder, and we fell behind schedule, so in the end it took us twenty-six days.

**Was it difficult to shoot in English with a cast from various countries?**
Fortunately, ninety per cent of my actors were well prepared. For example, Katrin Cartlidge made her own investigation/research; she met these women who were journalists in Bosnia, and she even came on set with the real clothes and jewellery that one of those women had carried in Sarajevo. It was almost embarrassing for me to be the director of certain parts of the movie, because I would do just one take, and it was perfect! The editing took just nine days, because the film had been carefully prepared prior to production. I cut the film with Francesca Calvelli, who did not speak either French or English or Bosnian, and I didn't speak Italian, so . . . ! Editing for me resembles music. If you play music, as I do, then when you meet somebody who understands the way you play, then it's simple. There is no need for words. Francesca Calvelli was someone who played the same jazzy music as I did.

**What was the reaction to *No Man's Land* in the former Yugoslavia?**
It actually won a prize at a festival in each of the six republics, which shows that everyone appreciated it. Not everyone agreed with the film, and I guess that if they had, we would have no more wars! After it appeared, I went back to Bosnia, and persuaded some of the officials in power to establish the film fund.

**What changes do you think have occurred in your film-making region over the past twenty years, and in particular, in Sarajevo?**
In 1988, Yugoslavia still existed, with a population of 20 million, and that constituted quite a powerful market. Today, it is much harder to make films. I think we have to unite in order to do so. The only good aspect of the situation is that because Yugoslavia just broke apart, Bosnian film-makers became more international than they had ever been. Suddenly they started connecting with Britain, or France, or Belgium, or Slovenia, or Spain, even Switzerland – asking for funding wherever they could get it, and trying to persuade people to help them produce their work.

Telephone interview by Peter Cowie on 7 November 2006.

**Danis Tanović** (born 1969 in Zenica, Bosnia and Herzegovina) made his first documentary, entitled *L'Aube*, for a Belgian producer. Five years later he wrote and directed *No Man's Land*, which won the Best Screenplay award at the Cannes Festival, followed by the same prize at the European Film Awards, a Golden Globe and an Oscar for Best Foreign Film, and a wide range of other awards. The following year Tanović made the 'Bosnia-Herzegovina' episode in *9.11.01*, and in 2005 he directed one of the screenplays originated by Krzysztof Piesiewicz and the late Krzysztof Kieślowski, *L'Enfer*, starring Emmanuelle Béart. In 2006–2007 he made *Tigrovi*, on location in India. He contributes music to his feature films.

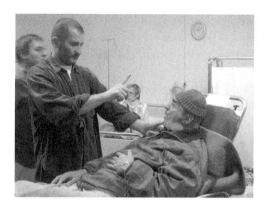

Cristi Puiu and actor
Ion Fiscuteanu

# A Question of Honesty

An interview with Cristi Puiu

*Cristi Puiu, director of* The Death of Mr Lazarescu, *has won various awards around the world. We talked to him about inspiration and responsibility and his home country Romania.*

**In the West, it appears as if Romania has mainly served as a projection space for more or less fantastic imagination. Has that influenced your work?**
Cristi Puiu: What I noticed during my entire life up to now is that Romania is a country searching for its identity. I think the main problem we have here is that we cannot find our identity. We're thinking about identity in a very opportunistic way and that's why I used to say that Romanians are suffering from this approach to identity. We don't know exactly who we are. Of course, it's easier to claim that we are descendants of Rome, of Latin heritage – that's much more comfortable because it's better to be a cousin of the French, Italians, Spanish, than to be the cousin of Slavs or Turks or whatever. But our identity is also defined by these influences – Slavic, Turkish, Armenian, Greek, or Jewish. I think we are confused and maybe that's

why we add this fantastic Vampire dimension to the Romanian identity – maybe it's easier for us to explain this confusion using these
fantastic and unreal channels.

**Do you see yourself as a cultural ambassador?**
When we are abroad, we discuss very often who we are and what we
are. But the problem is the kind of criticism I receive from those of my
people, the Romanians, who are saying that I'm not presenting the
proper image of Romania. That's not true. What I show is not ugly,
but I am not supposed to embellish [the truth]. From the start, I'm
against any kind of make-believe in relation to a story I'm telling. But
as far as I'm concerned, I cannot lie about the Romanian reality, be it
the social, political, or economic reality. In our daily life we are obliged
to lie from time to time because if you always tell the truth you'll hurt
people who are close to you. So you try to find the right way to tell
the things that are *not* nice. And this is really painful. But that's what I
force myself to do in my films, I tell the truth, whatever that is. Maybe
in a year or two I will think differently but if I want to present my
conception of a given moment, I have to be honest and believe in my
point of view. That's why there are these problems. When we're discussing my films, we're discussing cinema, not questions relating
to the image of a country or a people. And I find that reflects our
provincialism.

I have to talk about Romania and I like to talk about Romania
because I like to reveal things. Romania is a very special place with a
very special culture, and even for myself it is difficult to say that I
really know my country and its culture. It's hard to really know
something because to know it you have to define it. And trying to
define things can be really confusing. Romania, for example, is a
country where people are very kind and very warm and open, at the
same time they can be really criminal – and our history is full of
crimes. The first step we need to take is to look at our crimes and stop
thinking of ourselves as the most intelligent and beautiful and kind
people in the world like we used to do under Communism because of
the propaganda. I don't think that Romanians are different from the
French or Germans. I just think that we are in a position to assume

[responsibility for] our crimes and we are not ready to do it. And that's a problem.

**Does the area where you live, your environment, influence the stories you tell in your films?**
Of course, I think it's a question of honesty. An artist has to deliver himself when he's delivering an artistic object. The artistic object has to be an intimate part of himself, very intimately related to his biography. I am telling stories and I force myself to be honest telling these stories that I experienced. There is, of course, an important part that imagination plays in this process but the most important thing for me is to present a certain ensemble of elements which are social, economic, cultural contexts – things related to the individual, the most intimate part of ourselves, which belongs to the human being not to a certain cultural construct. When I say I'm Romanian, that's not false, it's true. But I'm also a human being and I'm interested in exploring that.

So, yes, my stories have a lot to do with where I lived – in a working-class neighbourhood with a very mixed population. During the Communist era, our block was surrounded by blocks where members of Securitate lived because one of the most important of the country's factories was in our neighbourhood. And Ceaușescu used to go there. That's why the neighbourhood had to really be inhabited by members of Securitate – just in case, you know. So it was a very mixed, there were some blocks with people like my family and some blocks with people from Securitate, the army and the Romanian police. That was then, but after the fall of Communism, they all left their houses and now they live in big beautiful villas around Bucharest. But in my class at school, people were coming from very different families. Some had fathers who were colonels and generals of Securitate and others common workers.

**In 2004 you won a Golden Bear and the Prix UIP in Berlin for your short film *Cigarettes and Coffee*; this included an automatic nomination for the European Film Awards. Has that made it easier to make your next film?**

No. I thought it would make it easier but it didn't. It has complicated my life in Romania extremely. If you get such an important award in the beginning of your career it confirms you somehow in your own eyes. But here in Romania, just after receiving the award in February, in April I submitted this new project, a feature, and in July I received a note that they wouldn't give me the money, they thought the script was stupid and I didn't deserve to be supported. So I challenged this decision and I went up to the minister of culture, and he said that somebody with these prizes deserves to have their next project financed. And that's how I received the money. But then the newspapers destroyed me, they wrote that Cristi Puiu is criticising the system but he's taking the money from it. It's very complicated. But that's how I started making *The Death of Mr Lazarescu*.

*The Death of Mr Lazarescu*

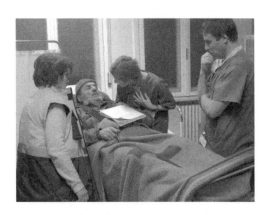

**You are planning six films about different kinds of love.**
Yes, *Lazarescu* was the first film of this project, like the first level of love. What I would like to achieve is the following: Usually, the audience feels that problems are solved, you can relax because there is a saviour – Jesus, or Buddha or Mohammed or I don't know who to save us. And I think that is a big lie, we are killing ourselves, we're killing each other. What's interesting is that people are killing each other with this so-called love – I love you, that's why I kill you. That's very strange. So, *Lazarescu* was the first part of this project, it was about love for your neighbour. This is in the Bible, love your neighbour

as much as you love yourself. In real life, people are not doing that, they are focusing just on their own interests. That's why the story is happening as it is, in a hospital, in this health care system context because doctors are supposed to take care of their patients without loving them and they are not doing it. So, it's the extreme of the extremes. There are people who receive money to care for their patients but they aren't. So, if you don't even get money, how could you possibly love or care for your neighbour? I think it's interesting to explore this, it isn't just a Romanian thing, I think it's universal. Now I am working on something related to the love in a couple, what is it, what is a marriage . . . I don't know if I'm moving in the right direction but I'm working on it.

**If you owned a cinema for one day, which films would you screen?**
Twenty-four hours? Ah, so first is *La Maman et la putain* by Jean Eustache. *A Woman Under the Influence* by John Cassavetes. *Ma Nuit chez Maud* by Eric Rohmer. And *Fear Eats the Soul*, Fassbinder. Oh, and *The Son* by the Dardennes. *Urgences*, directed by Depardon. I don't know, there are so many films I love so . . . Hitchcock's *Suspicion*. *Mouchette* by Bresson. *Trash* by Paul Morrissey.

Telephone interview by Pascal Edelmann, 29 January 2007.

Born in 1967 in Bucharest, **Cristi Puiu** studied painting and film directing at the Ecole Supérieure d'Art Visuel in Geneva, Switzerland. His short film *Cigarettes and Coffee* won the Golden Bear in 2004 and was nominated for the European Film Awards. His first feature *The Death of Mr Lazarescu* was screened in Cannes and nominated for the European Film Awards 2005.

György Palfi on the set
(Picture: Eurofilm)

## Being Hungarian

An email interview with György Palfi

**Do you remember your first film impressions?**
György Palfi: I suppose it was probably television ... My first film experience was something that came out of a television which was simply not turned off. I went to the cinema around the age of four or five – like almost every child at that time in Budapest – to watch cartoons and different animation films at a matinee (screenings before noon) in the Horizont cinema. You could arrive whenever you wanted to because the short films were shown continuously.

**If you think of European cinema, what has most influenced you?**
I'm influenced mostly by the really bad movies. Whenever I see one I feel such a big anger that I want to make my own film immediately.

**Do you feel that coming from Hungary you are looked at as something exotic?**
Hungary is a small country with a unique language, unfortunate history and a strange identity – even for us. Sometimes being Hungarian is exotic for us Hungarians too.

**Is it more difficult to get a movie financed than if you came from 'the West'?**
Of course – less networks, less money.

**In your latest film, *Taxidermia*, both food and sex are big issues. Why? What is your personal take on these?**
I just wanted to make a movie about the things I see all around me. About what I feel is important to talk about, about being human. And among these are sex and food.

**Food is one of the things that still distinguish areas in Europe from one another. What is your most absurd/bizarre food story?**
I think one of the most bizarre things is salami. It's a pig, whose flesh is put back into its guts. And what is more: it's tasty! Anyway, I can still remember the time, under Socialism, when we had to stay in long queues for more than two or three hours if we wanted to buy some bananas, for example. You could buy them very rarely and just during the winter.

*Taxidermia* (Picture: Eurofilm)

**As a final question we ask everyone: if you owned a cinema for one day, which films would you screen?**
In the morning, from 10:00 to 12:00, for the children, some very good Hungarian animation films.

12 to 4, for retired people, a Hungarian romantic film from the
1930s (*Fatal Spring*, for example) and a Chaplin movie (maybe *City
Lights*).

4 to 6 *Quest for Fire* by Jean-Jacques Annaud
6 to 8 *Paths of Glory* by Stanley Kubrick
8 to 10 Terry Gilliam's *Brazil*
10 to midnight Miklós Jancsó's *Szegénylegények* (*The Round-Up*)
Midnight to 6 am party with DJs, VJs, cocktails and food

Email interview by Pascal Edelmann in January 2007.

Born in Budapest in 1974, **György Palfi** shot to international attention
with his 2002 film *Hukkle* which received various festival awards and
won the European Film Academy's debut award, European Discovery.
His controversial feature *Taxidermia* (2006) was consequently invited
to the Cannes Film Festival.

4
(Picture: Phenomen Films)

## Thoughts from Russia
by Ilya Khrzanovsky

I don't like making films. The preparations and the shooting are always so trying. Yet I feel a strong inner need to try and share the experiences only I have, and which I think, may be both interesting and important for other people. Of course I don't believe in the educational power of film, but I do believe that for a thoughtful person, art may help to keep them as they are – as themselves, and at the same time to have an inner movement and to develop. When I watch certain films, and even more often, when I listen to music, read a book, or look at a piece of visual art, I experience a physiological feeling of change and movement within my personality, and this, as well as some moments of real life, allow me to remain myself and to be alive.

Film, as a collective art, allows the relinquishing of boundaries and gives the possibility of experiencing a life pulse that is not just localised, but that extends universally.

Making a film is difficult anywhere, especially when you are trying to make an artistic creation and not a formulaic commercial product. It is hard to finance films in Russia, as well as anywhere else. In my opinion, modern Russia is moving from a distorted reality based on

Ilya Khrzanovsky in Warsaw
for the EFA Conference 2006
(Picture: EFA / Andreas
Böhmig)

the model of socialism in the direction of a distorted reality based on the model of capitalism. Then again, socialism did not exist in Russia, and capitalism does not exist, and I am not convinced that it will exist here in the foreseeable future.

During the Soviet times there was a famous slogan: 'Our aim is to catch up with and to exceed America'. Many decades have since passed, and despite the fact that this slogan no longer hangs on red banners across Russian streets, it is still extremely relevant. In the realm of film the significance of the slogan, together with a great dislike for the US, gives birth to an ugly form.

The domain of art-house or independent film is increasingly limited while the power of commercial film is extending. Although the film industry is growing, there is no place for a serious analysis of important issues. I mean this in relation to the majority of investors, producers and television channels. Thankfully, there is the Federal Agency for Culture and Cinematography which finances films, including art-house cinema. Sadly, however, there is a lack of television backing for serious films, and systems of funding and film distribution are almost non-existent. This means that if a film is made, it is very unrealistic to think that the audience will have access to it. Therefore the budget of a film is limited to the sum of the government grant. And that means that involving a foreign producer is twice as important. Aside from the possibility of increasing the budget of the film, I see another extremely important element of such co-production, namely the possibility of testing your own project for its relevance and artistic credibility not just in the local territory of one's own country, but also in other places in the world.

Translated from Russian by Galina Kalinina.

Born in Moscow in 1975, **Ilya Khrzanovsky** studied at the Academy of Fine Arts in Bonn (Germany) and at the Moscow film school VGIK under M. Khutsiev. He made his first short film *A Bus Stop* in 1998 and his first feature, 4 (2004), was an international festival success and received a nomination for the European Film Academy's European Discovery 2005 award.

Eran Riklis on the set with actress Clara Khoury (Picture: Yoni Hamenachem)

## Slow Train to Europe
by Eran Riklis

Pack your suitcase, go over to the Tel Aviv central train station, buy a ticket and board the train. You are now leaving Tel Aviv, passing through Haifa, going across the old border between Israel and Lebanon, approaching Beirut (perhaps stopping for a quick, strong coffee), going further north through the western parts of Syria and then into Turkey. Lunch in Istanbul and then continuing into Europe – all the way to Paris where you have a meeting with some ARTE decision makers . . .

Yes, I know, you can also simply board a plane at Ben Gurion airport and land at CDG or any other airport for that matter – but the romantic notion of being close to Europe, of having a land link with it, has always been part of the Israeli dream (at least for some of us. . . ). Israel and Israelis have always been torn between Asia and Europe (in the 1960s we were champions of Asia in soccer . . . ), between East and West, between a Mediterranean, oriental culture and a European one. Society here reflects that in almost every facet of life and it's not an easy matter to cope with. I guess one could say that our heart is in the East while our body longs for the West – whatever that means if it means anything . . .

Israeli film-makers are no different in the sense that they are torn, perhaps blessed by this odd mixture. Do we go with the Chinese notion of film-making? Perhaps the Iranian one? Or is the former East European style our guiding light? Many Israeli film-makers of my generation went to film school in England – so do we follow the path of Mike Leigh and Ken Loach? And if you go back a while, say to my childhood which was a mix of growing up in Beersheba (the capital of the desert here in Israel), New York and Rio de Janeiro, then American cinema was everywhere and everything – as it was for so many film-makers around the world. So do you follow the trail of American stars that were burned into our personal and collective memory as kids, in small-town Israel, or do you follow the European trail? And do you go with Welles or Renoir?

Serious questions. . . and in the end, I can say for myself that I am a product of both landscapes, both cultures, both approaches – with an added touch of Chinese, Japanese and perhaps some South American spices. But aren't we all?

Anyway, this long introduction was just in order to establish the fact that the bottom line for me is that I am an integral part of European film-making traditions but I think I try to bring to it the unique flavour and touch of my region, my country, my people – which means I try to bring the Middle East to Europe and maintain my sanity while doing so – not an easy task . . . The Middle East – a haven of madness, joy, humour, tragedy, traditions, religions, fanatics, visionaries, hope, optimism, pessimism, breakthroughs, new horizons, a new day, the future, the past – all words used on a regular basis to describe the situation in a region that has seen it all, is ever changing and yet perhaps will never really change.

Combining all these words, all these ideas into films is a challenge but I feel it is also a duty, and I guess that is what also links me directly with European traditions of ensuring that films actually *say* something about us – wherever we are. Within the mounting pressures of pleasing the audience and the box-office, of satisfying the goddess of television, of choosing subjects that are both communicative and meaningful – the burden of doing the right thing, choosing the right path, becomes heavier and heavier. On the other hand, the sense of a pan-European film community seems to be growing every day and I always feel I have a virtual, possibly real connection with a fellow film director somewhere in Europe.

I mentioned soccer earlier – and it was not easy for Israel to become a part of Europe in sports, and possibly it is regretted as in Asia at least we used to win a bit more . . . but there are no regrets as far as cinema goes. Being a part of the European scene means you are part of a constant debate, an ongoing observation of how to take films a step further. I believe we have brothers in arms in that respect in the United States as well, around the world in fact. I don't think it's about nations and borders any more (despite the fact that some people seek to reinstate as many borders as possible), it's rather about concepts and ideas. And it's about emotions, since everything about cinema is about emotions. And in that sense the tradition that makes people emotional about things may differ widely between England, Italy and Israel. But in the end our audiences go for the same reaction – they cry with us, they laugh with us, they will go anywhere with us. And what 'my people' feel about my films does not, should not be different from what 'your people' feel about my films. I felt that very strongly when I made *Cup Final* years ago, I felt that even more strongly when I made *The Syrian Bride* more recently. And by the time this is published, I hope there will be the same feelings about *Lemon Tree*.

So again it seems I'm still at the introduction stage of this short essay – or am I? But going back to that slow train I boarded earlier – that train is still moving slowly. We are still far from being able to go to Europe across Lebanon and Syria, we are still far from resolving many things around here but as I said, we are getting closer to talking the same language of film – which, in fact, means we are developing rapidly our own style, our own statement. Because standing as a kid on the steps of the cinema at the centre of Beersheba, waiting for the 4 p.m. show to start was no different than standing in the centre of any city, any town, any village that had a cinema, anywhere across Europe, anywhere across the world. Today that unique experience is somehow reserved only for those places where the multiplexes have not taken over yet. In Israel it's already rare. In Europe too I guess, although as an art-house film-maker I am probably always destined to show my films in good, warm art-houses across Europe – and to keep the flame of these cinemas going somehow. It's a good feeling, sort of the eternal child in me always being able to go again to the warm embrace of the dark, intimate theatre, with no other films playing across the hall. And no popcorn available either . . . but I'm sure today kids will feel the same about the multiplexes one day, when they will be replaced by some other form of presentation, some other form of community experience, and their nostalgia will be for the multiplex just like ours is for the old *cinema paradiso* . . .

So where do we stand? We want to be local, we want to be international, not to mention universal (I hate using that word . . . ), we want to tell stories. It's always said that Israel is a gold mine of stories and ideas for films – and it is indeed. And not only because of what you hear and see on the news, it's because we are quite a unique blend of cultures which in fact brings Europe, Asia, North Africa, South America and North America into one condensed land, creating a new, diverse setting for great stories, as long as we know how to tell them. The bridge between us and the European film community helps us to tell these stories and to bring them one step closer to being part of European, universal (that word again . . . ) storytelling and culture. And hopefully that slow train ride is getting closer too . . .

Born in 1954, **Eran Riklis** has been active in film-making since 1975 as a director, writer and producer. After graduating from the National Film and TV School in Beaconsfield (England), he made his first film in 1984, *On a Clear Day You Can See Damascus*, a political thriller based on a true story. His film *Cup Final* was screened both in Berlin and in Venice, and, two years later, *Zohar* became a big Israeli success. His 2004 film, *The Syrian Bride*, was in the Selection for the European Film Awards 2005 and won various prizes, among them the audience award in Locarno and the FIPRESCI award in Montréal.

# 4  Acting European

*What would cinema be without its actors, without the people who laugh and cry and run, shout and suffer in front of our eyes? It is the men and women who get into a character, turn it into their own, who create a reality the audience can relate to, identify with. When they turn towards the camera, with the power of a minimal gesture they can change the mood of the film, make the audience laugh or flinch or move uncomfortably in their seats.*

*Actors and actresses in Europe are confronted with various different audiences with different tastes and languages. What are their experiences? What is it like to act in different languages? What motivates these people to dedicate their lives to audiences, to show their innermost, naked self?*

Liv Ullmann in *Skammen*
(Picture: © 1968 AB Svensk
Filmindustri)

## Being an Actor is to Recognise and to be Recognised
by Liv Ullmann

I believe that as an actor you are blessed. You get to travel, you get to meet wonderful people, and you get to be part of an environment which would never have been yours if you weren't a travelling professional. I have been an actress in the theatre and in films for almost fifty years. That's a lifetime. A quality life. The quality of this profession has been my possibility of ever-rediscovering, grasping, and revealing a reality, often far away from where I lived, far from what I was brought up to understand and accept. So much of my knowledge, of my empathy, I found watching a film in a dark movie house, sharing the experience with other people, people I didn't know. The faces and the movements and the voices from up there on the movie screen became to me – as a young girl – something more real than reality. I have a favourite film, *Umberto D.* by Vittorio De Sica, made probably so many years before most readers of this article were born. But I was born. The homeless man of the street, Umberto D., oh how well the thirteen-year-old, which I was, knew what he, the old man, felt. His pain was mine. His loneliness ran through my body. His fear made my heart bump faster. His love for his dog, and his sadness when they lost each other – that can still bring tears to my eyes. And this street where the homeless man Umberto D. lived, I recognised this as if it had been my own street. In spite of my being a little girl far from the North, protected and loved, Umberto D. and I, we were one. Even today, thinking about him, I identify, I recognise his story as my story as well. In my profession as an actor, my material is the life I am living and the life I am watching, the life I am reading about and the life I am listening to. That wonderful moment, when a ballet dancer does a leap and she stays in the air for seconds longer than is possible, that's my aim as an actor. That's what I watch for with other actors when I direct. To see something that may be possible. I wish to try for that leap again and again, and I want to be recognised, even when it fails. I wish to express something about humanity in my work as an actor, or as a director or as a screenwriter – something which may be a surprise when identified. I wish to convey a message that there doesn't have to be loneliness. That it is a human right for people to belong. So that those of us who thought we were on the outside can feel that we experience something together: A dark movie house – so good for shared feelings. To recognise ourselves, even if briefly. To recognise other people.

Most of my life I've been an actress. I've had a profession where I was always asked to share. As a child, when I acted, the only reality that existed was the pleasure of existing in this world of make-believe. I used to paint pictures. They just happened. And it never occurred to me that people and trees and houses should be depicted in any particular way if others were to recognise them and like them. My trees were violet and the sky was green. 'What is this?' the grown-ups would ask me. I didn't mind because my grandmother always said, 'What beautiful dreams you make, Liv!' The pictures were me. Later my roles were me. And some would recognise them, as my grandmother did. What more do I want as an actor? Maybe that my role – let us call her Nora – maybe that Nora plays Nora. In the best of moments that happens. The finest compliment I ever received came from a friend who quoted Zen: today you allowed the cloth to weave the cloth. The limitation of an actor is to have only yourself as an instrument, as a mean of expression. For me it is impossible, and even without interest, merrily to go through a complete change of personality from role to role. What I do allow is unknown secrets – so far from within myself that I was even unaware of them – such secrets to come forward, sparked by the shaping of my role, sparked by the experience of my life, sparked by the director. Acting for me has been stretches of happiness, when everything feels real. And even more so now that I can direct: to watch others when their soul and their life and their observation of a humanity and a human being is what they offer. The truth of imagination. A truth that, in this golden moment, is revealed for the first time to an audience. Because the actor recognised it, the audience will recognise it. A performance that makes us realise truth, at least the truth that is given us to understand.

I don't know what I prefer: the theatre or movie-making. Though I do know that movies have one thing that theatre will never have: the close up. For me it is like this, the closer a camera comes, the more eager I want to show a completely naked face. Show what is behind the skin, the eyes, inside the head. Show the thoughts that are forming. Working as an actress in a film is to go on a journey of discovery within my own self. Throw away the mask and show what is behind it. The camera comes close, so close, and the thrill is to allow it to capture what the eyes cannot see. Closer to the audience than in any other medium, the human face is shown on the screen. And the audience, in the moment of identification, should meet a real person, not an actor. Meet himself, a face confronting his. A soul to identify with. Yes, this is what I know about a human being, this is what I have experienced, have seen. This is what I'd like to share. There is no longer a question of make-up, of hair, or beauty. It is an exposure that goes way beyond because the camera doesn't only show a face, but also what kind of life this face has seen. Thoughts behind a forehead, something the face didn't know about itself, but which the public will see and recognise. Privately, we long for exactly this kind of recognition: that other people will be able to perceive what we really are deep inside. Yes, this is what I love as an actor and as a director. To paraphrase a little, no people are uninteresting. Nothing in them that is not unique in one excellent minute. Finally, this is why we actors are actors, directors, scriptwriters. The speeches of most presidents, and prime ministers and generals will surely be forgotten. But I know that Umberto D.'s pained face asking for mercy may change those who experienced it, be part of them for ever. Awaken their social conscience. It happened to me when I was thirteen.

We know, at least until this present moment, that the images and the visions of the cinemas from the most gifted creators will still fill people with a certain hope, hope that there is dignity to life. That there are possibilities, opportunities. The tragedy we film-makers are facing because of all the negative changes for creative workers in today's European policy making is, in fact, a tragedy for everyone. Not the least for the potential public. We have a world which to me seems to be governed by mindlessness. We, the cultural workers, may be facing the last moment where we still can make a difference. We can still lobby for greater issues, and be heard. Issues that deal with the mind and the soul, with the compassion and the dreams of a human being. Wars and TV speeches will never do this. But our acknowledgment of every person's uniqueness will. We are fighting for our identity. Belonging one way or another to the world of the cinema, we have an obligation because we are bearing witness to our times.

**Liv Ullmann** has worked all over the world – on stage in Scandinavia, on Broadway, in London's West End and in Australia. As a film actress she has starred in *Persona* (1966), *Scenes From a Marriage* (1974), *Autumn Sonata* (1978), to name just a few. She has received various awards, among them the European Film Academy's Achievement in World Cinema 2004. As a director, she has made five films, among them *Kristin Lavransdatter* (1995), *Private Confessions* (1996) and *Faithless* (2000) and as a writer she has written two best-selling books, translated into thirty-five languages, and several movie scripts.

*8 Femmes*
(Picture: BIM/Cinetext)

## Actresses Are Much More Intelligent
An interview with François Ozon

*François Ozon has within a short time established himself as one of the most intriguing and subtle auteurs in French cinema and, in particular, as an immaculate director of actresses.*

**You attended the FEMIS film school in Paris. How important do you think film schools are for European cinema?**
François Ozon: They enable you to progress faster, I think. I don't know about other countries, but in France there is a real culture – a tradition – of making short films. There are plenty of festivals throughout France devoted to shorts, and so, while it's never easy, there is nonetheless this sort of 'short film school'. Of course, many French directors have succeeded without attending film academies.

**What attracts you about the short film format? You began your career by making numerous shorts, and even at Cannes in 2006 your short, *Un lever de rideau*, was screened.**
I like shooting, and I don't like waiting around between projects. So working in the short-film field enables me to shoot more frequently.

**Is it possible to get shorts distributed in France?**
Often they are funded by television, and so find a slot there, plus they are screened at festivals. For example, one of my short films, *Une Robe d'été* (1996), had a lot of exposure [including a nomination for a César award], more so certainly than many shorts.

**Many actresses have received awards for their roles in your films. Do you think that it's easier to direct actresses rather than actors?**
They are much more intelligent. They accept that a man is looking at them; they accept that look and play on it. They accept direction. In any event, the actresses I've worked with have liked entering my world, they've accepted it, and they've had confidence in me. It is often more complicated with men, because they don't always have that feminine side that accepts a certain kind of domination. However, I don't think that I dominate my actresses, I think rather that there's an exchange involved. One's on equal terms, but one knows that the director has the last word – and actresses agree to that more easily than actors do.

  They're more used to seducing in life, and so they seduce the camera more easily too. Women are more accustomed to performing, they use make-up, they have their hair done, they beautify themselves for social purposes. They think more about clothes and how they'll wear them, so there's already something of an actress's work involved as a woman prepares to go out in the street each morning.

**How did you come to choose Charlotte Rampling for *Sous le sable*?**
From the outset, I wanted a woman in her fifties, someone very beautiful and who would agree to be filmed in a bathing costume on the beach! Very quickly, I realised that there weren't many women in France who'd agree to that. I met Charlotte, offered her the role, and she said, fine, no problem. As soon as we began working together, there was a chemistry between us. We understood each other almost without speaking. It was a pleasure, and during the shooting I realised that she became the subject of the film, and that to observe her was sufficient to tell a story.

**You relish a certain ambivalence in your films, and Charlotte Rampling seems to embody that to perfection.**

I really like the work that Antonioni did with Monica Vitti. I always like film-makers who fall in love with their actresses because an actor is good in a movie when he or she is loved by the camera and the director. And I like ambiguity – also mystery. I like things that are not black and white but rather more complex, grey, and I think that Charlotte can move from one extreme to the other.

*Swimming Pool*
(Picture: Fidelité Productions/
Cinetext)

**Was *Swimming Pool* an original idea of yours, or was it based on a novel?**

It was an original idea. I wanted to talk about how a book or a film could create itself, how the inspiration could emerge, and how one could start from either imaginary or real-life elements, so that the artist ends up by mixing these elements and becoming confused. I wanted to work again with Charlotte, and I offered her a role that she would have to create herself as opposed to just being herself, which she had been in *Sous le sable*. So she really did build this character in *Swimming Pool*, somewhat in the line of a P. D. James or a Ruth Rendell, this kind of English thriller writer who looks very 'British', someone respectable who, in fact, writes novels that include a lot of murders. I used this contrast. And the contrast works well with the 'little French girl', played by Ludivine Seigner.

*8 femmes* caught everyone's attention thanks to the performances of
the actresses, almost like a film by Altman or Bergman. Was it based
on a play?
Yes, on a stage play from the 1960s. It was not very interesting, a sort
of French whodunnit featuring only women. As I read it, I felt that
here was the chance to make a film about the cinema, about actresses,
and about women – an opportunity to make something playful while
at the same time rather cruel.

Was Danielle Darrieux in the original stage production?
No, I don't think so, but she had worked in the studios with the
director; the writer of the play had scripted and directed films during
the 1960s – completely idiotic pictures, notably one called *Patate*.

Your latest film, *Angel*, was the closing film at the Berlin Film Festival
in 2007. Was it based on a novel by the British writer, Elizabeth
Taylor?
Yes. I read it and fell in love with the female character who, as often
with the heroines in my films, is very contradictory. She's at once
charming and infuriating, someone who, as you say in England, 'you
love to hate'. I like English literature because of the interaction and
ambiguity that we don't have in France. French literature is more
about feelings, sentiments. . . . So, the writer who is most French is in
fact Virginia Woolf!
   *Angel* was shot entirely in English. I worked with a Franco-British
crew, and with Martin Crimp, an English playwright who translated
my screenplay (which was in French at the outset). It's a Franco-British
co-production.

Do you believe in the principle of co-production among European
countries?
Yes, I think that it's possible, but one must avoid the 'Euro-pudding'.
The director must have complete freedom in choosing his cast. So
long as directors are able to make their films in the way they intend,
that's fine, but they mustn't compromise and accept an Italian actor, a
Spanish actor, or a German actor just so that the co-production will

function. Everything must develop logically, and with justification. In the case of *Angel*, the film takes place in England, so there was a real reason for working with these particular English actors.

**Is there such a thing as 'French cinema', something that distinguishes French films from those in the rest of Europe?**
When one is in France, one realises that the French cinema is very varied. It involves films that are at once very popular, but also *films d'auteurs*, commercial movies, experimental films, and so on. So it's difficult for me, as I'm right in the middle, to have a real image of French cinema as such.

Perhaps there exists a tradition of European cinema that emphasises the importance of the auteur, but I think that probably stems from the New Wave, and the significance of the writer-director as such. In each country there are great figures – a Bergman, a Fassbinder, and now an Almodóvar – so we might say that European cinema is carried by its directors while American cinema owes more to its actors. So today we talk of stars like Brad Pitt, Tom Cruise, and Angelina Jolie, while when speaking of European cinema, one tends to say Ken Loach, Bergman, Almodóvar . . .

**Have you been tempted to work in Hollywood or outside Europe?**
I've had various offers, but I'm used to having final cut in France, so why would I work in Hollywood and lose that freedom? I think one can find quite a lot of money in Europe for co-productions, and I have managed to make my films without American financing. Perhaps it's more difficult, but one can do it. I don't want to be a prisoner of the guys who have the money, and who make certain demands on you. The more one makes films on a modest budget, the more freedom one enjoys.

Telephone interview by Peter Cowie, 6 February 2007.

**François Ozon** (born 1967 in Paris, France) graduated from the FEMIS academy in Paris and devoted himself to perfecting his craft through a series of excellent short films. In 1998 he made his feature debut with *Sitcom*, a disturbing and sardonic study of a bourgeois family and its secrets, and followed this up with the sinister, stylish thriller, *Les Amants criminels* (1999). His breakthrough on the international scene came with *Sous le sable* (2000), starring Charlotte Rampling, and in 2002 the cast of *8 femmes* won a Silver Bear in Berlin and a European Film Award. *Swimming Pool* (2003) confirmed his stature as a major French film-maker and also received a European Film Award for Charlotte Rampling. His latest film is *Angel*, shot in English and based on a novel by the British writer Elizabeth Taylor.

## Between Two Countries
### An interview with Daniel Brühl

*Already known in Germany for films like* Das Weiße Rauschen *(The White Sound) and* Vaya con Dios, *Daniel Brühl shot to international fame with his impersonation of the son in* Good Bye Lenin! *for which he received the European Film Award for European Actor 2003 and the People's Choice Award. Only twenty-eight years old, he has since starred in various European productions including* Joyeux Noël *by Christian Carion,* Ladies in Lavender *by Charles Dance, and* Salvador *by Manuel Huerga.*

**What does European film mean to you?**
Daniel Brühl: Well, my first influences and inspirations came from European cinema and my favourite films when I was sixteen, seventeen years old, were for some strange reason not *Pulp Fiction* or something like that but rather French and Italian films of the 1960s and 1970s. I loved Melville and Truffaut and Visconti. What I like so much about European cinema, and about Europe itself, is that there is such a big diversity because we have so many different countries and cultures on a comparatively small territory. You get a lot of different visions and

styles of cinema from all these countries. Every country in Europe has its own film culture and this is what makes it so fascinating. Also, I like the fact that money isn't everything, I like the way how Europeans, with the little money that they have, deal with cinema; how they focus more on the stories and the scripts. I also appreciate the different pace in films, as in French cinema which can be *so* slow compared to American cinema. The people rely on holding the moment, on somebody's facial expression, they trust in dialogue, and they focus on these things.

**Do you remember when you knew that you wanted to become an actor?**
It started when I was a kid, I am told. My mother tells me that when I was four I pretended to be dead in the bath tub. Of course, it was terrible for my mother, she started crying and then, when she realised I was just playing, she beat me (*laughs*). But I wanted to see the reactions and repeated this experiment several times and my mother, I don't know why, but she always believed it. So, lying was in fact my first passion, my first addiction; I loved it and the poor people in my family were my first victims, and then my friends at school and my teachers. Also later, I loved pretending to be somebody else or to be in a situation I wasn't in, like telling people that I was gay or that I had had a major operation which was not true. I think those were my first steps towards acting.

**But you never went to acting school. Did you ever regret that?**
No, not really. I mean, it's necessary never to stop learning. I hope I will never get to a point where I think I know everything because that would be really sad, in a way it would be the beginning of the end. But there are different approaches to acting and different ways you can learn how to act. Everybody should find out for themselves what the right way for them is. When I was twenty or so, after finishing school and my social service, I was in a state of mind where being in a school, an institution, for four years with so much competition, being among students who all want to become actors, and living with the egos of the teachers would have been the wrong thing for me. I probably wouldn't

have been tough enough to do it. So I preferred to travel the world and get to know real people and real life because for me that was an important lesson in acting. And I pretty much learned by working with actors who (*laughs*) have probably been to an acting school. My dream still is to have a mentor, an actor who I respect and admire who will be my personal teacher. But I haven't found the right person yet.

*Good Bye, Lenin!*
(Picture: X-Verleih AG)

**When you received the European Film Award in 2003 for your role in *Good Bye Lenin!*, that was almost the first time you stepped on to a European platform. What was that like?**

It was extremely important and I will never forget that moment because I received the award from the hands of Jeanne Moreau – she is one of my favourite actresses!

I grew up with two cultures, bilingually – my mother is from Spain and I was born there and I grew up in Germany, so I was always in between two countries – and my dream was always to work in different countries, with a special focus on Spain, of course, but also in France and in England. So, I was always waiting for a film that would be so successful outside of Germany that it would be my ticket to work elsewhere. Because I wouldn't have had the guts to just go there, to Spain for example, and present myself as a half-Spanish actor without having a film that people might know me from. So, *Good Bye Lenin!* and the awards helped me a lot.

**As you just mentioned, you are a bit of a European mixture yourself. Where and in what language do you feel most at home?**
Well, I grew up in Germany and I still live here, in Berlin, so I see myself more as a German than a Spaniard. But on the other hand, I have this huge passion for Spain because I miss that part of me, I haven't lived it. It would probably be the other way around had I grown up in Spain. It's funny because I couldn't even say what about me is German and what is Spanish. And to make it even more complicated, we also have family in France so as kids we grew up with this potpourri of languages. More than anything, I consider myself European. I could never say that I am exclusively German. But if I had to say what the strongest influence was, it was probably the German one.

**You have by now acted in various different languages. Which did you find most difficult and did you ever need a language coach?**
(*laughs*) Yes, twice. The first time in England when I had to play a Pole who cannot speak English [in *Ladies in Lavender*] and then starts learning it. So I had to speak English with a Polish accent – being a German! So I had a Polish-English dialogue coach. And then for the last film I did in Spain, *Salvador*. It is in Spanish and in Catalan and I was born in Barcelona and understand every word of Catalan because my mother speaks it but I never spoke it myself. Of course, it is a real story, and a real character, and this guy is from Barcelona, so I had to try – that was the challenge – to sound as Catalan, even in the Spanish that I speak, as I could. I had a Catalan coach here in Berlin, and in Barcelona, and it was quite tough because it's very different to Spanish.

**Do you think that people's impression of you changes depending on the language you speak?**
Yes, I think language changes the way you act because language has a lot to do with your gestures, with a certain way you express yourself. And German is definitely more restrained, and colder. When I speak German I don't use as much body language as when I speak Spanish. Also, the sound of my voice, that's something I don't notice but everybody who saw the Spanish film says that it's deeper than when I speak

German. Maybe that's trying to be more macho, more masculine, stronger (*laughs*). I don't know.

**Would you say that there are differences working in a French, Spanish or German film or are all sets the same?**
Well, there are differences. I mean, when it comes to the actual shooting it's pretty much the same but the surroundings, the preparations, the way people communicate, all of that is different depending on where you are. What I love about shooting in France or in Spain, for example, is that you get to drink wine with your lunch. That's something essential and I think it's great. We should do it here in Germany, it makes it much more easy-going for the whole crew, it makes everybody happier. I like that. Also, in Spain, the attitude towards time is different, they have more time (*laughs*). I have been shooting in Spain for ages and my agency here in Berlin was afraid that I'd never come back.

The Spanish, for example, tend to explain things in a longer, more extensive way, sometimes that might feel a bit redundant, but I like that, to say something and to repeat it two or three times. In Germany things are more efficient, there is a different way of communication between director and actor. Of course, it all depends very much on the person and I think you can easily end up with a cliché.

The other thing that I experienced in the films that I did is that the French and the Spanish are a bit more emotional, or they have less problems in showing their emotions in cinema than the Germans who always want everything to be very subtle, sometimes too subtle, I think. Anyway, I like to experience these different ways of acting.

**One of the problems of European cinema is that the films often don't get screened outside the country of their origin. That has to do with many actors not being known outside of their country. What do you think about the creation of a 'European star system'?**
That would be great! (*laughs*) In Germany we even have a problem trying to get the people to see our own films and I think we need stars to guarantee an interest, to get people to go to see their movies, to make them feel proud of their own film culture. I think the French do it

quite well, in cinema and in music. They have certain laws which say that a certain percentage of the films and of the music must be French. I think the star system in France works quite well, better than in Germany, and the percentage of people who go to see French movies in France is much higher than if you compare it to Germany.

We don't know enough about each others' film culture and there aren't enough European films we get to see from outside of our country. Therefore we don't know a lot of actors and directors from other European countries. I wish there were more international co-productions in Europe in the future because we have a lot of stories that we have in common, that could be told together. I talked to my father two days ago about the new film by Clint Eastwood, that war film he shot from two perspectives [*Flags of Our Fathers* and *Letters from Iwo Jima*]. That, for example, would also be very interesting in Europe, to mention an obvious topic, taking a certain incident during the Second World War, told from two or three or more perspectives.

The problem is that you get used to seeing a certain kind of cinema, and most likely it will be American cinema, with its money and its powerful industry, and the kind of promotion these films have. Of course, there are a lot of American films which are great and individual but in terms of mainstream cinema I don't think there is a doubt that these mechanisms work. The majority of people want to be entertained in an easy way but to fascinate people there is always an audience, even if it is maybe a smaller kind of audience. But it's difficult, even for German productions in Germany if they are slightly different than mainstream. I'm lucky, with all these awards and the 'Shooting Stars' programme, I am a bit known and can decide what kind of film I want to do.

It's funny, in Spain people now recognise me and that helps, it helps to have a standing. Right now people think that I'm a Spanish actor, they don't know that I am actually German, they ignore that fact – I'm Spanish, or, to be more precise, Catalan.

The Shooting Stars programme helped me a lot, even just by getting me in touch with people, with other European actors, and to exchange experiences with them. That was actually the best thing about the

Shooting Stars, that you do a tour with all these young actors to different festivals. The most interesting thing for me was to discuss with them their individual situation in their country and to see what goes on in their country film-wise.

**Do you think of yourself as a star?**
I like that (*laughs*), when the papers write that I am a European star! I like that but I have always had a problem with that term, *star*. I don't think that you can call yourself a star. Even real stars probably wouldn't call themselves a star. It has also something to do with time; it will be interesting for me to see if I can hold this up for a longer time, for some years. I would only call those experienced actors stars who after years and years still keep up a certain level of quality – not necessarily of popularity – people who do good work. Those are stars, so I would be a bit careful about using this word, I don't want to be a *falling* star. When we meet again in ten years or so, I might be more willing to see myself as a star, I don't know. You can ask me again.

**As a final question we ask at the end of every interview: If you owned a cinema for one day, which films would you screen?**
I think one of the first ones would be one of my favourite films, *Rocco and his Brothers* [by Luchino Visconti], then probably a Buñuel film, I don't know which, maybe *El angel exterminador*. I would show a Claude Sautet film, the one with Michel Piccoli and Romy Schneider, *Max et les ferrailleurs*. I would also show *High and Low* by Akira Kurosawa, and *The Shining* by Stanley Kubrick – I'd love to see that in a real movie theatre. And *The Wild Bunch* by Sam Peckinpah. Oh, and *Garde à vue*, in the original version by Claude Miller, and Oliver Stone's *Platoon*. Also, *Les 400 coups* by François Truffaut, a great film! And Murnau's *Nosferatu*.

Interviewed by Pascal Edelmann in Berlin on 24 January 2007.

Born in Barcelona, Spain, in 1978, **Daniel Brühl** grew up in Germany. After some radio plays as a child, he started to work in dubbing.

Before he started to work in film, his first acting was for television. Among his films are *Das Weiße Rauschen* (2001), *Good Bye Lenin!* (2003), *Was nützt die Liebe in Gedanken* (2004), *Die Fetten Jahre sind vorbei* (2004), *Ladies in Lavender* (2004), *Joyeux Noël* (2005) and *Salvador* (2006).

*La Double Vie de Véronique*
(Picture: Slawomir Idziak)

## Someone Has to Carry the Baby
An interview with Irène Jacob

*Irène Jacob enjoyed triumphant acclaim, at the age of only twenty-four, for her performance in Kieślowski's* La Double vie de Véronique *(1991). She went on to star in the Polish director's final film,* Three Colours: Red *(1994), and since then has acted in several European countries, as well as working in the United States. She divides her time between stage and screen.*

**What made you want to become an actress?**
Irène Jacob: Pleasure! (*laughing*) I started really being interested in becoming an actress when I was very young. I was part of various theatre groups while growing up in Geneva, writing things, improvising, and by the age of fifteen I had made small appearances on television in Switzerland.

**How did you get your first part on screen?**
At eighteen, I went to Paris, and entered a national school called La Rue Blanche, where every three months we would do a kind of show, with extracts from Chekhov, Molière, and so on in front of the people

we were working with. Casting directors would come to see these shows, and among them was the casting director for Louis Malle. They invited me to do a test for *Au revoir les enfants*. They needed an actress who could play the piano; I could play, and the casting director said, 'Oh, I know you come from Switzerland. Would you like to do our little interview with a Swiss accent, because we are thinking of using someone with an accent . . .'!

Louis really directed me very well in this film. I only had six days of shooting, and of course it was my screen debut. But he was very concrete with me. He told me to file my nails, and look at the window and yawn a bit as I sat at the piano. All the boys in the film were in love with my character, because she was the only woman around, and she showed her panties as she got off her bicycle!

**Do you find that you tend to be associated with the two great films (*The Double Life of Veronique* and *Three Colours: Red*) by Kieślowski, at the expense of your other roles? Have you been typecast?**
No. I think it was a great chance for me to work with Krzysztof Kieślowski, and these two parts were great roles in great films, and it's true that while I have done other parts in other movies that I like a lot, these two films are the ones that have been released everywhere, and that everyone knows. Krzysztof had an amazing talent in these films, and people still watch them today.

**Did he allow you to improvise at all during the shoot?**
The script was very specific, but he asked me to think of a personal dictionary of gestures, particular behaviour or attitudes. So he said that according to what the character feels in a scene, we can discover together how we can express concretely that feeling in a personal way. It could be a very small detail. Then, of course, he would express such feelings with the camera, with the light, and with the pace of the scene.

Krzysztof was not a French director, he was Polish, and I acted partly in Polish. So a lot of people thought I was Polish! And I have received offers from different directors in different countries, not just French film-makers.

**You have made films in the United States, and films in many countries in Europe. What's the main difference?**
I haven't done so many films in the United States. Working on *U.S. Marshals* was just like a visit; I knew the director [Stuart Baird], and it was fun to do. But I have not done really big films, although I've been offered parts of that kind. Instead, I tend to work on a more independent front, and I've acted for American directors like George Hickenlooper in his adaptation of Orson Welles's screenplay, *The Big Brass Ring* (1999) – films that were more European in character, where we had just five or six weeks to shoot the picture.

**How important is language? Have you suffered from the 'Euro-pudding' syndrome?**
What happens, I would say, is that with films that have many identities involved in the production, someone has to carry the baby at some point. You have to be careful that a film retains its identity. For example, the director Peter Brook always works with a multicultural crew – his actors come from everywhere, Africa, India, England, but this tends to give his work a great depth. It's very exciting to see these actors from all over the world, telling the same story in the same language with their accents and cultural differences.

It's a challenge for European cinema – what language is best for what story, combining different people from different places. As for Kieślowski, he also transcended borders, as it were. When he made *Blue, White*, and *Red*, he worked on the identity of the French flag: liberty, equality, and brotherhood. But one of the stories was set in Paris, one in Poland, and one in Switzerland. Yet these films were not 'local' in character – of course, *Red* was set in Switzerland, but we do not really care if the actors are French, Polish or English, or if they are talking French or whatever. Instead, there's a reality, a truth, that's beyond the specific country and its language.

**What was it like working with Antonioni on *Beyond the Clouds*?**
Beyond words! Antonioni could not really speak at that juncture. We had to communicate in sign language most of the time. I could ask him concrete questions, but he could respond only very modestly – 'Yes',

'No', 'Slow', 'Fast' . . . But the way he was setting up the shots could tell a lot about his intentions. Directors express themselves in the way they place their camera, and this does a lot for an actor. You realise, 'This is how the shot is going to be done, and this is how the bodies are going to move,' and suddenly there is a sensuality involved, a grammar that is specifically cinematic. It isn't just about telling a story. A director need not say much, because there are so many other ways in which you can feel his personality and what he wants. I really enjoyed working with him.

**Do you have more time to rehearse in Europe – or in any one particular country in Europe?**
It's not a question of countries. I really encourage this process, and I think some directors really love rehearsals, and love to improvise and discuss the characters with their actors. On *Othello*, which was my first film in English, we rehearsed for a week, and when I was working recently with Paul Auster on *The Inner Life of Martin Frost* (2007), we rehearsed for a week, on location, and it was very inspiring. Then there are other great directors who like to rehearse just the night before shooting, and then there are directors – apparently like Woody Allen – who don't tell their actors a thing, and yet the results are very good!

**How vital are the ties between theatre and cinema in Europe?**
It's two different kinds of rhythm. With theatre, you're rehearsing for a long time, and then suddenly you're playing every night, and each day you have this big appointment at night, as it were. I like this very much – this appointment with the public, this appointment with the play. It can last for six months. What's important is the truth, and through the truth comes the technique for an actor. More recently, during my two pregnancies I did a lot of theatre – it's easier for the insurance situation, too! I was able to appear on stage when I was eight and a half months pregnant!

**What do you like most about European film – at its best?**
Remember when Kieślowski said [at the first European Film Awards Ceremony in 1988], 'I hope that Poland is a part of Europe'? It was

very moving to hear that, because what makes it so important to be part of Europe? We need this exchange, really. Europe is rich in so many different cultural identities, and instead of trying to make a 'Europudding', we should celebrate, and understand, and encounter different ways of expressing ourselves. This is what European cinema tries to do – making it easier for Hungarian films to be shown in France, for example.

I have made films in many countries. I have done a film directed by Eldar Riazanov in Russia (*The Prophecy*), where I was speaking Russian. It was a very interesting experience for me, right after shooting *Red*. I'd seen all Riazanov's films, and I felt it was very nice to be a part of his new film. Of course I was dubbed afterwards, as I was for the Polish scenes in *La Double vie de Véronique*. And recently I made *The Education of Fairies* (*La Educación de las hadas*) in Spain. I told the director, José Luis Cuerda, that I did not really speak Spanish. But he said, 'It's adapted from a French book, and I really want you in the story.' So I had to learn Spanish, which was a hell of a job, because I really don't like it when it's not well done. Thank goodness I was not talking too much in the film!

I will always remember my first experience working abroad: spending six weeks in Poland in 1991. And because I was playing a Polish character, I asked if I could stay ten days with a Polish family, friends of Krzysztof Kieślowski, in order to experience a bit of normal life there. It was a genuine European exchange and a great chance for me.

Telephone interview by Peter Cowie on 10 January 2007.

**Irène Jacob** (born 1966 in Suresnes, France). Brought up in Switzerland, Irène Jacob studied acting in Paris, and auditioned successfully for the role of the piano teacher in Louis Malle's *Au revoir les enfants* (1987). Three years later, she was chosen by Krzysztof Kieślowski to take the lead role in *La Double vie de Véronique*, for which she won the Best Actress prize at the Cannes Film Festival in 1991. She made a second, equally impressive film for Kieślowski in 1994, *Three Colours Red*. During the past decade, she has acted in films in various countries, playing Desdemona to Laurence Fishburne's Othello and

Kenneth Branagh's Iago under the direction of Oliver Parker, and the 'Girl' in Antonioni's *Beyond the Clouds*. Her recent work includes appearances on the French stage, and also a major part in Paul Auster's *The Inner Life of Martin Frost* (2007).

Jalil Lespert with
Jean-Claude Vallot in
*Ressources humaines*
(Picture: Gilles Marchand)

## Talking to an Addict
An interview with
Jalil Lespert

*Be it as a journalist under the spell of an ageing president, a young man obsessed by the idea of sculpturing his own body to perfection, or a young police officer starting his first job, ever since he won the César for Most Promising Actor in 2001 for his role in* Ressources humaines, *Jalil Lespert has impressed audiences and critics alike.*

**You are often cast in roles of newcomers, of people moving from one part of society to another in (dis)orientation. What is your connection to these roles, what do you like about them?**
Jalil Lespert: Well, it's a bit like my life, I am close to these characters. I come from the middle of society, you know, not rich upper class, I'm quite working class. But I have learned a lot from cinema about culture and all kinds of things; I grew up with cinema, so I can manage in different parts of society, with the poor or the rich, I don't have a problem with that. Probably people see that in me, and I think I don't look like a rich guy, not very bourgeois or aristocratic, I'm just like the regular guy in the street.

**Do you try to get to know the different socio-cultural backgrounds for your roles?**

That depends a lot on the movie. For example for *Le Petit Lieutenant*, I didn't want to get too much into that because my character was only entering this world, so I had to be new in this environment every day. So, I met just a few cops and we talked but I didn't really go very far into that.

It was completely different for my character in *Ressources humaines*, here it was much more important to learn more about factory life, about capitalism in France, and of course about politics. It really depends on the character and on the movie.

Jalil Lespert in *Le Petit Lieutenant*

**How about your role in *Vivre me tue*? Did you prepare physically for that?**

Of course, yes. For this movie, it took about ten months. It was quite boring actually (*laughs*), but the character was great so I did it. It was interesting because this is really another world, where people do bodybuilding *every* day, it was a really special experience for me. I met a lot of them during these ten months which was interesting to build the character but quite boring for me personally (*laughs*). But it was good for the movie to be true.

**Is there a single role you found the most difficult?**

I don't think so. What is difficult for me is when I do something where I don't really feel anything. During the shooting I am sad because I don't feel I'm the best actor to do it or maybe it isn't my kind of movie. It doesn't happen very often but it did a few times.

For the movies that we talked about, it wasn't difficult because acting in cinema means you have a lot of people around you. And if the director is good and interesting and smart it's easy because you go through the adventure of making a film *together*. Everybody is working on the same thing. So you just have to be concentrated, especially when you have to cry or you have to die. But it's an easy job (*laughs*), you're just dealing with emotions. And if the director and the story are great, emotions come easily which is not the case when the movie is bad. So, the most difficult is to act in a bad movie (*laughs*).

**But how do you know, when you get a script, what divides the good from the bad?**
I don't know. It's something really personal and maybe it's a good movie for others but not for me. I mean, it hasn't happened so much to me, but in the few cases when it did, I knew from the beginning that it wasn't my cup of tea. But I said, I'll go for it anyway; it'll be an adventure, something different, maybe a popular movie. And in the end it's just boring and I am sad during the shooting, sad after the shooting, so it's not good for me, I cannot do that very often.

**You are also working as a director. Is that where you want to ultimately go or have you always wanted to be an actor?**
No, actually I wanted to be a lawyer (*laughs*).

**Yes, right. What happened?**
I don't know, too many dreams . . . No, I always loved cinema, I grew up with it, when I was maybe eighteen years old, cinema was my grammar, my language. But it was never my dream to be an actor. In the beginning I was just curious to see how you do a movie because for me it's fascinating how a film is created. People liked what I did and called me back and so I became an actor. It was really fun and it became a passion. And I love my job, it gives me great pleasure. I like to express myself but I don't know how to write a book or how to paint – the only thing I can do is cinema. And I love it! I love

working together with a crew, that's how I feel and that's why I'm doing it.

**So how did this move from acting to writing and directing happen?**
The first short film I did, I did with something like €1,000, with a DV cam. We just shot it and it was really fun to do it. So I wrote another one and it became more serious. In cinema I like to write, I like to shoot the movie, I like the editing – I like all parts involved in making a movie. It's my passion, I love cinema, I love to watch films, to act in them, to make them. For me it's a creative process like writing a book, where you think about the story the whole time, month after month after month. It's a bit of an obsession but I love it. I'm an addict!

**What role has European cinema played in your life?**
First of all, Europe means a lot to me. I am thirty and so I grew up with the idea of Europe. I did my first short film in the Netherlands and for me it is fantastic to go anywhere, well, almost anywhere, in Europe. It's bigger than your small town or country, it gives you a different perspective. And I hope that cinema will go that way and create a real European union, doing movies with each other, telling stories that we share.

For example I love English actors, or Almodóvar who I think is a genius. And I hope that one day Italian cinema will again be like what it used to be. Lars von Trier is another genius; there are a lot of great directors in Europe. And I hope that in the future we will manage better with the audience because in Europe we have a lot to say and a lot of talent to do it. It's sad that nowadays we only have a small share of the market, more than half of it is dominated by American films. I hope it will be the opposite and that we will have more European films in a few years.

**What about yourself? Would you describe yourself first of all as a Parisian, a Frenchman, or a European?**
As a human being, of course! (*laughs*) I'm all of that, I'm French and I love France. And I hate France. I'm Parisian, I hate Paris. And I love Paris. And I'm European. I love Europe because I don't even know all

of it, it's something bigger. So I want to become more European than French or Parisian.

**What about working in other countries?**
I haven't worked so much in other countries because people never asked me to. And I'm not so interested in working for a big American movie shooting in Paris – you know, like an American comedy about France and the French where you get a small part as the bad French guy or the French lover, a typical cliché. That's not very interesting.

**As a final question, we ask everybody: If you owned a cinema for one day, which films would you screen?**
Oh, my God! Let me see, there are so many films . . . Which one to choose? I'd say *La Dolce Vita*! Yes, *La Dolce Vita*! But there are so many, I would have to own that cinema for two years to show them all. I'd love that!

Telephone interview by Pascal Edelmann on 21 February 2007.


Born in 1976, after his *baccalauréat* **Jalil Lespert** started studying law. But in 1994 he accompanied his father, the actor Jean Lespert, to a casting for Laurent Cantet's short film *Jeu de plage* and consequently received his first acting engagement alongside his father. In 1999 he collaborated again with Cantet in *Ressources humaines* for which he received a César in 2001. In 2002 he impersonated the little brother who wants to be a bodybuilding hero (alongside Sami Bouajila) in Jean-Pierre Sinapi's *Vivre me tue*. Among his other roles are the journalist Antoine Moreau in *Le Promeneur du champs du Mars* by Robert Guédiguian and the young police officer Antoine Derouère in Xavier Beauvois's *Le Petit Lieutenant*.

# 5  Finding a New Approach: Dogma

*In 1995, a group of Danish film-makers rocked the film world, establishing a revolutionary set of rules for film-making, and invading film festivals and cinema screens with a distinctive, rough and not always comfortable look. Thus Dogma was born. Not everybody liked it and not everybody has to. But without doubt it has exerted a strong influence on film-making and has set an astonishing example for film-makers all over the world, demonstrating that it is possible to make successful films on a low budget, in a small film nation, and without a tripod.*

# A New Wave in Danish Cinema
## by Henning Camre

Evolution is regarded as the reliable road to progress, but this is not necessarily the case for art. In the late 1980s, Danish cinema had evolved nicely: two Oscars for best Foreign Language Film and a Palme d'Or at Cannes. Who could ask for anything more?

From an artistic standpoint the films of the day did not break new ground in either aesthetic terms or general ways of working. They did not trigger a new direction or 'tendency' to which one could either adhere or against which one could rebel. These were isolated works, as had been many films in previous decades, perhaps providing inspiration but not leaving any tracks.

Graduates of the Danish National Film School had been smoothly absorbed into the industry throughout the 1970s and 1980s but it was evident that there was a mis-match between the ambitions of the talent coming out of the school and the lack of ambition and the complacency of a production environment reluctant to take on board fresh ideas and ideals.

As the director of the Film School at the time, it was my vision not only to train our students to a high level of professionalism but also to expect and demand of them that they go on and revitalise Danish film and change the industry.

It took a young rebel and his fellow students to drive that change and to apply the film school's ideals to the industry, and it took a new and alert public film body to capture the fire and build it up through a sharpened and updated national film policy that would be instrumental in bringing about renewal.

The creation of Zentropa in the early 1990s, followed closely by the setting-up of Nimbus, changed the situation for good. It marked the necessary break with the past. The initiators were all film school graduates and they shared if not the same interests and aesthetic sensibilities, then at least a language in which to communicate, understand and disagree. Leading the change were Lars von Trier and producer Peter Aalbæk Jensen, by any measure an odd couple. But the Zentropa hub turned out to represent a creative and organisational synthesis, an irresistible and provocative challenger to the old world order.

At Zentropa, von Trier as a co-owner could have it all his own way. The working conditions were shaped to optimise his creative capabilities but the ambitions went further than merely establishing a company for the sake of one film-maker. Von Trier and Aalbæk Jensen wanted their talented contemporaries to join them. Many did, attracted by the company's commitment to collectivism and to the merging of creativity and business sense.

The first several years for Zentropa were characterised by a lack of focus and direction. Only a few Zentropa films were successful, but the establishment of a viable creative space was decisive for what was to come.

Nimbus emerged as an ally as well as a competitor. It was headed by two producers, Birgitte Hald and Bo Erhardt, and by director Thomas Vinterberg, all of whom graduated from the film school in the same year. Nimbus and Zentropa, physically located under the same roof, soon became the hotbed for the entire talent pool that was to become the 'Danish New Wave'.

Lars von Trier had already made remarkable films: *The Element of Crime* and *Europa* made his name in Cannes and all over the world.

Neither of the films was commercially successful, but it was obvious to everybody that here was a film-maker of a different calibre. However, he had nowhere to go. An obsession with Dreyer and Tarkovsky and confidence in his own talent were not enough to persuade anyone in Denmark to give him the backing he needed. His trademark was the expensive aesthetics that threatened to become his own worst enemy.

It's notable that, being such an eccentric and uncompromising director, von Trier diverged sharply from the traditional *auteur* stereotype: starting at the film school, he always worked closely with co-writers, cinematographers and editors throughout all stages of development and production.

His first two feature films, *The Element of Crime* and *Europa*, are filled with grand, visually refined tableaux but they come across more weakly on the psychological level. The actors are quite clearly relegated to the role of mere appendages, subordinated to the complicated technical set-up.

Letting loose this elitist film-maker on a television series for the national broadcaster, Danmarks Radio (DR), was either the result of momentary madness or the consequence of a synergy that was developing between TV drama and the cinema world. In any case, it marked a shift whereby television, which had traditionally used in-house people, now invited an outsider, von Trier, along with key members of his team and Zentropa, to take charge.

The carefully calculated and often cumbersome set-ups of von Trier's previous work are absent from his television series *The Kingdom*. Again, several members of his creative team were involved in developing a new aesthetic, this time a major departure from both orthodox TV aesthetics and von Trier's own: jump-cuts, available light and hand-held camera had taken the place of precision-choreographed, monstrous camera movements and demanding lighting set-ups.

Von Trier had allied himself with one of the realistic masters of Danish cinema, Morten Arnfred, who brought experience in working with actors and in setting them free to contribute with their talent. A new sense of humour arose alongside the artistic ambitions. It seems that von Trier had found a release through breaking down the division between serious art and popular appeal. Much to Aalbæk Jensen's delight and relief, it had become 'acceptable' to von Trier to have an audience.

With *Breaking the Waves*, von Trier advanced further, experimenting with hand-held, this time on 35mm. His new interest in the actors entailed his offering better access, contact and intimacy. He had clearly started a vigorous process to free himself of the heavy technical apparatus upon which he had been so reliant, and he would now be able to fully exploit other, more essential, cinematic means of expression.

## The Great Break with the Past

It was in the inspired, individualistic yet collectivist atmosphere of Zentropa and Nimbus that the design of what was to be a huge shock to wide circles of the film world, came into being. Von Trier and Vinterberg drew up the Dogma rules. First seen as a provocation, then ridiculed, they were finally almost forgotten, except by the Dogma brothers.

The rules, or 'commandments', were seen as inappropriate. Why did there need to be restrictive rules of any kind? Surely they would only hamper creative freedom, ruin the film language and lead to the demise of cinema. Wouldn't audiences turn their back on this kind of crap? To those familiar with the Danish National Film School's working and learning methods, however, rules were fundamental to creation. The school's basic philosophy about teamwork – about all key members of the film team being contributors to the storytelling – was, though simple, also important and distinctive from the traditional ways of working.

Dogma may be seen as the logical outcome of a slow maturing of several factors, sometimes working in sync, sometimes out of sync, that led to the new conditions and a new basis for film-making in Denmark.

Without the lucky coincidence of a fair number of significant and charismatic individuals, the impact of the film school and the public film support system, there would have been no Dogma.

The first four Dogma films, however, almost did not come about. The Danish Film Institute of the time could not find a way of supporting the productions or any reason for doing so, and it was actually DR-Television that backed the first productions, presumably in return for the success of *The Kingdom*.

The notion of a Danish New Wave was born in Cannes in 1998 when the two first Dogma films, *Festen* (*The Celebration*) and *The Idiots*, were selected for the main competition.

In the ten years following, Danish film has gone from strength to strength. The ten Danish Dogma films were to achieve both artistic and commercial success, travelling all over the planet. Dogma gave the film-makers a sense of dignity and self-reliance: they were able to make films without having to spend years scrabbling for investment. The later Dogma films (such as *Italian for Beginners*, *Open Hearts*, *Kira's Reason: A Love Story*) were given basic funding by a re-structured Danish Film Institute that was now able to support the films without reducing their artistic freedom.

The Dogma rules were widely copied all over the world. However, the fact that they do not represent a success formula for film-making is evident from the lack of artistic and commercial success of Dogma films produced outside Denmark. Dogma was much more a mindset and a way of working, and it could not easily be replicated by film-makers with a traditional film background.

Dogma was never meant to be *the* new way of making films but rather a necessary purification process, a cleaning-up of film language to bring it back to its most essential components: story and actors.

Dogma was from the outset conceived to be shot on 35mm film, but economic constraints led to the majority of the films being shot on digital. This offered a new-found freedom to working with actors without limitations. This in turn led to a dramatic change in acting style and an increase in performance intensity.

Dogma meant a change in the fundamental attitude towards film-making in general, and as more films came out, it opened up into a big diversity in expression and style, even in genre, a term that paradoxically was banned by Dogma.

Dogma inspired, provoked and challenged everything, and those who did not surrender to Dogma had to find other ways to keep pace. The Dogma directors all went on to do other, non-Dogma films but I believe that none of them went on unaffected.

## The Talent Pool, the Film School and Public Film Policy

It is the aesthetic, intellectual and spiritual fellowship of a whole generation of film-makers, growing up together at the Danish National Film School, which has created the fabric of modern Danish film production and film culture. Other people, of course, coming from other walks of life, took part but, in so doing, they too subscribed to the underlying ideas and ideals.

When the new Danish Film Institute was established in 1998, it was only natural to see it as a continuation of the ideas, hopes and demands that had shaped the Danish Film School. It was now possible to develop a proactive and interventionist film policy that could secure the conditions for film-making and for a generation of brilliant film-makers that would be able to realise their potential to the full. A critical mass of talent had already been assembled, changes in the production sector were well underway, but more options for producing films needed to be found. A massive new injection of public funding made this possible.

The new policy was built on quality, volume and diversity. Understanding that the investment in talent needs to be followed through includes the will to take big risks. The frequency with which an individual gets to make a film must be high: nobody improves by making a film only every four or five years. Active development support to optimise projects has underpinned the production support schemes.

The newest addition to this active film policy has been the establishment of New Danish Screen. It was created at the point at which Danish film was considered universally successful. New talent was to be given the chance to gain a foothold and established talent to take on new challenges. New Danish Screen is based on low-budget thinking. Not expensive films made cheaply, but projects developed according to the available budget: pure film-school thinking. A string of films have come out: *A Soap, Princess, Off Screen*, all accomplished festival films. In New Danish Screen, the conventional has no place, and experimentation – in the best meaning of the word – is mandatory. It is about new form, new aesthetics and new ways of conveying content. But at the end of the day, it is content over form.

In the last ten years we have seen the closing of the traditional gap for European cinema between film art and 'mere' entertainment. The idea that art films were synonymous with films not having (or needing) an audience, while entertaining films did not deserve to be counted as real films, has divided film-makers, critics and audiences in Europe for decades. What has happened in Denmark shows that the traditional barriers can be broken down and that Art + Commerce is an option.

**Henning Camre** (born in 1938) started out as a cinematographer, becoming head of the department of cinematography at the National Film School of Denmark in 1971. In 1975 he became the school's artistic and executive director. From 1992 on he was director, later chief executive, for the National Film and Television School in the UK. Henning Camre became the chief executive officer of the Danish Film Institute in 1998.

*Open Hearts*
(Picture: Dansk
Filminstitut/Cinetext)

## A Curse and a Blessing

An interview with Paprika Steen

*Paprika Steen is one of Denmark's liveliest and most successful young actors, and has appeared in some of the key Dogma films, under the direction of Thomas Vinterberg, Lars von Trier, and Søren Kragh-Jacobsen. Since 2004, she has also gone behind the camera, directing the much-acclaimed* Aftermath, *and following it up with* Till Death Us Do Part *in 2007.*

*Aftermath* by Paprika Steen
(Picture: Erik Aavatsmark)

**What made you want to become an actress, and can you say something about your training?**

Paprika Steen: I became an actress because my mother was an actress! And my father was a musician, and my four brothers are musicians, and my stepfather was a painter. Of course I reacted briefly against all that when I was a teenager – I wanted to be a dentist or a photographer – but that lasted about a month! I was nine years old when I decided to become an actress, and I've followed that dream ever since.

I went to theatre school at the age of twenty-three – that's a pretty average age in Denmark for that course – after having tried for a long time to be accepted. I did not know whether I wanted to be a serious actress, or act in comedy, but I knew that I wanted to make films. My generation in Denmark was the first to be so utterly focused on film. Before that, the emphasis had been on theatre and television plays and the drama schools weren't that hot on films. In fact, we only had two weeks of film education out of four years!

I was fortunate, however, because in my third year at the theatre school I was allowed to work with the Danish National Film School, and one of the students in the class was Thomas Vinterberg. We became friends, a whole group of us, and we appeared in film school films. Theatre was also very important for us but with hindsight I can see that in my heart I knew I would act in movies. But at the theatre school, people told me that I would never do well in the cinema because I was too expressive, too loud, too eccentric.

For the first few years of my career I concentrated on comedy, and I was regarded as 'the funny woman' of Denmark! I was doing sort of *Saturday Night Live*-type shows every Saturday, and I was working with three other people and we started mostly underground and then eventually broke into television.

**Why do you think that Dogma proved so successful?**

I think that the big breakthrough came when we started to concentrate on the screenplay. Before that, the scripts weren't that good. If you wanted to make something natural and real, you had to improvise because the lines were always very heavy, very theatrical. Of course someone like John Cassavetes had been doing that more than twenty years before us, but that was my inspiration as an actress – Gena Rowlands was my great idol, and I was anxious to follow that path. But I didn't see how I could do so in Denmark, because we almost only made movies about young, teenaged people – really great movies, but often with amateurs and real youngsters – so adult films, as it were, only rarely emerged from our studios.

So improvisation was something we did because we didn't know how to make things work otherwise. This was at theatre school and on stage, before Vinterberg and Dogma came along, not forgetting Nicolas Winding Refn who made *Pusher* three years before Dogma . . . Then I worked also with various new playwrights, who were trying to develop the language.

**What were the limitations placed on you as an actress by the Dogma directors? Did they tell you, 'You can't do this, you can't do that'?**
Well, in *The Celebration* nothing was improvised, except for one scene – where I'm studying the letters from my sister. There's also one scene where Thomas Bo Larsen and his wife are having an argument. We knew each other so well by then – Thomas Bo Larsen, Ulrich Thomsen, Trine Dyrholm and I had been working with Vinterberg on his first feature film (*The Biggest Heroes*, 1996), and several of us had worked with him at the film school. We were friends, and we were inspired by the same movies, loved the same scenes – so when we came together that summer we knew what Thomas wanted. We all liked *Fanny and Alexander*, we all liked Cassavetes, and we all liked Robert De Niro, and *The Godfather*, of course.

What I liked about *The Celebration* was that it looked at what it was supposed to do, and the story became what it was because of the Dogma rules, and the same applied to *The Idiots*. I always remember the scene when we are going downstairs to have our own private party to avoid the really gross guests who have turned up for the dinner. And I take a glass and I say, 'I hope it's not a Disgusting One's glass!' Actually an improvised one – I delivered the line in a very Danish way, so it's difficult to translate. But it became one of Mogens Rukow's favourite lines, and when you ask students at the Danish Film School, what line do you like best in Danish cinema, I've heard that some of them choose 'The Disgusting One!'

**Is there a relationship between a Dogma film like *The Celebration* and a typical Strindberg play, in which the characters tear each other to pieces?**
Definitely. The new wave of Danish social realism is very much related to Bergman and Strindberg, and Ibsen – and the Swedish playwright Lars Norén. We are coming from a cold country, and all our emotions are 'indoors'. A lot of our tradition stems from that, you know, the 'baiting' at the dinner table, and the way people start drinking and then the truth comes out . . . I think it's the Scandinavian way. We are Christian and yet not Christian, but we don't have the temperament of the south and its difficult to sit and meditate outside in the streets having a coffee in this cold freezing part of the world. On the other hand, we don't have the John Osborne tradition, but in the UK they have this working-class/upper-class thing. Being intellectual about how you feel is, I think, extremely Scandinavian – maybe because of our famous welfare state.

**You appeared as Pernille in Søren Kragh-Jacobsen's *Mifune*. Søren's technique was more classical up to that point. What was it like working with him, and on that film?**
Well, Lars von Trier, Thomas Vinterberg, and Søren Kragh-Jacobsen are as different as black and white and brown! They are all very, very Danish. For many years, Søren was *the* one. During the 1980s, he was the one who made things come alive on screen, and he was my idol in the days before von Trier and Vinterberg. We all knew him as the warm, Big Brother guy. So when Dogma came along, Søren, as the Golden Boy of our cinema, had to do a Dogma movie. I was only on *Mifune* for five days. For some strange reason during the mid–1990s, I was the actress, like Elaine May, who directors like to call to read their scripts, asking me to suggest who should act in a film, wanting my opinion on the story – because I'm very opinionated! When Søren met me for coffee and we were discussing the screenplay, he said, 'Well, you've been in the first two Dogma movies, you should

be in this one, too!' So it was becoming a sort of tradition for me to be in the Dogma films, maybe for luck and superstition.

The difference between Søren Kragh-Jacobsen and Lars von Trier is that Søren wants the warmth and the poetry to emerge from the characters. You can be a cold character but you always have to find some kind of hope in his movies. He's not so cynical on screen. I wouldn't call him sentimental, but he's looking for the light and hope in every story he directs. He likes it to be very lively – things can be very raw but he wants the emotion and sweetness in his characters to show.

**Do you feel that Dogma has enabled actors to reveal more of a character? For example, in *The Celebration*, the emotions are exceedingly raw and unforgiving.**
For me, it was paradise. I had only been on television up to that point, and in a couple of children's movies where one played a little melodrama, slapstick or comedy. But *The Celebration* for me was my school, and it was only at that juncture that I realised I wanted to make *real* movies, that this was the right way for me.

**Your debut as a director, *Aftermath* (2004), attracted widespread acclaim. Was it based on anyone you knew?**
It was based on a script written by Kim Fupz Aakeson, but of course it was also influenced by a lot of personal experience – not with children dying in my family, but dealing with sorrow, because I'd had a lot of sorrow in my life and it was important for me to find out how to deal with it. Kim sent me a story outline, and I fell for it because I could relate to it. And of course I made a lot of suggestions as to how the story should develop, but he wrote every word.

**Do you adhere to the Dogma commandments in your work as a director? If not, why not?**
I wanted to do a movie that was completely different to Dogma. At that point, I was sick of the hand-held camera and video, and I wanted to do a beautiful movie, with lots of silence, quiet sound –

which you can't do under the Dogma rules. I wanted to dwell on situations, not use a lot of words, with no improvisation at all. I wanted to make a very controlled film! And definitely not a movie for everyone.

I see the Dogma wave as both a curse and a blessing for Denmark. It's been really hard to get out of it, but it has also helped us a lot. I loved what we did with those first Dogma films, but I don't like the idea that everyone's going to make a Dogma film just for the sake of it. We have to refer to that 'wave' for the rest of our lives, which is great, but it's also a curse – which explains why, when I moved to direction, I wanted to embark on something totally different to what I'd been doing as an actress. Of course I had learned everything from those Dogma days, and working with so many different directors – Susanne Bier, for example, on *Open Hearts* (2002).

**This year you are directing a second feature film, *Till Death Us Do Part*. You are not acting in it. Would you find it difficult to direct yourself? What made you so eager to go behind the camera?**
It's a very dark comedy. I am not acting in it; I think I'm too shy to appear in my own movie. I'm very Danish in that respect. But maybe I will direct myself in the future. Certainly in my first two films I did not feel the urge to do so, I wanted to be behind the camera, and have a visual concept. But I'll never say never.

**Are there any directors who have inspired you as a film-maker?**
My first film was inspired by Sean Penn's *The Pledge* (who *did* direct himself in his first movie, by the way!), and by Ingmar Bergman, and by Paul Thomas Anderson. Also Todd Solondz and Ang Lee. I think that *Happiness* and *The Ice Storm* are two of the greatest films of the 1990s. Of course my roots are in Scorsese, Cassavetes, and Coppola and that generation. But also in Bergman and Bo Widerberg, and the classic Italian films. The funny thing is that whenever I'm talking about what an actor should be wearing, or how he should look, I keep returning to the French New Wave. I want all my female characters to be in trench coats, and in high heels and looking beautiful – although my new movie is very far from all that.

**Do you feel that Dogma has changed the face of film-making in Europe, or even further afield?**
In northern Europe, yes. I don't think that southern Europe will ever take it on board. They are so much more into colours, temperament, emotions and they have their religion also; personally I think they are much more influenced by the Almodóvar style, and by painters and music. But then I don't like to generalise.

**Have you been tempted to work outside Scandinavia?**
I worked on a small role in the United States (in *Forty Shades of Blue*). And I would actually love everyone to call me from all over the world, because I know so many different languages, and love to be a stranger 'lost in translation'. One must understand that Denmark is a small country, and although I won all the national acting awards in 2004 for *Open Hearts* and *Okay*, I have not really been offered any major parts in Denmark since. It's as though you have your limited spell here, and maybe my time will come again sometime. So now I'm working a little in Germany, a little in Sweden, and directing of course.

**How do you mix theatre, film and television in your work in Scandinavia, where it's such a tradition to do all three media?**
If you do too much television work, you notice it when you start acting in movies. With TV, you work so fast that you never have time to get deep into your character. Stories are told on television so that everyone can understand them, and that can rub off on the movies, although a company like HBO in the States is doing some really great work. I feel that for the next five or ten years television in Denmark will continue as it is, with very easy-to-understand metaphors and so on, and then will come a point when they have the courage to probe more deeply into a story and develop the characters more richly and dangerously as in *The Sopranos* or *Six Feet Under* and that kind of great character-driven TV. I love theatre, and I've done quite a lot, but on stage you have to grab the audience, you have to *perform* so much . . . I like to appear in one play every year or every other year.

Telephone interview by Peter Cowie on 15 January 2007.

Added by e-mail:

**If you owned a cinema for one day, which films would you screen?**
My list of a day in the cinema would maybe look like this:

*The Dictator* Charlie Chaplin
*Nashville* Robert Altman
*The Conversation* Francis Ford Coppola
*Jaws* Steven Spielberg
*Roma* Roberto Rossellini
*Love Streams* John Cassavetes
*This is Spinal Tab* Rob Reiner
*Raging Bull* Martin Scorsese
*Manhattan* Woody Allen

As you see I'm very indecisive, and very mixed taste . . . but very old school ☺.

**Paprika Steen** (born 1964 in Copenhagen, Denmark) studied drama and film in her native Denmark, and made various TV appearances as a comedy actor before taking the part of Helene in Thomas Vinterberg's *The Celebration* (*Festen*, 1998). In the same year she had a small role in Lars von Trier's *The Idiots*, and in 1999 appeared in Mifune's *Last Song* (*Mifunes sidste sang*). She won the Danish Academy Award for her acting in *The One and Only* (*Den eneste ene*, 1999), and three years later earned a nomination for a European Film Award in the bittersweet comedy *Okay* (directed by Jesper W. Nielsen). She took two Danish Academy Awards – for *Open Hearts* and *Okay*. Since 2004 she has combined directing her own films – *Aftermath* (*Lad de små born*, 2004), and *Till Death Us Do Part* (*Til døden os skiller*, 2007) – with acting in Germany, Sweden, Denmark, and the US.

# THE VOW OF CHASTITY

'I swear to submit to the following set of rules drawn up and confirmed by DOGME 95:

1. Shooting must be done on location. Props and sets must not be brought in (if a particular prop is necessary for the story, a location must be chosen where this prop is to be found).

2. The sound must never be produced apart from the images or vice versa. (Music must not be used unless it occurs where the scene is being shot).

3. The camera must be hand-held. Any movement or immobility attainable in the hand is permitted. (The film must not take place where the camera is standing; shooting must take place where the film takes place).

4. The film must be in colour. Special lighting is not acceptable. (If there is too little light for exposure the scene must be cut or a single lamp be attached to the camera).

5. Optical work and filters are forbidden.

6. The film must not contain superficial action. (Murders, weapons, etc. must not occur.)

7. Temporal and geographical alienation are forbidden. (That is to say that the film takes place here and now.)

8. Genre movies are not acceptable.

9. The film format must be Academy 35 mm.

10. The director must not be credited.

Furthermore I swear as a director to refrain from personal taste! I am no longer an artist. I swear to refrain from creating a "work", as I regard the instant as more important than the whole. My supreme goal is to force the truth out of my characters and settings. I swear to do so by all the means available and at the cost of any good taste and any aesthetic considerations. Thus I make my VOW OF CHASTITY.'

Copenhagen, Monday 13 March 1995

On behalf of DOGME 95

Lars von Trier
Thomas Vinterberg

# 6 European Success Stories

*The French auteur cinema, the recent success of German films, the career of Bernardo Bertolucci, the power of Almodóvar's imagery, or the rising star of the documentary genre . . . Every so often, European cinema has brought forward impressive stories of success. What is the secret behind them, and who are the people facilitating these developments and careers? And what are their motivations and aims? This chapter takes a closer look at some of the many success stories in European cinema.*

# Dedicated to Auteur Cinema

## An interview with Margaret Ménégoz

*Margaret Ménégoz is president of Unifrance Film, the institution charged with the promotion of French cinema throughout the world. She is also an experienced producer, having worked notably with Eric Rohmer for many years.*

**As head of Unifrance, what do you think sets French cinema apart from other European film-making countries?**

Margaret Ménégoz: There are several reasons, which are in fact very pragmatic. Angela Merkel, the German Chancellor, asked me the same question in Berlin last year. She asked if it was because the screenwriters in Germany or in other European countries were not so good as their French counterparts – or was it that their actors, their directors were not so good? I said no, but that in France we have constructed a system that allows 250 films to be produced each year. We revere our *auteurs*, and we have established legal rights for *auteurs* very different to those in other countries, not just in Europe, but throughout the world. We are very far advanced in this respect where copyright is concerned, for we believe that an *auteur* has an inalienable right to his work, and that nobody can interfere with his work, not even the producer. So it's the sovereignty of the *auteur* that remains important in France.

What distinguishes French cinema from the cinema elsewhere is this position given to the *auteur*, and our total belief in variety. We don't just support a particular kind of film-making; rather, we have focused on retaining the widest possible variety in production and creativity.

**France produces regularly about 250 feature films per annum. What proportion of these is exported?**

When the European Film Academy was created twenty years ago, the French cinema was adored by everyone. All one had to do was to arrive at a festival or a market, and distributors from around the world would raise their hands and say, 'I want it, I want it, I want it.' Then some very serious competitors arrived on the scene – first the British cinema, because the best directors had been working for the BBC up to that juncture, and had not had so much chance of working in cinema. So French film lost something of its appeal by comparison with the British cinema, with directors like Stephen Frears, Ken Loach and others forging their reputation. Then we had another huge competitor from Asia, namely South Korea, which now features at all the festivals and in all the movie theatres, and is very sought after by distributors. So we have had to struggle against our competitors, and of course Unifrance is not neutral, any more than similar organisations in Europe like Filmitalia for Italy, German Films for Germany, and so on, even if they do not have the same tradition or resources as Unifrance.

**Is it easier to get French films screened in the United States than it is in some parts of the European continent?**

It's not easy. But we have established, since we've been battling for decades between the *cinéma d'auteur* on the one hand and the commercial cinema on the other, that there exists a third genre which we call the 'travelling *cinéma d'auteur*'. This consists of films which are indeed personal, but which have a commercial appeal, and these are the films that best penetrate the American market. They are films by Jacques Audiard, Patrice Leconte, Michael Haneke – films made by great directors that please the American taste and mood. Within Europe, the prime market for French films can be Germany one day, Italy the next. Outside Europe, if one speaks of separate territories, then it would be the United States.

**You are president of the *Franco-German Rendez-vous*. Has this initiative helped to get more French films shown in Germany, and vice versa?**

More than anything else, it has enabled us to get French films more widely circulated in Germany, and to contribute to a better distribution of German films here in France, because the aim of this initiative is to increase co-productions between our two countries. It goes hand in hand with the creation of what we call the 'mini-treaty', whereby a film produced in this way can be sure of distribution in the other country. So we are seeing more German films in France and the Germans are seeing more French films in Germany.

**Your work as a producer with Michael Haneke illustrates a kind of European collaboration which has proved very fruitful – an Austrian director working in France, to the point at which many audiences assume that Haneke is French.**

Yes, of course, because he works in French, with French actors. The first film I made with Eric Rohmer was *Die Marquise von O* (*The Marquise of O*, 1976), shot in German with Edith Clever and Bruno Ganz in the leading roles. Then, on account of my knowledge of German, we co-produced Wim Wenders's *The American Friend* and Fassbinder's *Chinese Roulette*. So I have a natural leaning towards German-speaking directors.

**But *Caché* takes place in Paris, and not in Munich, Haneke's native city. Was it like that already in the screenplay?**

From the start, the film was set in Paris and intended for the two principal actors [Juliette Binoche and Daniel Auteuil]. To our great surprise and delight, the territories where the film had the largest audiences were the English-speaking countries – the United Kingdom, the United States, and Australia.

**At Les Films du Losange, you have also been involved with Eric Rohmer, a film-maker who is quintessentially French. How do you explain the success of his films?**
I think it's quite the contrary to Haneke's situation, because Rohmer's films have their roots deep within French society, and what interests spectators throughout the world is not a story that could take place anywhere, but a story that is for them synonymous with life in France: the sophisticated banter between the characters, how one gets caught up in a romantic situation, how one becomes suspicious, themes that are close to the French people.

Where the budget's concerned, Eric has always told me that the vital thing is his story. He used to say a long while back that if there were enough money to make it in colour, so much the better, but if not, he'd make it in black-and-white. If we couldn't make it in 35mm, well, we'd have to shoot it on 16mm, or 8mm, or on video, but the key thing was the story. The luxury of film-making for him was simply to tell the story.

**Long before Kieślowski came to France, you were instrumental in setting up the co-production of Andrzej Wajda's *Danton*. Is it easier to make these arrangements today than it was a generation ago?**
In fact the film benefited, I dare say, from the political conflicts of the time because at the outset we'd planned for financial reasons to shoot the crowd scenes in Kraków. Then the conflict between Solidarity [Solidarność] and the state broke out, and we managed to extract the film from Poland and make it in Paris. Rightly so, in fact, given the story, but we were obliged to find other funding, to restructure the screenplay, and to shoot the film differently. So, as far as the film was concerned, it was a pleasure to shoot in Paris rather than in Kraków. It's true that at that period things were more difficult because the Berlin Wall was still in place, and there existed co-production agreements with many other countries that were in the Soviet fold – with Hungary, with Poland, even with the USSR, although we had to fight against something very problematic, and that was censorship.

**What are the most effective ways of exporting European cinema?**
We arrange festivals in New York, in London, in Shanghai, in Tokyo,

in Budapest, in Mexico and so on. Of course European films are not unknown to foreign distributors, because of the major markets in Berlin, Cannes, and Los Angeles (AFM). One can't say that our films are unfamiliar to the buyers, but if for whatever reason one doesn't find a buyer for a film, in a territory outside Europe, the one thing that can prompt a distributor to buy a picture and release it in their country is for him or her to watch it with a local audience. At markets, they are on their own, with colleagues or rival distributors, and other buyers from all over the world. But if they see that same film in Mexico, for example, with a Mexican audience, and that audience laughs, cries, or is especially gripped by what's happening on screen, that can decide a distributor to buy something he or she may have ignored at one of the markets.

**Do you offer an 'after sales service' at Unifrance, and do you follow the progress of a film once it's been sold abroad?**
No, as far as 'after sales service' is concerned, it's the rights-holders who do that – in other words, the sales company and the producer. We are not involved in the business side. We promote French cinema. For example, for a film that has not been bought for the United States, one needs a good review in the *New York Times* or another newspaper because it's the only country in the world where the critics still have an influence over the buyers. In the other European countries, unfortunately, that's not the case because the reviewers usually simply describe the film in amusing terms and say if they like it or not.

Therefore it's vital for Unifrance to send the films abroad, and to help with their promotion. We give them the chance of finding a buyer, and after that it's the rights-holders who watch over the way it is released. What we do is to enable the talent involved to travel to the opening in that country – we pay the air tickets, we persuade the director and actors to accompany the film when it goes abroad – and that takes a lot of work because often the actors are at work in the theatre, or already involved with shooting another film. After all, two years after a film has appeared in France, it can seem rather irrelevant to start trumpeting it all over again. I frequently use the argument that you are not just performing an after-sales service, but you are promoting yourself and your career, you're gaining a profile abroad.

In spite of the problems among major television concerns like Canal Plus in recent years, are the circumstances of production and funding still something of a paradise in France, as most foreigners believe?
Well, it's more difficult to find funding for production. That has forced us to look for money outside of France, to increase the level of co-productions, certainly with all European countries, also with Russia. What we are lacking in France, we try to find with co-productions involving Germany, Italy, Spain, Great Britain, Belgium and Russia. We're obliged to pack our bags and convince our partners ahead of time of the value of our scripts.

Telephone interview by Peter Cowie on 20 February 2007.

**Margaret Ménégoz** (born in 1941). President of Unifrance Film and also an experienced producer in her own right, Margaret Ménégoz became a production assistant to Eric Rohmer on *Die Marquise von O . . .* in 1976. She soon established herself as Rohmer's regular producer at Les Films du Losange, where she also produced or executive-produced the work of other European directors such as Wim Wenders (*Der amerikanische Freund*), Barbet Schroeder (*Koko le gorille qui parle*), and Volker Schlöndorff (*Un Amour de Swann*). She produced Wajda's *Danton* and Agnieszka Holland's *Europa Europa*, and in 2005 was producer on Michael Haneke's award-winning *Caché*. She has served as a member of the jury in Berlin (1990), and Cannes (1991).

Pedro Almodóvar (Picture:
Paola Ardizzoni & Emilio
Pereda/El Deseo D.A., S.L.U.)

# All About Almodóvar
by Vicente Molina Foix

Rarely does a film-maker embody an entire country for audiences in the rest of the world, and the nature of Almodóvar's films makes the phenomenon all the more extraordinary. His films emerged on the fringes of the industry, took inspiration from the outer reaches of Spanish reality and never aspired to social allegory or the depiction of customs. Almodóvar is nourished from within and creates in his films a characteristic world, yet managing to make an overwhelming connection with the audiences farthest from him, with the most remote, even the most opposed audiences. Or perhaps the relevance, the appeal, the success of his films – always more acclaimed outside Spain than within, at least in the early days – are rooted precisely in his daring invention of a country desired and admired by outsiders? It would not be an exaggeration to say, in this respect, that for many outside Spain, Almodóvar is Spain.

All artists create their own landscape, but first they must ride the tide of tradition, in the context of their contemporaries, before a public who tend to favour known satisfactions over the giddiness of the different. Almodóvar's invasion of the Spanish film industry is fixed by time and date: the night of 27 October 1980, when his film *Pepi, Luci,*

*Bom y otras chicas del montón* (*Pepi, Luci, Bom and Other Girls Like Mom*) was shown at the Peñalver cinema in Madrid. This was a screening without spotlights or limousines in a (now closed) film theatre outside the normal circuit of the capital's big cinemas, where you could, however, witness the move from private dream to public lights, from the 'underground' to the cosmopolitan, represented by Almodóvar's first 'commercial' film. A film-maker was born and, at the same time, the daring, lucid and sparkling spirit of La Movida cultural movement.

What was happening in the Spanish film world at the end of 1980? General Franco had been dead for five years and, at that time, Spain had a new head of state, King Juan Carlos, a new constitution, voted in by a majority, and an opposition containing Communists. And the film world had a dream: the dream of all Western countries awaiting the emergence of great explosions of our new democratic spirit made incarnate on film, arising from our film industry liberated from the Fascist yoke. And certainly during those years several films impossible to make during the dictatorship were produced. Some – such as *Camada Negra* (*Black Litter*) and *Sonámbulos* (*Somnambulists*) by Manuel Gutiérrez Aragón, *Raza, el espíritu de Franco* (*Race, the Spirit of Franco*) by Gonzalo Herralde and *La Vieja Memoria* (*The Old Memory*) by Jaime Camino, all four from 1977, or *El Proceso de Burgos* (*The Burgos Trial*) by Imanol Uribe and *El Crimen de Cuenca* (*The Cuenca Crime*) by Pilar Miró, from 1979 – explicitly or metaphorically referred to the 'long night' of Franco's years. Others obliquely reflected the 'dark matter' of that same suffocating reality: *El Desencanto* (*The Disenchantment*) and *A un dios desconocido* (*To an Unknown God*) by Jaime Chávarri (1976/1977), *Los Placeres Ocultos* (*Hidden Pleasures*) by Eloy de la Iglesia (1976), *Bilbao* and *Caniche* (*Poodle*) by Bigas Luna (1978). However, Almodóvar is, in my opinion, the Spanish film-maker who, without ever producing political or testimonial films, has borne witness in the most revealing way to the profound social changes taking place in Spain over the last thirty years.

So are Almodóvar's films inherently Spanish? I would say so since, although the artistic influences come from literature by Dorothy Parker, Truman Capote and 'beat' novels, and from films by

Fassbinder, Cocteau, John Waters and the New York and Californian underground movements (Warhol, Anger and Markopoulos), he fully embraces, both personally and artistically, the imagery and popular music of the so-called 'Eternal Spain', and a formal apprenticeship in the Spanish humorist tradition: a tradition of 'soft' surrealism and a sort of comedy of the absurd practised by Edgar Neville, Buñuel and Fernando Fernán Gómez, an actor-director for whom Pedro Almodóvar has openly expressed his indebtedness and admiration. Nor should we ignore the ethnic connotations in his films, drawn from La Mancha, the central region of Spain in which Pedro grew up and where some of his family continues to live. The Manchego references, ranging from the sentimental to the comic, from local customs to the fantastic, used to be an important feature, as for example in the local dance scene in *La Flor de mi Secreto* (*The Flower of my Secret*), and are of course an essential component of his latest film to date, *Volver*.

*Volver*
(Picture: Paola Ardizzoni &
Emilio Pereda/El Deseo D.A.,
S.L.U.)

But La Mancha is also the mythical-realistic land of Don Quixote from the novel by Cervantes, typified by a rough and absurd humour constantly merged with the pathetic, a language very rich in popular terms and expressions, and a marked liking for narrative within the narrative, for detours from the main story, by introducing parenthetic stories and mini stories into the main plot line, all very typical elements of Almodóvar's films. I do not believe that the Cervantes model has

ever been emphasised relevantly, in terms of the narrative freedom –
and even anarchy – of Almodóvar's films – and of the characteristic
stamp of his ironic dramas; both the sixteenth-century writer and the
twentieth and twenty-first century film-maker are torrential storytellers and frequent cultivators of a narrative *mise-en-abîme*, but their
fusion of the sublime and the grotesque, the popular and the cult,
belongs uniquely to them. And fuses them.

However, whether consciously or unconsciously Manchego, what
cannot be said about Almodóvar's films, and which for me represents
the highest praise, is that they are localised, inward-looking,
traditional. Traditionalism is the great blemish of Spanish art and, in
my opinion, is evident more in film than in literature or painting.
The philosopher Miguel de Unamuno, in his excellent essay 'On
Traditionalism', wrote: 'The term "breed" is normally applied to pure
races or varieties of species of animal, particularly domestic ones,
and thus a dog is referred to as "of good breeding", which originally
meant that it was of pure race, whole, without any mix or hybrid.
"Traditional" has come to mean pure and without the inclusion of
foreign elements.' Using sometimes indigenous and domestic elements,
Almodóvar practises gloriously impure, mixed-race, 'open' cinema.
And cinema very orientated to the 'feminine side'.

Emphasis must be given to the agitating and destabilising elements
of that profile of the film-maker marked by a new sensitive female cut
as he hurtled into the Spanish film world. His films went beyond the
boundaries of not only sexual mores and the social landscape but also
of the very semantic pattern of femininity. And while Almodóvar's
heroines appeared to us so different from the norm, they were even
more surprising and transgressing to audiences in other countries,
where this unexpected film-maker gained in standing, this film-maker
who spoke (sometimes very locally) about Spain but with the dis-
ordered, digressive freedom of the Eastern narrators of *1001 Nights*.
Almodóvar has been the Scheherazade of a tale in which the women's
voices managed, in each new film, to interrupt, with their art of persuasion and enchantment, the execution of a masculine decision. It
seems to me reasonable to consider him, from this point of view only, a
'director of women'.

For a long time people spoke of 'Almodóvar's girls', who represented a young, indomitable, shameless, 'pop' spirit, at first linked, to a greater or lesser degree, to the ambit of La Movida in Madrid in which Almodóvar was a key player and indubitable revulsive. Those 'Almodóvar girls' were central characters of the first work *Pepi, Luci, Bom and Other Girls Like Mom* and reappeared in the characters of Sexilia (Cecilia Roth), Queti (Marta Fernández Muro) and Angustias (Concha Grégori) in *Laberinto de Pasiones (Labyrinth of Passion)*. They could also be images of the voluntarily ambiguous personality exhibited by Pedro during the La Movida years, with his rock concerts in drag. However – and perhaps the passage of time in the life of the director himself has something to do with this progression – 'Almodóvar's women' have recently acquired greater importance in his films. Marisa Paredes, for me the 'Almodóvar woman' par excellence, brought to the three films they made together, starting with *Tacones Lejanos (High Heels)*, the exact degree of dishevelled gravity, of serious delirium, achieved in Pedro's stories of the 1990s. Intense, grief-stricken, with the appropriate grandiloquence required by the roles of actress and writer, Paredes dominated at all times that primordial feature of the film-maker's great female characters: using humour to detract from tragedy.

*Todo sobre mi madre (All About My Mother)* involved the second female apogee in Almodóvar's canon, after *Mujeres al borde de un ataque de nervios (Women on the Verge of a Nervous Breakdown)*. In this film, Cecilia Roth, with admirable restraint, smoothly resolves the dramatic quality of the key character of the mother, Manuela Coleman. The director confessed he had modelled the mother's character on that of Myrtle Gordon, another actress with 'fantasy' problems, interpreted by the extraordinary Gena Rowlands in *Opening Night* by Cassavetes, a film cited and paid tribute to in another part of *All About My Mother*. Five more women accompany Cecilia Roth in her drama, in a formidable quintet which veers from the natural sense of comedy of Rosa Maria Sardà and Antonia San Juan to the genuine sentimentality of Penélope Cruz's missionary. Not to mention an earlier outbreak of real histrionic genius: that of the lesbian couple formed by Huma Rojo (Marisa Paredes) and Nina Cruz (Candela Peña).

*Women at the Verge of a*
*Nervous Breakdown*
(Picture: Macusa Cores/
El Deseo D.A., S.L.U.)

Maternal figures are present in Almodóvar's canon, in one guise
or another, starting with *¿Qué he hecho yo para merecer esto!!* (*What
Have I Done to Deserve This?*). They appear in a rich range of
variations from the egotistical and absent mother in *High Heels*
(undoubtedly inspired by that tormented and damaged former
prostitute in Hitchcock's extraordinary masterpiece *Marnie*) to the
phallic mother in *Matador*, the parasitic one in *High Heels* or the
dedicated loving one in *All About My Mother*. This group has of
course been greatly enhanced by *Volver*, where the emerging conflict
of the lack of affection by Raimunda (Penélope Cruz) and the disap-
pearance of Irene (Carmen Maura) form the centre of action, branch-
ing from that suggestive mother/daughter nucleus into a rich series of
real or imagined mother and daughter relationships.

In any case, I am sure that Pedro has not yet said everything about
the mother, about mothers, about women, to whom he will certainly
grant a reprieve in order to penetrate that comparatively unexplored
territory of his films: men. *La Mala educación* (*Bad Education*) constituted an exercise in the observation of the sliding registers of
masculinity. But we would not be surprised if one of these days
Almodóvar surprised us with 'All About My Father'.

**Vicente Molina Foix** is a renowned novelist, playwright and film critic.
In 2001 he wrote and directed the feature film *Sagitario*, starring
Angela Molina, Enrique Alcides, Eusebio Poncela and Bob Wilson.

## A New Kind of Scene

An interview with Dieter Kosslick

*Dieter Kosslick has been director of the International Film Festival Berlin for the past six years.*

**One of the undoubted success stories of the past few years has been the resurrection of German cinema. What's the explanation for this? Is it the screenwriting? The choice of subject matter? The acting?**

Dieter Kosslick: I remember when I was starting the Hamburger Filmbüro for the Cultural Film Fund in 1983. At that point people were making films in the usual manner – in other words, deriving money from public funds – and sometimes, but on the whole very rarely, they were successful, and sometimes they ended up having just one screening at a festival. There was usually one film during the year that attracted an audience, but in general it was a lousy period.

We launched the European Low-Budget Initiative in 1986, with the focus on distribution, because at the time nobody invested in distribution, and nobody was seeing the films. There was a big lack of almost everything – except directing. We had more than enough directors; everyone wanted to direct, from his own story, with his wife in the main part, and his brother as main producer! And fortunately enough, he had an uncle with a cinema! A whole chain. So there was not a lot of money devoted to screenwriting. That all started to change with the American script doctors, such as Frank Daniel, who came frequently to Europe in the late 1980s, and Robert McKee. I was building up a distribution network with EFDO in Hamburg at that time (1988–1990). So the two poles of film-making were gradually established, after a long time, with the emphasis on enhancing screenwriting on the one hand and distribution on the other.

Then I moved to the NRW Film Foundation in 1991; this was not just a funding agency, it was already constructed in such a way as to be able to do a lot of different things for film in general – education, training programmes, supporting specialised cinemas, and so on. We opened a film school in Cologne (not an academic institution so much as a skills programme – today's International Film School Cologne, IFS), and put a lot of energy into training young people and bringing them into contact with professionals. We wanted to develop certain neglected areas – sound, costumes, set design etc. This was functioning almost alongside the MEDIA Programme, with its initiatives such as EuroAim, or SCRIPT, or EAVE. There was a tremendous effort on a regional, a national, and a European level to improve all the departments that are involved in film-making.

All these activities generated a new kind of scene, in which creativity and entrepreneurial abilities could grow and could be nourished. Fortunately for me, therefore, when I arrived at the Berlinale in 2001, I had the opportunity to select some of the films that had emerged from this fresh climate in Germany. Before that time, the running had been made by the Danes, and prior to that by the British.

**The last great period of German cinema was probably the 1960s to 1970s, with directors like Schlöndorff, Wenders, Herzog, and Fassbinder coming to the fore. In what ways are the directors of today in Germany different to that previous wave?**
It's a completely new generation, a new breed, even if you do find some directors who have their roots in the previous wave. When I first saw Margarethe von Trotta's *The German Sisters*, when I was living in

Hamburg in the early 1980s, I came out of the cinema feeling that I had just seen a masterpiece about my contemporary reality. By the same token, I believe that many of our current film-makers make films about our reality today even if the subject-matter comes from the past. Sophie Scholl has been a big figure in German modern history, and the movies made about her, whether by Michael Verhoeven or Marc Rothemund, show what it takes to be against a dictatorship. *The Lives of Others* [which won the EFA's European Film 2006 award and the Oscar for the Best Foreign Film] has been successful chiefly because it's a good film, perhaps more than because of the debate that it has aroused.

You can make a film about contemporary reality that ends up in a vale of tears, but what these new film-makers are doing is showing the tears but at the same time rendering the story in entertaining terms, with some kind of real catharsis. It's really astonishing that with Tom Tykwer's *Perfume: The Story of a Murderer*, you have the proof that a German director and a German producer can make a world-class movie from a work of literature. Tom and I met in the early 1990s, just after he had made his first film, *Deadly Maria*, which was screened at the Hof Festival. I was a big fan of *Winter Sleepers*, and supported it at Filmstiftung NRW. I remember Tom sitting next to me in the first row of the Castro Theatre in San Francisco, where the film was being presented, and he whispered to me, 'Aren't you upset that the film has sold only 173,000 tickets?' I replied, 'No, because when the curtains open, I'll be looking at one of the best films I've seen.' Tom later brought box-office and high artistic value together in films like *Run Lola Run*.

**How has the Berlinale helped the cause of German cinema during your five years at the helm?**

Well, for me, coming from a funding background, it seemed quite natural to prove what we had always believed – that many of the German films were better than people thought they were, but that they had not been properly marketed. Just as in Robert Altman's *A Prairie Home Companion*, you can say that some films take the highway to the airport, and others take a kind of detour – and yet can arrive at their destination just as quickly. Besides, under Moritz de Hadeln, the Berlinale had also been a national film festival, not just an international event, with the difference that we have perhaps shown the films in a mood of more optimism – the glass is half full, not half empty. I believe that the Berlinale is the natural place to show the variety of themes and styles in German cinema.

**Do you think that European Cinema has changed or mutated in any significant way during the past twenty years?**
There is a different kind of cinema, but more importantly there is a different kind of behaviour among the members of the different European film industries. Within the past fifteen years we have expanded from twelve countries to twenty-seven – more than double. Whatever one cares to criticise about the MEDIA Programme, or Eurimages, or European film bureaucracy, one has to admit one thing – that the money was really used to enable everyone to get to know each other. When we started with the European Film Academy, and with EFDO – basically during the same years 1986 to 1988 – the European film industry looked like an elementary school class, in which everybody was sitting and writing in his own little notebook, shielding it so that others couldn't see what figures were being written down. But now there is more openness: we have the figures, we know how the film industry works, and we know that, incidentally, eighty per cent of all the movies are low-budget. And during the years since 1988, I think that Europeans have learned the need to make films that appeal to audiences in different countries – but without introducing elements from all those different countries, a practice that resulted in the so-called 'Euro-pudding' productions, which never found an international audience or a pan-European audience, and indeed lost their national audience too, because they had relinquished their identity. So, people learned to finance movies in the classic manner, finding partners and distributors in other countries, partners who would not, however, be part of the artistic side of the movie.

The European Film Academy went through some tough times, in particular the wonderful staff, which had to organise the awards with less and less money. We had to 'Europeanise' the event, and this led to the system of staging the awards in a different European city every other year, which made it complicated and often difficult. The presentations have been on various levels – some have been very good, some not so good. We underwent an incredible change from 99 members at the beginning to around 1,800 today, which raised some questions – for example, how many members are there in a particular country, and are those members likely to vote for a film from their own territory? But I like that we went to Warsaw last year, and after a bumpy time I think that without the European Film Academy, the community would not be so close to each other. It may take another fifty years until everybody is proud of their artists.

**Do you think that the Central European, formerly Communist countries, will be able to recover the great days of Wajda, and Forman, and Jancsó as a result of joining the EU and its film-financing structures?**
I'm completely convinced that the Central European countries, and former Communist nations, will not make the same mistakes as the Western European countries did at first as far as co-financing is concerned. As you cannot *buy* creativity, an association like the European Film Academy is much more important than everything else, because the EFA was and is the home of *all* the European countries, and became a kind of big refuge for film-makers, for artists, for creativity, and for the awareness that there is a family of which you can be a member. For the Central European countries, formerly Eastern European countries, the funds are of course important, they help one to work, but they cannot replace the sense of security that film-makers had in those territories under the old system – and when that's all replaced by the wild capitalist system, how can you habituate yourself after fifty years of being trained under another system? So the EFA is a kind of community to which they can belong, and that's why it remains so vital and so indispensable.

Interviewed by Peter Cowie in Berlin on 11 December 2006.

**Dieter Kosslick** (born 1948 in Pforzheim, Germany) has been a crucial authority in German and pan-European film policy. He studied communication, politics, and education in Munich. In 1983 he became involved in film funding, as head of the Hamburg Film office, and three years later began his vocation as a crusader for wider release of quality European film, when he co-founded EFDO (European Film Distribution Office). In 1992 he was appointed head of Filmstiftung NRW, and in the ensuing years made Nordrhein-Westfalen a focal point for the production and financing of films from numerous territories. In 2001 Dieter Kosslick left Filmstiftung NRW and took up his duties as head of the Berlinale, a post he continues to hold.

Bernardo Bertolucci at an EFA Meeting in 1989 in Berlin (Picture: EFA/ Kristina Eriksson)

# A Mirror of the World We Live in

An interview with Bernardo Bertolucci

*Bernardo Bertolucci received a Golden Lion in recognition of his career at the 75th Anniversary of the Venice Film Festival in September 2007. Each of his films, from* Before the Revolution *in 1964 to* The Dreamers *some four decades later, has been an event in European cinema. He won two out of nine Oscars for* The Last Emperor *as well as the Italian David di Donatello award, the French César, the BAFTA for Best Film and a Special Jury Prize at the inaugural European Film Awards in 1988.*

**You have worked through the past forty years in European cinema, starting with the golden age of the 1960s. How would you compare the films of that period and the films emerging in the first years of the new century?**

Bernardo Bertolucci: I think that cinema has both a privilege and a condemnation in mirroring the world. The changes that we have seen during this long period are very much reflected in the movies. I remember Pasolini saying that 'Cinema is the language of reality.' So films are the medium that the twentieth century has chosen to speak about itself.

**You've made all your films in Europe or the Far East, but always with a European post-production base – in Italy or in London. Why have you resisted the siren calls of the Hollywood studios?**
Well, if you look at my filmography, you'll find that I haven't made that many movies – around seventeen features – so I do only what really 'calls' me. I do only stories that intrigue me, and up to now I haven't found anything in Hollywood that inspired me, like I have found in China, or in India, or in the Sahara [*The Sheltering Sky*]. But that's the only reason – I certainly wouldn't have a problem about working in Hollywood, if only I were to find a subject that engaged me, or a story that I really wanted to tell.

When I did some big movies like *Last Tango in Paris*, or even *1900*, in some way I was feeling that I was challenging the Hollywood cinema on their own turf, using Hollywood actors like Marlon Brando, Burt Lancaster or Robert De Niro. In other words, I was using Hollywood talent in Europe, rather than going the other direction.

One of the factors behind Italian film-makers using so many American actors during the 1950s and 1960s is that in my country we do not have a great tradition in sound technique. Therefore we focused on the images, and not the voices, so it was really only half the experience of cinema. Traditionally, everything has been dubbed in Italy, something I've been trying to fight over a long, long period – not always successfully. For about the last thirty years – let's say, since *Last Tango in Paris* – I've tried to insist on an original soundtrack. Of course all my movies are dubbed in Italy, otherwise they will not be released. And that's an admission of a great, great 'black hole' in Italian cinema and the way films are released here.

**Is it necessary to shoot films in English in order to achieve a widespread distribution?**
I think that when English is used simply to attract a wider audience, it's an old, big mistake, that nobody makes any more. When you have in fact a story that justifies the use of English, then I think it's quite normal to shoot in that language.

*The Dreamers* returns to the period of intellectual confusion and debate in 1968. Is there still room for political films?
In the sixties and seventies politics was physiological in our movies. Today, if I want to do a political film, I have to deal with a total lack of political passion in the viewers. That is a problem.

**And why is it that Italian cinema no longer occupies such a central position in Europe?**
As I said earlier, cinema cannot be isolated from reality, and it corresponds to the complexity of our real world. So throughout the 1950s we had neo-realism, with that wave of film-makers, which included Rossellini, De Sica, Visconti, etc. The 1960s were an especially French period, thanks to the Nouvelle Vague, which was very important and a model for everyone. Since then I think that cinema has been floating in a kind of semi-agony. I cannot tell you the reasons, but they must be found in Italian history of the past thirty years. We still make political films, as witness Nanni Moretti's recent *Il caimano*.

**The central personalities in your films are always changed by the end of their journey or their experience. Would you say that's a central theme of your work?**
For me, change, or changing, is one of the most interesting things that can occur during the shooting of a film. The period when you shoot a film is a very special one, and I always try to do everything to find a dynamic which takes the characters from one point to another – as it happens in real life. I'm not the same being I was a few hours ago, especially because of my method of shooting, where I leave plenty of room for improvisation. That's why I am obsessed with screenplays that are done and then repeatedly re-done because then, if I'm sure of the story, I can perhaps allow myself to forget it. As far as my actors are concerned, I can tell you that my relationship to them comprises my way of looking at them, and 'spying' on them. At the end of the day, cinema is a voyeuristic medium. So this change is almost inevitable. It's *there*.

**Will you be using digital technology on your future productions?**

I am extremely curious about what one will be able to do with digital technology. Even if I haven't been really able to understand it technically – but then it's the same with film, I've never been a great technician! Sometimes, when I am in discussion with an audience, I remind them that I'm unable to take a good photograph.

**You have worked with the same producer, Jeremy Thomas, since *The Last Emperor*. Can you say something about what makes him special?**

His father was a film director, and his uncle was a film director, and he was raised virtually in the studios around London. So cinema is his life, he's been in love with film since he was born. On the other hand, he is somebody with an incredible curiosity for films that are very risky. He's not a producer who is looking for simple economic solutions. He's always fascinated by the same things that fascinate me, by stories that might on the surface seem difficult for an audience – and that makes us a team. He's always attracted by the potential quality of a film.

**How do you think that the enlargement of the European Union will effect European cinema?**

I see what's happening as a cultural enrichment. After all, one of the reasons why the European Film Academy was born was to serve as a kind of fence, or protection, against the overwhelming power of American distribution, and it's very important that national European films can be released with more care. I am against protectionism as such, I think it's completely obsolete in the contemporary marketplace, but I think that one should find a kind of protection from Hollywood colonialism.

**If you could programme an art-house for just one day, what film (or films) would you like to screen more than anything else?**

Without a moment's hesitation, I'd choose *La Règle du jeu*, by Jean Renoir.

Telephone interview by Peter Cowie, 19 February 2007.

**Bernardo Bertolucci** (born 1940, in Parma, Italy) attended university in Rome, and, in the footsteps of his distinguished father, the poet Attilio Bertolucci, made an early impact as a writer. In 1961 he served as assistant director to Pier Paolo Pasolini on *Accattone*, and the following year directed his maiden feature, *La commare secca. Before the Revolution (Prima della rivoluzione)* followed in 1964, but was only released in the United States in 1971, to great acclaim. *The Conformist (Il conformista*, 1970) influenced an entire generation of American directors, and *Last Tango in Paris* (1972) confirmed his place among the greats of European cinema. He reached the zenith of his career with *The Last Emperor* (1987), which swept the board at the American Academy Awards. Since then he has made films in Africa, the Far East, and France and Italy, notably *The Sheltering Sky* (1990), and *The Dreamers* (2003).

## A Cinema for Our Time: the Documentary
by Thierry Garrel

Twenty years ago, on the founding of the European Film Academy, no awards had been planned for documentaries. It was only the following year that this oversight was corrected. Twenty years on we can see that the last decade of the twentieth century was, in fact, the first decade of a century which would clearly be the century of the documentary.

In the overwhelming accelerated maelstrom of sounds and images, information and 'data', the documentary has become a special genre from which 'citizens of the world' can try to reconstruct a rich and committed relationship with an increasingly complex universe. In taking the time to share, sensitively and in depth, an experience which is essentially marked by its desire for truth and experience, the documentary appears as the best weapon against omnipresent information, this 'grim fourth rider of the apocalypse' that Luis Buñuel talked of, which only generates angst and indifference.

For twenty years, the documentary has left what one documentary maker called the 'paddling pool' of direct cinema, to swim in the 'open seas' of ideas, in the depths of the human soul. If increasingly diverse and rhetorical procedures are now used each time, if increasingly rich styles and *écritures* are affirmed, prompting the effects of comprehension through aesthetic effects, the aim is always to serve an invincible double truth: the truth of beings caught in the processes of life; the truth of the view of those observing and questioning them.

The most tragic events in history, or the minuscule destinies of the anonymous, epiphanies of joy and love, upheavals in globalising societies, are all subjects which contemporary documentary makers have not hesitated in grasping, with rage and passion, emotion and poetry.

Documentary cinema has established its pedigree, it has its consecrated authors. In cultural history, the 'documentary revolution' – like the revolution that shook up the nineteenth century with the appearance of the novel – seems to promise new horizons for man.

The love for the documentary which unites directors and audiences, resounds like the sound of a humanity wishing – in a shared contemporaneity – to keep questioning its own diversity as its *raison d'être*.

Translated from French by Bernard Reeves.

**Thierry Garrel**, Directeur de l'unité de Programme Documentaires ARTE France.

Nino Kirtadzé on the set

## The Fiction of Reality
by Nino Kirtadzé

'Man is in the world, facing the world and looking at it like a puzzle to be solved,' said the Russian philosopher Nikolai Berdiaev.

This is where the documentary may be said to start.

It is born from a question, from a view of a place or a face. Yet while it explores the reality in front of the camera, the documentary goes further. It does not just narrate what it sees, but also describes what cannot be seen directly. It unfurls in time, moves forward in space and often goes beyond the point at which reality meets the universal. Only this personal and subjective view exploring the depths of the reality in front of the camera can achieve the universal.

Documentaries talk of nothing and of everything. When they talk of nothing, they talk of us, of the world, of the universe, of the great puzzle of life, which is the subject of philosophy. This is because documentaries are a viewpoint on the world.

And since the enigma of the world is so complex and inexplicable, first one film is made about it, and then another. Questions proliferate and we move forward through contradictions.

A few years ago I was determined to make a documentary on death, which while remaining within the framework of death would transform it into a hymn to joy and praise for life. I wanted to tie extremes together. I dreamt of a film which would be full of energy, force and vitality, which through death would talk of life.

It is said that when Johann Sebastian Bach learned of the death of one of his children, he fell to his knees and prayed, 'Lord, do not let me lose the joy of life.'

Seeing humankind in all its splendour, in all its vulnerability in face of the mystery of death, where mourning becomes a celebration of life, is something which fascinates me.

The project I wrote was essentially based on my childhood memories: on images which have stayed in my mind of funerals in Georgia, where I was born and where, according to the customs of certain regions, the living keep strange links with their dearly departed and continue living as if they were still alive.

The title of the film *Dites à mes amis que je suis mort* came from an epitaph, which I found in a graveyard, when I was looking for locations in western Georgia. The 'owner' of the epitaph was represented by an enormous life-size portrait on his tomb. His chest was covered with medals in recognition of services to the state, of which he was clearly proud. His epitaph, in the first person, invited all his friends to sit near him and take a drink. The deceased asked them to come and see him often and to sing him his favourite songs so that he would not get bored all alone in his grave, as life – his life – went on.

There was something surrealistic about this reality I was seeing, something incredibly strong about this way of facing death, about this joy for life which emerged from these incredible epitaphs and this cemetery. Imagine this place, which looked like an open-air gallery with portraits of the dead smiling, life-size, each one sending out invitations to sit down by them on the benches and seats for visitors around each grave. Some graves even had a television set brought by families so that they could gather around a loved one and watch a football match 'together'.

When I started preparing the film, I told my assistant what I was planning on doing and he looked at me as if I was crazy.

'How are you going to do the casting?' he asked.

The difficult thing about the film was the absolute impossibility of preparing anything. We did not know how to find our main character, who had to be deceased, or how to get the family's permission to film what we felt essential. The long preparations for the funeral, which seemed so much like preparations for a wedding, the condolence ceremonies reminiscent of images of the *commedia dell'arte*, the solo lamentations, which are always so surprising in their theatricality and can go very far in terms of improvisation, the wake with memories and funny stories about the dead person's life, and where, for an instant, uncontrollable laughter eclipses mourning.

The biggest question was how to introduce a film crew into this world without disturbing it, how could we place a camera in the family's intimacy without causing a catastrophe. It was mission impossible, or almost.

'It would be a wonderful drama film,' my producer said, 'but can you make it as a documentary?'

'Are you sure that what you're saying in the project is really true?' the television channel asked when they read it.

I shook with fear and desire to make this film. I left for a month to find locations and stay in the region I wanted to film in. And this time was very precious for what was to come.

I will never forget how I was glared at when I started going to see people, asking them the most unlikely questions. Over time, I got to know all the cemetery managers (as they are called) in the region, almost all the families, who came regularly to see their dear departed, bringing fresh fruit and cakes, reading them the newspaper, or simply spending time with them. They came with their children and grandchildren, so that the dead could see the little ones grow.

Step by step I moved forward in this funny, poetic and totally surrealistic world of contrasting extremes: amusement and the deepest grief, joy for life and the mystery of death. Their cries were like open-air arias, condolences like lines from a play, and death as part of life. As if everything was connected, as if there were no separation, as if life celebrated its victory over death.

I often saw incredible scenes in the cemetery: I saw a young man come to his grandfather's grave to present his fiancée, a beautiful young woman carefully dressed and made up for this strange introduction. When they went, they left photos of their recent holidays, so that grandfather 'could have them close to him'.

Young people and local musicians came to celebrate the birthday of a deceased friend. The musicians set up their instruments on the grave and started singing rather unsuitable songs into their mike. There was disco, jazz, folk music, all sorts of styles that the deceased liked.

I witnessed bizarre quarrels, including one in which a man was unhappy that someone else had grown a large plant on a neighbouring grave, blocking the deceased's view: 'He can't see anything,' he complained. The plant's owner did not want to give in to the neighbour's demands: 'When my father was alive he loved to rest in the shade of a tree, why should he change his habits now?' Tempers rose, the situation degenerated and a real fight started in front of these life-size portraits, as if the village of the dead was observing the quarrels of the living.

It was with great relief that I saw that what I had written or imagined was pale and insipid compared to the reality. The fiction of the real went way beyond whatever I could imagine. It taught me a lot. And forever. It taught me never to underestimate the fiction of reality, not to stifle it with prepared ideas, which can sometimes stop you discovering what you did not anticipate or plan. Reality, vibrating and breathing in front of the camera, is full of signs and metaphors of contradiction. It is both real and surreal, it is visible and invisible, transparent and opaque at one and the same time, and demands patience and humility.

I have understood that you must be ready for the most improbable surprises, the most dizzying changes. As the philosopher said: When we face life, we face an enigma. We try to understand it, but its secret comes to the surface.

*Dites à mes amis que je suis mort* is at once the most paradoxical and the craziest film I have ever made. That is why I have such fond memories of it. It was a real challenge for all of us, for the crew, the producers and the channel. Its success with audiences at festivals, its

Fipa d'Or and its Cinéma du Réel award are a tribute to the fiction of reality, a tribute to this real and surreal world, where laughter and tears mingle, where joy and mourning live together, where life and death are one.

The most surreal thing in the story is that the most precious permission to film was given to me by my main hero, the deceased person himself. When I arrived in the house where the father had just died and I explained to his wife what the film was about, she looked at me for a long time and then said, 'I can't decide without asking him first.' I did not immediately understand who 'he' was. She took me upstairs to a large room where her dead husband was lying. She sang to him, explaining why I was there and asked him what he thought about the idea of me making a film 'with him'. There I was, sitting beside her, wondering if what I was seeing was reality or fiction. And at the same time I was very worried about what the deceased would 'say'. After a while, the woman turned to me to say that her husband had agreed to film with me.

Even today when I am asked what this film is about I do not know what to say: is it about life or death? Mourning or joy? Love or immortality? I still don't know. But I am happy to have made it.

I would like to wish a happy birthday to the European Film Academy, which puts the spotlight on documentary creation, which preserves it, strengthens it and gives it its rightful place in European cinema.

European cinema needs documentaries and documentaries need cinema. Today, when we are witness to the mixing of genres and the merging of styles between documentary and drama, it is all the more clear that first and foremost when you make a film you are creating cinema, be it a drama fiction or a documentary. Cinema that surprises, overwhelms, moves and creates dreams.

Translated from French by Bernard Reeves.

Born in 1968 in Tbilisi, Georgia, **Nino Kirtadzé** has worked as consultant to the Georgian president and as a journalist covering armed conflicts. Among her films are *Il était une fois la Tchétchénie* (2001) for ARTE, *Dites à mes amis que je suis mort* (2004), also for ARTE and *Un dragon dans les eaux pures du Caucase* (2005), winner of the European Film Academy Documentary 2005 – Prix ARTE.

The Georgian cemetery
(Picture: Nino Kirtadzé)

# 7 Out of the Closet: Queer Cinema

*Man loves man, woman loves woman – that in itself doesn't appear to be a particularly interesting, much less scandalous concept. Love and sex are basic desires that influence our lives, our stories and our films. Yet there are people who experience discrimination and hatred because of their sexuality. And this doesn't only happen in some abstract, uncivilised and far-away place, it happens everywhere in Europe all the time. Queer film-makers have enriched our film culture portraying gays and lesbians, their struggles, their romances, their lives. Meanwhile, a whole new set of classifications for sexual identities has stepped into the limelight – transgender, transsexual, androgynous cross-dressing drag kings and queens, and their families. Who tells their stories, who makes these films? How has queer film changed and can films make the world more tolerant?*

## Things Can Change

## An interview with Wieland Speck

*Wieland Speck has been working for the Panorama section of the Berlin International Film Festival for over twenty years and he was one of the initiators of the Teddy, the queer film award at the Berlinale. We talked to him about the developments in queer cinema.*

**When you started, the Berlinale was the only big festival with a section actively looking for queer films as part of the official programme. How would you describe the situation today?**
Wieland Speck: Well, even if Western countries seem to live favourably, if not comfortably, with the queer part of their population, that's not the case in most parts of the planet. Quite a few officials in countries I travel to are astonished when I ask where the queer work is. Sometimes they will then have a secretary coming in to do some research because they simply don't know. And that, of course, is already an interesting little procedure in itself.

When we started, there were rarely any queer film festivals, and all of them were quite low-key and didn't reach out much to the outer world. It was more work for the subculture created by the subculture.

Of course we've seen changes in the wake of liberation. But it's still a process, and it will remain a process for ever because we're talking about a minority and a minority is always positioning itself against the majority so it will never be finished. But at least we have better conditions for queer people to live these days and also to be presented in the arts.

**What about the way queer films are received, has that also changed?**
The audience has changed tremendously. In the beginning, it was *really* a family gathering and nothing but that. And if you still have that today with some of the films we show, it must be a film that does exactly what I mentioned before – it's a film from the subculture for the subculture. What I mean is that the specific conditions of living as a member of a minority creates certain ways of handling life – in public but also in private. And to develop that further you need communication with other members of that minority – that is subculture. Also, today, many non-queer people are interested in queer film, which is great.

**As someone who has been campaigning for queer cinema, how do you feel about gay or lesbian characters being inserted into mainstream film just to attract an additional audience?**
In general, I appreciate the appearance of queer characters in cinema as such. It's a sign of emancipation because that is what the world is like – when you get on the Underground, a certain percentage of the people on your train is queer. It was simply very unnatural that for decades and decades this percentage of people was never presented on screen. On the other hand, the political importance of queer cinema, which was very strong and in a fighting position in the 1980s and late 1970s, is much less dominant today. That's partly because television has taken over the function of representing the population; on television you have a lot of queer characters and that takes away from the public's need to see queer film.

You can also compare it with pornography: why is pornography so popular? Because sexuality is not portrayed in other films. So basically you have to see pornography in order to bring together in your head the films you have seen without sexuality and then sexuality only and only then do you get the complete picture, the portrayal of human behaviour on this planet.

**Has there been a change in the kind of stories that queer cinema tells?**
Coming-out stories obviously play an important role because they describe an experience shared by many queer people. But the first generation of cinema-goers that went to the cinema to see queer films in the eighties was naturally tired of seeing coming-out stories ten years later. By then, their own coming-out lay so far behind them that they didn't want to see the same story over and over again. But the issue of awakening sexuality will always remain a top theme. If you look at French cinema, it has been telling the same stories for decades and decades and decades. The period of awakening sexuality has simply remained one of the most fascinating moments in a human's life, when you are basically complete – and then sexuality steps in and sheds a totally different light on everything you have ever seen up to that point. Of course, it also generally coincides with the biggest sexual attractiveness of people, it's so blossoming and full of excitement and charm and questions.

I think that queer cinema brought in the question of sexuality in general, how it is lived and how attraction can work not only male – female, but also in all other kinds of directions. And that also led to a new view on heterosexual sexuality as we can see in Catherine Breillat's films, for example. She really goes into observing exactly what is happening; she wants to tackle those open questions which can often be very provoking and harsh. But in my eyes it goes hand in hand with working on the portrayal of humans in cinema which cannot exclude sexuality as such. So I think it's not so much a question of what does queer cinema do and what does non-queer cinema do. I think they meet at some point and also get inspiration from each other.

The other thing is that we now see films about people between the genders. It may be a person who feels they have the wrong gender and they change it, get an operation and think that all their problems are solved. Most of the time that's not true. This is a very socio-political issue because many societies force one gender on to a person and if it doesn't fit into that drawer they'll make it fit into the other drawer. It's about being what you are. There are inter-sexual people who were born with genitals of both sexes and they got operated, which is the standard in our world today; usually it's an operation to cut the male away and create a female. But then you have a physically created woman and at the age of fifteen, sixteen, seventeen, when sexuality starts, it turns out that that was the wrong decision – it's not a woman. And this leads to people who are unhappy and who reclaim the right to be what they are – between the sexes. It leads to an amazing tangle of psychology and philosophy because it questions dualism. And when you question dualism that makes it difficult for everyone. But it's only a concept and it's not working. So, I think we can learn a lot about our view of the world from that.

**The Teddy award is by now an essential part of the Berlinale. How did it come into being and how do you view its development to today?**
The Teddy was possible because after six years of showing queer work, many people working in queer cinema came to Berlin from all over the world. We had all these amazing individuals here and started to organise gatherings where people could exchange information and get to know each other. Out of these gatherings we developed the idea of the Teddy as an award. The idea wasn't so much to have a contest or anything like that. But I had won a few awards with my own films by that time and that inspired me because it had helped me, just a line here and there, that the film had won such and such an award. So the idea was to create a queer film award to help films to get acknowledged, to get seen.

It was a PR idea in the beginning and also the idea to bring together people in the festival, where everybody runs around like crazy. We would have a gathering at the end of the festival, to celebrate what we just experienced, and hopefully to also create a network that exists for longer than just ten days.

**When the Teddy was started, it was a few people sitting in a bookstore, now it is a televised gala event. What kind of compromises did you have to accept to get there?**

Well, we had a few years where the gala had become so big that I wasn't sure what kind of thing I was attending. Was this the same thing we had created back then? Was this still *my show*? On the other hand, the producer of the show said that we have to get the attention of the media – otherwise the idea of the Teddy wouldn't be fulfilled, namely bringing attention to queer cinema. Basically, the question always is: do we want to celebrate ourselves and be happy with that or do we want to reach out and move something. The decision was to go bigger and so we brought in some gay and lesbian TV stars and tried combinations with that. In the end, every single Teddy Awards ceremony is completely different from all other ones. It is always experimental and we always try to find out and set the tone anew.

A big change is TV. Now we have the right television. In the years before we had commercial channels lining up; at one point there were eighteen TV channels in the show, all of them just looking for pictures, wanting to feed their audience with 'the weirdest wig'. None of them had any interest in the content or the movies. Last year we finally found a TV channel that suits us really well, namely ARTE, which covers several countries and is the most sophisticated channel we have.

**What do you see as the Teddy's biggest achievement?**
What you see at the Teddy Awards is an amazing mixture of people – age groups, nationalities, but also sexualities. This is something I totally adore – the Teddy was able to create a true atmosphere of tolerance. If you go into the subculture today, it is more or less commercially divided according to taste with a strong separation of age groups and you don't have that many other people there. The Teddy, on the other hand, brings everyone together which was the idea from day one: to bring things together that might not have been together otherwise. And this really culminates in the Teddy party right after the awards ceremony, one of the best Berlinale parties.

When we started the Teddy, it was a unique thing which was great but it's kind of sad that today that's still true. Of course, other festivals are opening up, they are trying, they feel they have to, but – if at all – it's still hidden away somewhere. But I think they realise that this is an important part of cinema culture that can deal with issues, aesthetically and content-wise, and I am very proud of seeing that happening.

**There used to be the slogan 'We're queer, we're here – get used to it'. Today, it seems – at least if you're in London, Berlin, Paris – that everybody is used to it so much, that even the queers are bored by it. Is there anything left that's worth fighting for?**
Well, I think everybody should be bored by someone being gay because it's not very exciting. It's just as exciting as being heterosexual. Sexuality is an exciting thing for the individual, but the difference between sexualities shouldn't be an issue to get excited about.

Of course, it all starts with an individual experience, an experience which is connected to how the socio-political surrounding is. And this will change immediately once you leave the city, but also within the city it can mean completely different things. If you look at Berlin, a huge part of the population has an Islamic background. How do they deal with different kinds of sexualities? We cannot assume that everything is fine just because in Berlin the majority of white Christian German citizens may happily attend a queer festival. Problems are everywhere, at every corner. And when you leave the city, go thirty-five minutes east, to Poland, you have a situation where the president of the country calls out to his citizens to beat up gay people when they dare to demonstrate for their rights – in 2006! If you don't see this, it's because you don't want to see it.

We are now trying to create something called Queer Academy which means we're trying to bring all the Teddy-winning films into the Internet to be available, particularly in countries that don't have the money and the means to establish a queer film festival so that people can download films and create their own festival. When you speak to people from countries where it is more difficult, very often they will say how we live in such great places where you can do what you want. Here, they insist, nothing will ever change. And I can say, I have seen it change in the twenty years of the Teddy. And I was part of it, so the news I can bring to these places is that things can actually change.

That's still the main message – things can change and you can enjoy
your life.

**One last question: If you owned a cinema for one day, what would you
screen?**

That's a great question! I'd start with a matinee at eleven of *Ludwig* by
Luchino Visconti – the long cut. Then, at one I'd continue with *From
Here to Eternity* by Fred Zinnemann, for the happy few. At four,
*Im Himmel ist die Hölle los* by Helmer von Lützelburg, at six a documentary, *Ich kenn keinen – Allen unter Heteros* (Talk Straight: The
World of Rural Queers) by Jochen Hicks. And, at prime time, eight-
thirty, *Nicht der Homosexuelle ist pervers, sondern die Situation, in
der er lebt* (It is Not the Homosexual Who is Perverse, But the Society
in Which He Lives) by Rosa von Praunheim. And, as a late-night
screening, *Myra Breckenridge* by Michael Sarne at eleven-thirty.

Interviewed by Pascal Edelmann in Berlin on 19 October 2006.

**Wieland Speck** was born in 1951. He studied German literature,
drama and ethnology at the Freie Universität Berlin and then started
working on video and film projects and as a writer and publisher. In his
work he focuses on the men's movement and homosexual identity.

As a director Wieland Speck started out with several video documentaries. From 1979 to 1981 he studied film at the San Francisco Art
Institute. He is director, author and producer of numerous TV and film
productions and has worked for several film institutions and events,
among them the Filmhaus Berlin, the Filmbüro Baden-Württemberg,
and the Berlin European Short Film Festival.

Since 1982 Wieland Speck has been working for the Panorama
section of the Berlin International Film Festival: 1982–1992 as
assistant to the former director of the section, Manfred Salzgeber, and
since 1992 as director of the Panorama section.

# A Journey Through Twenty Years of Lesbian Film
by Silke Brandt

'Twenty Years of Lesbian Film' seems an innocent enough title, but the term 'lesbian film' itself persistently evades definition. Closely connected to twenty or more years of heated discussions on gender roles, sexual politics and social implications of 'woman' and 'female', any opinion on what really makes a film lesbian will never go uncontested. Keeping in mind that there is a legion of exceptions to this rule in the context of this article alone, let's assume that a film is a 'lesbian film' if it has one or more lesbian characters or female characters in any kind of sexually/romantically motivated relationship with other women, and/or if the film-maker is a lesbian. This article will also mention films that do not fit into this definition because they might be of interest for a lesbian/bi/trans or gay audience.

## The Early Days

Lesbian or bisexual characters date back to the silent film era, and in particular to German Expressionist cinema. The most (in)famous being *Die Büchse der Pandora* (1929) by G.W. Pabst from Wedekind's controversial play *Lulu*, starring Louise Brooks – who also collaborated with Pabst in the same year for *Tagebuch einer Verlorenen*, partly set in a girls' correctional home and featuring the inmates' friendship as a subplot (the film was censored and re-released in a cut version in 1930). The actress quickly gained iconic cult status epitomising 'the modern woman' (also a synonym for 'lesbian') with her bob haircut and independent lifestyle.

Leontine Sagan's *Mädchen in Uniform* (1931, also banned but re-issued uncut) is set in a girl's school, dealing with one girl's unobtainable love for her female teacher that finally leads to a suicide attempt. The moralistic tone hasn't changed in the 1958 remake.

These early films featuring lesbian roles – or women with lesbian desires – already set the tone for years to come: The characters, being unstable, irrational or just pitiful, often criminals, drug addicts or prostitutes, are driven to nervous breakdown or suicide or are murdered. Even if we jump continents and move ahead some twenty years, we still get the same picture: e.g. *Ai nu* (*Confessions of a Chinese Courtesan*) shot in 1972 in Hong Kong shows a lesbian love story set in a brothel, and the movie ends with one woman killing the other by cutting off both of her arms with a sword; or the German movie *Die Bitteren Tränen der Petra von Kant* by Rainer Werner Fassbinder, a depressing tale of sexual dependence and emotional abuse, also released in 1972.

## From the 1980s to the Early 1990s

Finally, the second Women's Movement with it's exploration of sexual identities created a new assertiveness and independence which allowed lesbian audiences to long for – and demand – positive characters in film, enabling directors to create movies around positive and/or more realistic lesbian roles.

The iconic artist Derek Jarman not only revolutionised on-screen gay love, but was also first to cast extras who were obviously dykes – as in *Caravaggio* (1986) or *The Last of England* (1988). French director Jacques Doillon cast stars Jane Birkin and Maruschka Detmers as lovers in a nervous bisexual ménage à trois (*La Pirate*,

1984), while in *Egymásra nézve* (*Another Way*, 1982), Hungary-based Károly Makk tells a tragic lesbian love story set in the Stalinist society of the late 1960s.

By this time, with 8mm or even 16mm cameras more readily and cheaply available, independent film-makers were able to tell their stories without committing financial suicide, and soon a multitude of shorts, also by lesbian directors, was released. Very obviously coming from this experimental background, there was the first feature film by and with lesbians in 1995, the trendy urban love story *Go Fish!*, shot in black and white and boldly using its 'homemade' look as a chosen style. The film itself, as well as leading actress Guinevere Turner and director/producer Rose Troche, gained cult status in the lesbian community, for this was not only the first lesbian film that combined independence and commerce, but it also depicted lesbian characters which weren't that different from its audience.

Likewise, a German TV production from 1995, Angelina Maccarone's *Kommt Mausi raus?*, was one of the first German commercial feature-length movies by a lesbian director, followed by her feature *Alles wird gut* (1998), also a love tale. Maccarone returned to a lesbian plot in *Fremde Haut* (*Unveiled*, 2005).

Jasmin Tabatabai and
Anneke Kim Sarau in
Angelina Maccarone's
*Fremde Haut (Unveiled)*
(Picture: MMM Film
GmbH)

With the surge in lesbian (short) films and the demand for more adequate entertainment, the first genre film festivals were founded: San Francisco's International Lesbian and Gay Film Festival in 1976, followed by the first Festival de Films de Femmes in Créteil, France in 1983, just to name the oldest and most important ones. There are also three exclusively lesbian film festivals: Lesben Film Festival Berlin in Germany (since 1984), Festival International du Film – Lesbien and Feministe de Paris in France (since 1988) and Immagenaria in Bologna in Italy (founded in 1993).

## The Late 1990s and 2000s

The late 1990s saw a fragmentation of the women's and especially the lesbian movement: questioning sexual and/or gender identity, as well as trying to include or exclude as many personal, social and cultural features as possible was the new fashion. Also, lesbians dissatisfied with the traditional women's movement or the new conservative lesbian community opened up to a new 'queer' identity. Crossing gender lines and social stereotypes never seemed to be so easy. Likewise, identities from cultural backgrounds other than white US/European emerged more prominently in political debate as well as in film. At the same time, lesbian features became more commercialised as heterosexual mainstream cinema picked up on the trend.

A major influence came from US American film-makers – not only for the sheer number of genre movies released, but also for groundbreaking concepts by artists such as Barbara Hammer and Julie Dash before her. Still true to independent cinema, Cheryl Dunye shot the first lesbian feature film by an African-American woman, the 'mockumentary' *Watermelon Woman* (1996). In the same year mainstream audiences were introduced to the first truly hip lesbian couple in *Bound*. Directed by the Wachowski Brothers who broke gleefully with tradition and rewarded the criminal couple with a happy ending, both leading actresses – Jennifer Tilly and Gina Gershon – not only gladly became lesbian pin-ups but also keep playing quite unorthodox characters.

These were followed in 1997 by Lisa Cholodenko's *High Art*, evoking Fassbinder's *Petra von Kant*, and the surreal-philosophical sci-fi film *The Sticky Fingers of Time* by Hilary Brougher.

Jamie Babbit, like Angelina Maccarone, is one of the few directors who keep coming back to lesbian storylines. Her 1999 premiere feature *But I'm a Cheerleader* was an instant hit, and both *Stuck* (2001) and *Itty Bitty Titty Committee* (2007) bear a lesbian plot. She creates lesbian subtexts in the short *Sleeping Beauties* (1999) and the feature *The Quiet* (2005) while directing episodes for TV series such as *The L Word, Alias* and *Nip/Tuck*. Babbit also worked on the script of *D.E.B.S.*, Angela Robinson's lesbian version of *Charlie's Angels* (2004). It's still pre-Bollywood-craze, but films by directors with Indian background are already becoming fashionable: following her documentary *Kush* (1991), openly out British director Pratibha Parmar releases *Nina's Heavenly Delights* in 2006, a lesbian romance set in London's Indian community. *What's Cooking* (2000) is also a love tale by Gurinder Chadha – whose *Bend it like Beckham* (2000) was also adopted by the lesbian community for it's dyke subtext. Films with Asian background are limited to the US, with the exception of British director Kim Longinotto. Her documentaries *Dream Girls* (1994) and *Shinjuku Boys* (1995) explore the world of female-to-male crossdressers.

France brings us the highly controversial *Baise-Moi* by Trinh Thi (2000), featuring two les/bi women on a killing spree, lots of sex and raped men. Beautifully shot, the Belgian *S.* by Guido Henderickx (1998) also deals with desperate love, (self-)abuse and violence against men, while Iceland confirms the stereotype of weird Northern European films: in Baltasar Kormakur's *101 Reykjavík* (2000) a mother has an affair with her Flamenco teacher while her son also falls for the sexy Spaniard. Pirjo Honkasalo's *Tulennielijä* (*Fire Eater*, 1998) from Finland tells the story of twin sisters – named Vladimir and Iljitsch by their Socialist grandma – who grow up among circus performers in post-war Helsinki, sustaining an erotically charged preternatural bond. The Swedish cult hit *Fucking Åmål* (1998) by Lukas Moodysson deals with more down-to-earth problems as a teenage girl's coming out in a narrow-minded small town community turns out to be an experience more bitter than sweet.

Rebecka Lilleberg in Lukas
Moodysson's *Fucking Åmål*
(Show Me Love)
(Picture: Åke Ottosson/
Memfis Film AB)

Spectacularly, there are also films from countries with a long history
of repression: the first lesbian feature from Iran, *Daughters of the Sun*
directed by Marjam Shariar (2004), and also from China: Li Yu's *Fish
and Elephant* (2001), as well as the noteworthy early documentary on
lesbian life in Russia by Natasha Sharandak, *To My Women Friends*
(1993).

## Today: A Broader View

For some years now, programmers of genre festivals have mourned the
decline of feature films or professionally produced documentaries by
lesbian directors. At the same time mainstream cinema seems to be
fed up with girl-on-girl stories. It's true that we now have TV series
like *The L Word*, and a multitude of mainstream films that feature
lesbian (supporting) characters as positive and desirable role models.
But the era of groundbreaking 'first of' lesbian/bi/trans feature
films seems to be over. Where does the lesbian audience turn to for
cinematic entertainment – or shall we say, where does it *return* to?
Reading lesbian subtexts into heterosexual films and claiming hetero
characters as objects of lesbian desire is an old game we've always
loved to play, even if no longer strictly necessary. Does this mean we
have to stretch our definition of lesbian cinema to include any film
which – for whatever reasons – could be of interest for a lesbian
viewer?

The fact is that various lesbians from different backgrounds wouldn't cite 'real lesbian movies' as their favourites, their answers ranging from 'every film starring Jodie Foster', *Lara Croft* and Captain Janeway in the TV series *Star Trek: Voyager* to any Hong Kong martial arts movie. Speaking as a consumer and not as a festival programmer, my favourite 'lesbian film' is Marcus Nispel's *The Texas Chainsaw Massacre* with Jessica Biel – not only because she's a real hottie, but also a feminist role model of self-preservation.

In the year 2007, the reality remains that despite a bigger choice of older and more recent lesbian films, we still tend to prefer substitute characters for entertainment, or non-genre movies, when parting with our money at the box-office. As film-makers, producers or festival programmers, how can we deal creatively with this gap between private and professional (or political) demands?

Born in 1967 in Wiesbaden, Germany, **Silke Brandt** has been living in Berlin since 1989. After her studies in English philology, art history and politics, she worked as a freelance journalist, published texts for Claudia Gehrke's *Mein heimliches Auge* and financed/organised the photo exhibition *Lovers and Warriors* by lesbian artist Susan Stewart. She has been with the Lesbian Film Festival Berlin since 1996 as programmer, organiser, press officer and moderator and, as a day job, has been conducting market research on home entertainment and cinema.

Constantine Giannaris

# Reinventing Yourself
## An interview with Constantine Giannaris

*Constantine Giannaris has become recognised as one of Europe's foremost queer film-makers, and has won the Teddy Award at the Berlinale on two occasions. Internationally considered a 'Greek' film-maker, in Greece his work has stirred quite some unrest, some of it being considered scandalous.*

**Do you think of yourself as a Greek film-maker, a gay film-maker, or are such categories simply insufficient?**
Constantine Giannaris: Some people say my work is closer to British avant-garde film, some say I'm a gay film-maker. I believe that there are all sorts of elements in my work, but I think my film-making has more of a queer trajectory than a mainstream gay trajectory.

**Has financing a queer film become easier since you started your career?**
I think it is easier. It's become more 'normal' to do a gay comedy, a gay love story. Almodóvar has been absolutely seminal to this. So has the Panorama in Berlin, with Wieland Speck and Margaret von Schiller, and before that of course Manfred Salzgeber. I had made a kind of mad

film on Super 8mm for the Arts Council in London for about £500, around forty-five minutes long, influenced by Derek Jarman. It was rather overlong I admit, with this ten-year-old boy reading extracts from Genet's *Thief's Journal* and *Miracle of the Rose*. Lots of homo-erotic images running over the reading. I did not think anything more of it, until I got a call from Manfred, whom I didn't know from Adam, and he said, 'I run a section called the Panorama in the Berlinale, and I want to give you the money to blow this film up to 16mm and I want to screen it in the section "Young, British, and Gay".' I told him I was not technically British and didn't feel very gay as such, but he said that didn't matter, the section was about work coming out of the UK. Well, I and the other film-makers (apart from Derek) were booed in Berlin. They were hurling all sorts of insults at us, accusing our films of being too indulgent, too male, too homoerotic. Too arty. It surprised me because I had always thought of Berlin as being rather a liberal place, open to more unconventional and difficult work. I was very mistaken. Tough lesson.

It was a traumatic experience – in that even the gay audience turned their back on the film. They were more interested in formally more conservative things. And, in the end, 'gay or not gay/queer or not queer' people like a beginning, a middle and an end. They want a definable pace and trajectory. Who can blame them?

My second short film shot entirely on Super 8, *Trojans*, won the gay Teddy Award in 1990, and received all sorts of awards – in Ireland, Italy, all over. Paradoxically, the only place where it was completely rubbished was in Greece itself. The Short Film Festival in Drama utterly ignored it at the time. That was I believe because of its low-budget Super 8 form. At that time in Greece, and even now, they make a fetish of 'proper' cinematography, 'proper' technical input into a film. It was unconceivable that someone could make a film for so little and actually *want* that very grainy black-and-white look! It was a 'snobbery' which came out of the previous technical backwardness of the Greek film industry, which it was desperate to put behind it. Iron-ically, it was keeping them away from some of the most exciting things that were happening in the rest of Europe. *Trojans* was a much more structured, much more rigorous pseudo-documentary, looking at the

life of the Greek poet Constantine Cavafy. In fact, it was all a metaphor for AIDS, talking through the verse of Cavafy, who is my hero
poet of all time. I tried to bring him to a younger queer generation,
because he was in vogue during the 1930s and 40s and was revered
by people like E. M. Forster and W. H. Auden. This is another of the
reasons the film was ignored in Greece. Cavafy is still a bit of a
*national* figure. Something Greeks can hold up to the rest of the world.
His queerness and 'hellenistic promiscuity' is something that still
shocks, believe it or not.

I came back to Greece from the UK a few years after I shot my first
feature *3 Steps to Heaven* in 1995. It was made for the late British Film
Institute Production Board and Channel Four. It was picked up by
Cannes and was in competition for the Caméra d'Or [first feature
prize]. Lo and behold, the Weinstein brothers at Miramax picked it up
for $1 million. Probably to stop anyone else getting their hands on it.
So everyone in the UK was very curious about me. The BFI sales people
at that time were ecstatic, because the Institute had never made so
much money out of one of their films.

*3 Steps to Heaven* was a black comedy, not at all politically correct
at a time when everyone was so po-faced about women/gays/-
minorities (hypocritical rubbish actually) and it was trying to blend
art-house with commercial. I was moving towards a more recognis-
able, narrative style of film-making. It was a risk since it was not
pleading for liberal PC acceptance and hence would not earn any
brownie points for 'goodness'. It was out on a limb. Despite the critical
recognition at Cannes and the money from America, I found a lot of
hostility at the top at places like British Screen when it came to developing my second feature. And I didn't want to be in London for ever. I
did the round of agents in LA on the back of the film, but somehow it
didn't quite click for me. I couldn't *get it*. So I returned to Athens in
order to reinvent myself. To the periphery if you like. I kept remember-
ing what Derek Jarman had told me once, 'If you want to make films,
get a fucking camera and go out and make' em and don't wait for these
people to give you the money. They are just going to keep you in
"development" for ever.' That was the wisest piece of advice I ever got
from a fellow film-maker. I adored him. He was the last link in the line

with classical British education. A brilliant cultured tolerant man. It took Derek years to get the money to make *Caravaggio*, and it's such a beautiful, controlled piece of work.

**How did you establish your career back in Greece?**
I reinvented myself. I changed. I started doing things impossible to do in London. It was a very exciting time, the late 1990s in Athens. I met an enterprising young producer who asked me what I was doing. I told him about this bunch of guys living on the slum outskirts of Athens. I was hanging out with them. They were really fantastic, very sexy. I said I'd written the script for a short inspired by them. He read it and said, 'Make it feature-length and I'll get you the money.' So I sat down and wrote a screenplay in about five weeks (*From the Edge of the City*, 1998), and within three months we were actually shooting. I used a mixture of non-actors and professionals and it was all a bit chaotic, because these guys had no idea of discipline, didn't know how to turn up at a set time so as not to keep the crew waiting and kept being busted by the cops and so on. I had to drum that discipline thing into them during a five-week rehearsal phase. Nobody had tackled this youth culture overlap with immigrants theme in Greece before, so *From the Edge of the City* I believe was a hallmark for film-making in the country. It stuck two fingers up at the old stuffy academic 'lefty' film-making so prevalent here since the fall of the dictatorship in the early 1970s. It sold all over the world, and had a theatrical release in London, Berlin, Italy, and even in New York.

*One Day in August* (2001) proved much easier to set up as a result, and it was almost all privately financed by the major distribution company, an advertising firm and the Greek Film Centre helped as well. It was a hopeful time for Greek cinema. Things were happening, audiences were coming back, and they wanted a crossover film. I said, 'Well, I can't do a genuine crossover film, but I can do one that's pretty queer.' *One Day in August* proved a critical success and allied to the fact that it was in competition at the Berlinale in 2002, helped gain it an audience much bigger than for *From the Edge of the City*.

The film takes place in August, on the last Bank Holiday of the summer. The entire 'native' population of Athens abandons the city and returns to their origins, their islands and villages – a mad pilgrim-age, very Dionysian, very Christian, nostalgic and very dangerous, with loads dying on our famous roads. I was trying to capture that atmosphere. The film fans off into different road movies following three families who leave the same apartment block in downtown Athens. At the same time a *lumpen* young angel (Costas Kotsianidis) burgles the entire block and rifles through their homes and secret lives. He brings a mood of threat into the proceedings.

In a way I'm very proud that every summer on August 15th the film is always shown on some national TV channel at prime time.

**You have frequently worked with non-professional actors. What can they contribute to a film that a professional actor will not, or cannot?**
I like what I'd call the *veracity* of the screen presence. It brings a second level of reality, a kind of 'documentary' realism that you know has not been acquired at drama school. So the audience recognises that this is not just a film, there's something behind it, there's a *life* that invades the screen. These non-professional men or women can come alive on the big screen in a way that even the brilliant professional actor can-not; they can bring to the table a freshness and a naivety that's brilliant in itself. I work with them for weeks and weeks in rehearsal, before we arrive at the point of shooting. I don't allow improvisation; everything is very controlled, but they bring their own experience to bear so that the work doesn't appear contrived or fake.

**When you first started working with Stathis Papadopoulos, did you foresee that he would become somewhat of a gay icon?**
When I discovered him upon my return from London he was a wild card. We formed a very close bond. He is an ethnic Greek, from the Pontus (Black Sea) region of Turkey. But with the ethnic cleansing of the 1920s, his family – instead of coming here to the Greek mainland – escaped to the then Soviet Union. Of course Stalin deported them all to Central Asia during the 1940s and 1950s. Many died or suffered ter-rible hardship and torture, and when the Soviet Union collapsed in the early 1990s Stathis came to Greece. His family settled on the outskirts of Athens. So he carries within him all these interesting influences –

Kazakh, Central Asian, Pontian, Greek, Soviet. He was very rough when I found him. He had absolutely no training as an actor. But I could see that he could become a 'gay' icon. He's a very instinctive, almost a reptilian kind of actor.

*Omiros (Hostage)*

**As an openly gay director, do you feel part of a European film family (being part of the EFA) or are you always on your own when making minority/controversial films?**
I certainly know lots of people in the 'industry', but do I feel part of the family? I think I probably feel slightly marginalised, and that my concerns are actually different from what the European 'film establishment' wants to do. I hold Pasolini and Fassbinder as models. They both come from a kind of post-Marxist, political and cultural disillusionment but were searching for a utopia, I believe (especially Pasolini) that's very different to what exists now in Europe or the US. I believe that one should not worry about finding a mass audience on the spot, because, who knows, your real audience might be fifty years from now. You should never ever lose sight of the fact that it's *you* doing the work – in a sense you're talking about yourself. However good, however bad, or however indifferent that may be, that's what you're stuck with and don't feel ashamed of it.

I think Europe is not so much a film industry as a series of workshops. We clearly don't have an industry on the level of Hollywood. We have no linguistic homogeneity and we have no stars any more. On one level, that's a huge drawback. On another, we have a freedom to create, and to investigate other ways of making films. There's a kind of solidarity in the cross-border financing in Europe. But films must be organic, and not just bureaucratic production hybrids. Sometimes these co-productions work well, other times they can make your flesh crawl.

**If you owned a cinema for one day, which film or films would you screen?**
Probably Pier Paolo Pasolini's *The Gospel According to St Matthew* (1964). I love the fact that he found this non-professional actor, Enrique Irazoqui, to play Christ, and his mother plays the Virgin Mary, and he uses his friends as he did in *Accattone*.

Telephone interview by Peter Cowie on 15 December 2006.

**Constantine Giannaris** made his debut as a film-maker with a fine documentary (*Trojans*) on the life and work of the Greek poet Cavafy in 1990. Both this film and his subsequent short, *Caught Looking*, won the coveted Teddy Award in Berlin. He turned to fiction with *North of Vortex* (1991), set in the United States, and attracted widespread attention in 1998 with *From the Edge of the City*, dealing with the youth in a poor suburb of Athens. *One Day in August* (2002) was screened in competition at the Berlinale, and *Omiros* (2005) dealt with a hostage situation in northern Greece, and was also shown at the Berlinale. All three of his latest films have been part of the selection for the European Film Awards.

*Life on the Edge*
(Picture: Pere Selva/Els Films de la Rambla)

*Food of Love*
(Picture: Pere Selva/Els Films de la Rambla)

## Going Independent Was the Best Idea
An interview with Ventura Pons

*Ventura Pons is a Catalan who has been directing and producing feature films steadily since the early 1980s. His work deals with both queer and straight characters, and he has remained loyal to his homeland throughout his career.*

**When you made *Ocaña, an Intermittent Portrait*, in 1977, the gay scene was not as relaxed or liberal as it is now. Was it difficult to get that film accepted at first?**

Ventura Pons: No, in fact it was not. This is a very special movie. I had been working in theatre for some ten years, but I was fascinated by the cinema, and so I felt that I should start by making a documentary, as a kind of exercise. I wanted to find out how the camera functioned! So I looked around for a good story, because I believe that even in a documentary the story is very important. I knew this guy, José Pérez Ocaña, who was performing a drag show in the Ramblas of Barcelona. He did so, because he wanted to get the attention of the audience. He was a very pleasant, naive painter, and he wanted to attract the public. So I made my portrait of him on film in just five days, and it became a fairy tale because it was invited to Cannes. Whenever people mention the Barcelona, the Spain, of the late 1970s, they talk about my film because it's a reflection of the spirit of that period. Of course it had a gay theme, as do many of my movies.

**There's a gap of several years in the early 1980s between your feature films, *El Vicari d'Olot* and *La Rossa del bar*. Any particular reason?**

When I did *Ocaña, an Intermittent Portrait*, it became an international success, and went to festivals all over the world. It did very well in the cinemas, but nobody gave me a job as a result. So I thought, well, they assume I'm a documentarist, a man from the theatre (and stage work was paying me well at the time). So this is the reason that it took me such a long time to make another movie. I wanted to move into fiction and shoot feature films. So I made *El Vicari d'Olot*, a comedy with a gay theme within it, about the right to diversity. That too proved a great success, and attracted larger audiences than any of my previous films. It was radically different to my previous work, too, in that it was fiction, not documentary, it was a comedy not a drama, and it dealt with several characters, not just one.

People wanted me to do a sequel to that film, but I didn't want to, and I had fruitless talks with various producers. So in 1986 I decided to establish my own production company, because I needed the freedom to work in my own way. My first film under this banner was *The Blonde from the Bar* (*La Rossa del bar*).

Going independent was the best idea I've had in my career, and I was able to make a film almost every year – films that I like, passionate stories.

**Can Catalonian films find distribution easily in other parts of Spain?**

Most of my films have been in Catalan, although I've done one in Spanish and another in English (*Food of Love*, from David Leavitt's novel *The Page Turner* in 2002). But all my films have been screened outside Catalonia. Like American films, they are screened in a dubbed version in the bigger theatres, and with subtitles in more specialised venues. I hate the dubbing, but what can I do? It's the same for Woody Allen as it is for me! And it's a problem we share with Germany, France, and Spain.

**Can you describe the film scene in Barcelona, or in Catalonia, and how it differs from Castilian cinema?**
I can only speak about my own films. Of course we have a different culture and a different language compared to the rest of Spain, but that's a little like saying Denmark is different to Sweden. There *are* differences, but we are all part of the bigger picture. Perhaps we also have a rather distinctive approach to living. As everywhere, cinema reflects society.

Catalonian producers are involved in more than just local cinema. For example, *Perfume*, directed by Tom Tykwer, was co-produced by a Catalan company, and Woody Allen is due to come here in 2007 to shoot a film, and it will have Catalan participation too.

**In *Actress* (1997), a budding actress interviews other, established figures in her profession. Was there a queer element that appealed to you in this story?**
It was based on an excellent play by Josep Maria Benet i Jornet called *E.R.* My previous film to that was called *What It's All About*, consisting of fifteen sketches, each with a different tone – realistic stories alongside fantasy stories. It was about will-power in life, and also about doubt – in work, in love, in everything. It was very popular and ran for almost a year on screens here in Barcelona. It was also appreciated in Paris. So after that film, which was so difficult to do, I felt I had to do something more intimate. So I chose this play, featuring just four actresses. In a way, I moved from a big orchestra to chamber music! The theatre became a metaphor for life. The key question was: do you serve society with your work, or do you take advantage of society for your work? I like this kind of film, because my cinema is primarily based on ideas.

*Beloved/Friend* (1999) focuses on the self-destructive urges of its protagonist. This is a theme that appears in much of your work, and also in Almodóvar's too.

The most important thing about that story is the sense of life's continuity. If there's an inheritance, who's the heir? Is there such a person as an heir in a gay world? That's the reason I made the picture, and it's one of my best, I feel.

*Anita Takes a Chance* (2001) is actually a straight film, right?

Yes, but it's special in that it deals with a woman in her fifties. She has been so correct from a social point of view, and has worked for many years as a cinema attendant. Then the owner of the movie theatre wants to tear it down and have it replaced by a multiplex. She falls in love with a worker on the construction site, and starts a new life, saying to herself, 'Even though I'm fifty years old, I have the right to live, and I have the right to live like myself.' I enjoyed making *Anita Takes a Chance* because it describes the world of the actual cinema, and I like talking about that.

There are three themes that I always repeat in my movies. The first, and most important, is the need for the other, 'the other' whom one loves and with whom one can share life. It's a theme that runs through so many films, gay, straight or whatever. The second theme concerns friendship, like another kind of family relationship (I never talk about the traditional family!); friends being another kind of social conscience. And the third theme concerns death – one's relationship to death. So in all my films, gay or straight, documentary or fiction, it always boils down to love, friendship, and death.

*Food of Love* (2002) brings people together from Spain and the United States. Did you shoot much in the US, if at all, and what was it like directing actors like Juliet Stevenson in English?

A little bit in the States, but mostly in Barcelona. The English actors were marvellous – Allan Corduner, Geraldine McEwan, Kevin Bishop, Paul Rhys. I was happy during the making of this film, because I liked the story so much. And I have to fall in love with the story, otherwise I can't make the movie!

*Crazy Love (Amor idiota, 2004) seems to indicate a fondness for Dogma-style camerawork.*
It follows the desperate progress of this man, searching for his woman, and so we decided to write the story from his point of view, which explains my choice of shoulder-held camera and so on.

**How strong is the temptation to work in America, or at least outside Catalonia?**
I'm not in a hurry to move, because I have the freedom and the independence to do whatever I like in my country. It's a great privilege, and of course in Barcelona we feel very European. I grew up loving the American cinema, but in recent years the American cinema has become really terrible. It's been responsible for deterring so many adult people from going to the cinema, you know.

**As a final question: If you owned a cinema for one day, which films would you screen?**
I would start very early, screening the films I like by Visconti (*Rocco* or *Il Gattopardo*), Mankiewicz (*All About Eve, Letter to Three Wives*), Allen (*Annie Hall, Husbands and Wives*), Bergman (*Summer with Monika* or *Fanny and Alexander*), Buñuel (*Viridiana, Simon of the Desert*) . . . There are so many great films in the history of the cinema!

Telephone interview by Peter Cowie on 24 November 2006.

**Ventura Pons** (born in 1945 in Barcelona, Spain) began his career as a documentarist, but then ventured into fictional feature film-making. In 1980 he directed *El Vicari d'Olot*, and after an interval of some years, established his own production company. His main films since then include *The Blonde from the Bar* (*La Rossa del bar*, 1986), *Actresses* (*Actrius*, 1997), *Beloved/Friend* (*Amic/Amat*, 1999), *Anita Takes a Chance* (*Anita no perd el tren*, 2001), *Food of Love* (2002), *Idiot Love* (*Amor idiota*, 2004), and *Life on the Edge* (*La Vida abysmal*, 2007).

Olivier Ducastel and
Jacques Martineau
(Picture: Eve Petermann)

## No More Drama, Please!

An interview with
Jacques Martineau and Olivier Ducastel

*Olivier Ducastel and Jacques Martineau are a unique film-making
ensemble: A couple in private life, they have developed, written and
directed films together for several years. Their work stretches
from a musical about AIDS (*Jeanne et le garçon formidable*), a
coming-of-age road movie (*Drôle de Felix*), and a video diary (*Ma
Vraie Vie à Rouen) to the summer comedy* Crustacés et coquillages.
*We talked to them about their work and the role of queer cinema in
today's world.*

**Can you remember the first queer film you ever saw and what it meant
to you?**
Jacques Martineau: A real queer film, you mean, not like *La cage aux
folles*? It was *L'Homme blessé* by Patrice Chéreau, in the mid-eighties.
It was probably the first queer film I saw and I must confess, I was
quite impressed, even if I think it isn't exactly the kind of queer movie
I'd like to see today, it was something really exciting, as a teenager . . .
Olivier Ducastel: You were not a teenager! (*laughs*)
JM: I was not a teenager? How old was I?

OD: (*laughing*): Twenty!

JM: I can't remember!

OD: Well, for me – I *was* a teenager – I saw *A Bigger Splash*, by Jack Hazan, it's a film about David Hockney. I remember that I was particularly touched and impressed by the fact that it was a love story between guys, most of the characters were guys and there were really beautiful kissing scenes between the guys.

**How do you think that the expectations to queer film have changed?**

JM: I think it used to be a lot about suffering and being gay as damnation, something very dark and sinister. In *L'Homme blessé* there are some cruising scenes that are very dark, it's a very dramatic story. It's an old-fashioned way to show gay people. I knew that I was gay at the time, but I wasn't so clearly out of the closet so I found it touching. Well, actually what I think I found touching is that there is a blow-job in the movie.

OD: There are real sex scenes in the film, not just a blow-job; I mean, they fuck.

JM: No! Oh my God! I saw it with my mother!

(*Both laugh*)

JM: For me, those movies were about being gay, they were about what it is like to be a homosexual; nowadays we want to see movies with gay characters and gay stories but not movies about the fact of being gay.

**Is there one (queer) film or film-maker you would say had the biggest impact on your work?**

JM: Don't look at me!

OD: It's quite complicated, but I think I can say that a big influence on our work is Jacques Demy; and for me, his cinema is very gay even if most of his films were with heterosexual characters. Maybe Jacques has a more gay answer?

JM: No, because I don't think about specific directors. Usually, when we think about a script for a film, I think of all the queer movies I saw which I think are really bad and I try to do something else. Maybe I am not so convinced by gay movies.

OD: No, you can't say that. There are films you like very much, by Almodóvar for example, or Fassbinder.

JM: Fassbinder, of course.

OD: We very much like Almodóvar and a lot of Fassbinder movies, but if they have an influence on us, it's more unconscious. I could even mention George Cukor, because those were the classic movies we saw when we were very young; at that time I wanted to do films and of course these directors had an influence on me, but Jacques Demy is the most conscious influence.

JM: Well, there is one queer director we like very much, Gus van Sant – not only because he made gay movies. And I don't know if I can speak about influence. I mean, he's such a great director. I'm sure that *My Own Private Idaho* was the first queer movie I saw which convinced me in a very incredible way and I was really moved.

**From your point of view, is film-making first of all a creative activity or a political one?**

JM: Wow!

OD: I can try, as we say in France, a Norman answer, meaning it's neither yes nor no. I think it's a little bit different for each film that we did. When we decide to make a film, the aesthetic project and the fact that we want to tell a story is the most important thing, but of course we are also conscious of the political message implicit in the film. For me it's important to be aware of these political issues but that's not the main object. Do you agree?

JM: Yes, but I can try a coward's answer too. I don't really understand the concept of entertainment. I think that making a movie, queer or not, is always something political. You make a movie and you put it out in theatres and you want people to come to see it – it is always part of a social activity, it always means something. Even people who say they're not making politics, they're making entertainment, are political because of that statement. And they're dangerous because they may not be conscious of the fact that making entertainment is making politics. If you want people to come to see your movie, it's better to think of it as something political.

*Drôle de Felix* **came out at a time when most films dealing with AIDS typically portrayed tragic figures, victims. Was that part of your decision to make it a positive, happy film?**
OD: Jacques?

*Drôle de Felix*
(Picture: Canal Plus/Cinetext)

JM: Ah, Olivier says that the question is for me, so . . . yes, the way we conceived the project was very private in a way because previously we had done *Jeanne and the Perfect Guy*, a tragic love story about AIDS. It was released in '98 and we thought that we had to add something different, especially now that there was treatment which was quite new at the time. We felt we should do another movie with an HIV+ character, not because we wanted to explain anything but because we wanted to show that something had changed. You know, I was an activist in the Paris Act Up group for six or seven years, and what I tried to take from this experience when I wrote the script, was to de-dramatise the HIV issue. Not to forget the tragedy, but to try to put on the screen an HIV+ character without building the entire story up around that fact, to try to find a new way to portray HIV+ people. It's a big deal, of course, but it doesn't mean that HIV+ people can only be portrayed in one way.

**The film received the Teddy award at the Berlinale. What did that mean to you and did it help the film's career?**
OD: It was very important for the international career of the film to get those two prizes in Berlin. In fact, it completely changed our image

outside of France. As our first movie was a musical, it was distributed a little in foreign countries but it was not a real success. It was difficult to add good subtitles for the songs. It was really *Felix* that was our first film well distributed in the US or Germany or in Great Britain. Maybe the most important thing for us was that we discovered all these queer film festivals all over the world; the film was even screened at some festivals in countries where the film was never released. It was a really great experience to be considered as gay directors. The fact that the film was a gay film became more important than the fact that it was a French film. That was our first great surprise.

JM: It also meant a lot to us personally to get the Teddy award because two years before we were in Berlin with *Jeanne and the Perfect Guy* and we discovered the Teddy ceremony and I madly wanted a Teddy but we didn't get it! When we got the Teddy in 2000, we were really very happy . . .

OD: . . . and proud . . .

JM: . . . But I must say I was really pissed off when we didn't get the Teddy two years ago with *Crustacés et coquillages*. I really madly wanted a second one!

OD: Next time!

JM: Yeah, next time.

OD: They also have to give the Teddy to other directors, you know?

JM: Ah! Why?

**In places like Berlin or Paris a queer film doesn't stir much controversy as such. What has your experience been filming in provincial cities and touring the country with your films?**

OD: I'll tell you a story about the shooting of *Felix*. At the end of the film, Felix and his boyfriend meet on the steps in front of the Marseille railway station – it's a very crowded place, even if in the film it looks quiet. There were a lot of people watching, especially teenagers – a lot of teenagers of Arabic origin from the suburbs of Marseille. And, of course, they saw an Arabic guy playing, so they were very interested, some of them knew the actor. When they saw the two guys kissing, I think they were very shocked and they wanted to know if the actor was gay or not. And when he said, no, I'm heterosexual, they wanted to know why he would agree to kiss a boy in front of the camera. In the beginning we were a bit afraid that it would lead to an ugly situation. But it didn't, probably because of Sami Bouajila, who is very generous and curious about people, and was receptive to discussing it with those teenagers. I don't know if they changed their minds about gays, but they probably learned a little bit about what it means to be an actor.

JM: We never had problems with the shooting. I suppose that in France people wouldn't dare to display a homophobic attitude. Well, it's a bit complicated because, on the other hand, when we try to get authorisation to film in public locations, the production manager usually makes a special, lighter, version of the script. We always find that ridiculous, but it always happens so we lie sometimes. When it comes to showing the films, personally we've never had any problems and we've travelled a lot, both in France and in foreign countries. For example, *Felix* wasn't shown in big theatres in France because the people who decide on releases on the big circuit decided not to show the movie because it would be shocking. So, personally, we never had any problems, but we know that there is a kind of censorship, even in France. And it was the same with our last film, *Crustacés et coquillages*, because the major companies boycotted the film during its release. In foreign countries it's difficult to say because when we go to foreign countries to show our movies, it's in the framework of festivals, it's a special space and in international film festivals people are usually open-minded.

*Crustacés et coquillages*
(Picture: Eve Petermann)

**Have you ever encountered any problems casting gay roles?**

OD: No, we never had any problems. For example, for both *Felix* and *Crustacés*, we got our first choice actors. The first actors we sent the script to, Sami Bouajila and Gilbert Melki, both accepted. So we never had the experience of an actor saying no because it was a gay character.

JM: It's probably because we asked straight actors and they don't care or they think it's good for their career. Sami is also very nice and I think he loved the experience. It was obvious on the set that he loved to kiss all the boys; it was really incredible, we never had so much kissing on the set. He really wanted to kiss everyone.

**You have worked in very different genres. Do you normally start with a genre in mind or with a story?**

OD: I think most of the time when we start on a new project we have both in mind – a story, and a genre which allows us to tell the story. And it's probably when we have a good combination between the two that the project really starts rolling. This is particularly true with *Crustacés et coquillages*. At the beginning, in my mind, it wasn't necessarily going to be a comedy, it could have been a little bit more dramatic. It was really when we started to discuss it and Jacques began to write that the idea of a comedy emerged more and more clearly. And the longer we worked on it, the more comic it became.

**Generally you portray happy queers with supportive family backgrounds. Does this reflect your own experiences?**

JM: Probably, yes, we are almost happy. And we don't have fathers (*laughs*), so yes, our characters are very close to us. Well, except for the fact that they are much, much sexier than we are but . . .

OD: Especially Sami.

JM: Well, except for the fact that because we are two, everything gets a bit muddled. Even I am not sure exactly what comes from my background and what comes from his because since we speak so much, we mix our stories. Although I am probably happier than Olivier is. Well, he's getting better.

OD: I agree with Jacques, but maybe I would say it a bit differently. I think it's also a political decision. There are a lot of dramatic stories with queer characters and we are not always completely convinced by this drama. So when we began to make films, we wanted to show positive, happy characters – even in dramatic situations – I mean, maybe with a little bit more of a positive approach to situations and life in general than we see in our lives or in the lives of people around us. I think it's something quite conscious and it's connected to the influence of Jacques Demy on our work. It's a decision that you take, to be optimistic in your films, it's not something that just happens.

JM: I agree, but now we're working on a new project which is much more dramatic, we decided to do something much more dark. And it was really difficult for me when I wrote the script. I don't know why but it comes naturally to me that when I write a very dramatic scene, it immediately becomes funny and I really had to work hard to stay on the dramatic track of the project.

**Do you believe that it is still more difficult to make a successful queer film?**

OD: No, I don't think so. I don't think it's a question of queer movies, it's more a question of the budget – with a small budget project it will be difficult to get a bigger audience.

JM: That's very optimistic, I think. But it also depends on what you call a queer film. A real queer film with a queer look doesn't have a big chance to have much success. We've seen people who say that they have heard that this is a queer film but since they are straight they won't watch it, which is ridiculous. It's very difficult to make a big queer film with a lot of money because producers know that it won't be a big success that makes much money.

**When you work, is it always Jacques writing, Olivier directing? Or how do you work together?**

OD: Well, before Jacques begins to write, we discuss it, decide on the general direction of the story and the main characters; I make sure I'm okay with the general direction he's taking. We work together. Jacques likes to write in a very expansive way so that the first draft tends to be far too long and I'm the one who cuts it. After the first draft, we decide together how to re-organise the story. That's how we work on the script.

JM: Well, we live together (*Olivier laughs*) . . . You know that! It's horrible but what can we do? So, we speak about the project all the time. It's not that he isn't involved because I'm writing or that because Olivier is a real director I'm not involved. Olivier is the one who says 'Action' and 'Cut', that's right. But I'm always on the set, I talk to the actors a lot.

OD: It's true, I went to film school, I've had some cinematographic background, so – at least in the beginning – I had more technical experience. But with Jacques on the set, I can always ask him what he thinks. We both speak with the actors, not necessarily at the same time; he spends more time with them before the shooting and I talk more during the shooting. But now we're really working together, we can both communicate in a complimentary way.

**As a final question we ask everyone: if you owned a cinema for one day, what films would you show?**

JM: Jacques Demy's movie *Une chambre en ville*. And *Nosferatu* by Murnau, in the original version – my favourite film. It's probably the most beautiful movie ever. And I just found out that Murnau was gay! I never knew that!

OD: I would probably like to see a classic too, because nowadays the audience has very few chances to see old classics on a big screen, maybe *La Règle du jeu* by Jean Renoir.

JM: And *My Own Private Idaho* by Gus van Sant.

OD: But you can only say one.

JM: No, we have a full day.

OD: Oh! I didn't realise that.

Olivier Ducastel later added the following films to his list by e-mail:

*La Chambre verte* by François Truffaut
*La Geule ouverte* by Maurice Pialat
*Le Petit prince a dit* by Christine Pascale

*Les Parapluies de Cherbourg* by Jacques Demy
*Playtime* by Jacques Tati

Telephone interview by Pascal Edelmann on 27 December 2007.

Born in 1962, **Olivier Ducastel** has studied film studies and research after graduating from the Paris film school IDHEC and has worked in sound, as an editor and as assistant director before starting to make his own films.

**Jacques Martineau** was born in 1963. He has studied literature and taken singing classes at the conservatory in Boulogne-Billancourt. Together they have made *Jeanne et le garcon formidable* (1998), *Drôle de Felix* (2000), *Ma vraie vie à Rouen* (2003), and *Crustacés et coquillages* (2005).

# 8   A Regional Matter: Local Heroes

*In many regions in Europe, if you travel for a few hours people speak a different language, the food is different, maybe the houses look unfamiliar – sometimes without you having crossed a single border. Although each of the communities that make up Europe is itself a fascinating and unique collage of cultural tradition, international modernity, and neighbouring influences, many of them have little chance of building or maintaining a functional film industry without the co-operation of others. Sometimes this leads to big, European plots, multi-national casts and international enterprises (and not only the much pilloried 'Euro-pudding').*

*But, like a sculptor in his workshop at the edge of the village, there are film-makers who seem unimpressed by the financial allure of the international marketplace. They concentrate on the authenticity of a particular story – be it the contrast between two cultures, the harsh reality of prostitution, or the bleakness of long-time unemployment. Whether their stories take place in Galicia, Scotland or Valonie, the films often impress with their particular intensity, and surprise audiences across Europe and beyond because the individual experience of a human being can be understood regardless of national identity or cultural proximity.*

Ken Loach in Warsaw for the European Film Awards 2006 (Picture: EFA/Andreas Böhmig)

# A Touchstone of Reality

An interview with Ken Loach

*Ken Loach has been making committed feature films for some forty years, and has won a European Film Award on three occasions (for* Riff-Raff, Land and Freedom *and* Sweet Sixteen*). He remains Britain's most uncompromising director, the true heir to Lindsay Anderson and the provocative cinema of the 1960s.*

**Your films express the need to fight to retain our minorities, our cultures, and our local languages . . .**

Ken Loach: Basically, it's a question of the language – the language of working people. Posh people might say that they were born in Scotland, but as far as one can tell, they might as well have been born in Sussex! For ordinary people, their humour, and their experience, and the work they do can be heard in their language. You can hear the *detail* of everyday life. The language is very particular, and varies from region to region. It's enormously rich; the rhythm of the language expresses the humour, and makes you smile. People are funny, and sharp, and thoughtful, whether they're from South Yorkshire, or Glasgow, or Liverpool.

**You have shot a majority of your films on location. What attracts you so much to that style of shooting?**

Well, mainly because studios are completely sterile. What's attractive about film are the things you can't plan, the people you find, the things that you would never dream of including. They just happen to be there, and so they become part of the film. Part of the challenge is trying to capture the richness of life on the streets, and in people's homes, and the details of the buildings, and the interiors – things that you would never create in the studio.

Nothing was shot in the studio for *The Wind That Shakes the Barley*. I've never really shot in a studio. And nothing was post-synched, either, apart from the odd word, or maybe a crucial phrase that might be hidden. I've worked with a terrific sound recordist named Ray Beckett for fifteen years, who has just refined the business of location sound, so that it's a mixture of personal mikes and the boom, wherever possible, just to keep the ambient sound. Obviously, you may add to the dub things that are missing, but by and large all the sound is recorded on location.

I think it's very important for the actors, because all around them they have a kind of touchstone of reality. So they just have to be there. Whereas, if you put them in the studio, it becomes like the theatre, and a different set of responses comes into play. If you really are in the streets, then you have to be like everyone else in the streets. So it's not just about what it looks like, it's the circumstances in which you create the fiction.

*Sweet Sixteen*
(Picture: Joss Barratt/Sixteen
Films)

Going back to the regional issue, on *Land and Freedom*, set during the Civil War in Spain, I remember we had people from many different countries coming to Spain. They were speaking Catalan, Castilian, French, American, Scouse English, West Coast Scottish, German, and so on. But in a country like Italy, where films are dubbed, all these different languages ended up in Italian! The multiplicity of languages was an acknowledgement of the internationalism of the campaign, and the effort to understand, and the effort to translate, was part of the story.

*Land and Freedom*
(Picture: Paul Chedlow/
Parallax Pictures)

**In an age when politically committed film-makers tend to go for the documentary, you go for fiction.**
I think you can just go deeper with fiction. It should inform what you do, rather than determine it; it should inform how you see families living together, and the work they do. You can make wonderful documentaries, but fiction is a deeper challenge. You've got to deal, for example, with a whole family, the psychological background, the inter-action, the conflict, the resolution – all the basic elements of dramatic structure. You may fall a long way short, but what you have in your sights is the process of being human in a social and political situation.

The screenwriting and pre-production process are vital. The actual filming is working through that, and living off the people who come into the film. There's always a great space for them. They have to bring their own person into this, and if you get it right, when they reveal themselves, they also reveal the characters. So you're trying to touch profound things in everyone who performs, that will bring to life that pattern which my screenwriter Paul Laverty has written and that we've both been talking about.

**Is it easier for you to raise the funds for a film than it was twenty years ago, when the Academy was founded?**
Yes, it is. We have access to more European funding, and I think that European co-productions are the way to go. But the big, abiding problem is that we do not have access to our cinemas – and that's particularly acute in the United Kingdom. We can make good films, or mediocre films, or bad films, but in a way it's academic if most of the people cannot see them. Will the digital age change all that? I don't know, but I don't really think so, because there are vested interests where the cinemas and the studios are concerned, and they'll protect that revenue. The onus is on the politicians to deal with that, but they won't because basically the European Union is a club for big business, and I don't think they'll tangle with the Americans, who decide what appears in our cinemas.

Nevertheless, I continue to make films for the cinema, because I find that television is constraining in that the tempo at which you've got to cut, and the style you have to adopt to keep people tuned in, is too frantic. There isn't space just to hold a shot and look into someone's eyes. It won't have the impact on the small screen. Everything's got to be close-up, cut fast and bang-bang, and that limits what you can say and the way you can explore a subject. Television executives have used the advent of the digital camera to dispense with all the cameramen. I learned everything I know from Chris Menges, the cinematographer who had learned everything in his turn from great documentaries. He taught me to look at light, and to have a sense of framing and images. Today those executives regard a project as a one-person shoot. The director has to do a home video, and the craft of cinematography is suffering, just being lost.

Interviewed by Peter Cowie in Warsaw on 3 December 2006.

**Ken Loach** (born 1936, in Nuneaton, UK) began his career in British television, and received excellent reviews for his full-length study of a young woman at the mercy of society and her own unfortunate choices, *Poor Cow* (1967). His breakthrough came in 1969 with the much-loved *Kes*, and *Family Life* (1971) underlined his commitment to social change. During the 1990s he established himself as a world-class director, with a succession of outspoken political fiction films: *Riff-Raff* (1990), *Hidden Agenda* (1990), *Raining Stones* (1991), *Ladybird Ladybird* (1994), *Land and Freedom* (1995), and *Carla's Song* (1996). More recently, he has focused on films set in Scotland and Ireland, among them the award-winning *Sweet Sixteen* (2002), *Just a Kiss* (2004) and *The Wind That Shakes the Barley* (2006), which won the Palme d'Or at Cannes.

Jean-Pierre and Luc
Dardenne
(Picture: Les Films du
Fleuve/Cinetext)

## An Opportunity to Resist

An interview with Jean-Pierre and Luc Dardenne

*With a background in documentary film-making, the Belgian brothers Jean-Pierre and Luc Dardenne are committed political film-makers who portray the lives of ordinary people in modern society.*

**Your films are very character-driven. Where do you find the ideas for these characters?**
Jean-Pierre Dardenne: Work! It doesn't happen by itself. It is fed with our experiences, what we see, what we read, what we talk about, the people we know, and also the intuition we get from the film. Our life is our first source of inspiration.

**How important is the location for your work?**

J-PD: It's always the same place. Maybe we'll stop on the day we work out *why* we keep filming in this place (*laughs*). I could give you lots of reasons, like our childhood here. But I don't know if that's relevant. As someone said, I don't remember who, 'The only scenery is that of childhood.'

**You work a lot with amateurs or unknown actors. Why is that?**
J-PD: It's basically due to the fact that we work with teenagers. In Belgium, there are very few teenagers who are professional actors in cinema or theatre. So we have to look for them anyway. Take Olivier Gourmet, for instance; he was already a professional actor in theatre when we met him. However, we like to have this mix of experienced actors and others who are making a film for the first time, like we did for *L'Enfant*. For Jérémie [Renier] it was, of course, not the first time but it was the first film for Deborah François. This mixture creates a certain energy on the set. Sometimes tension too, but that produces something interesting.

*L'Enfant*
(Picture: Les Films du Fleuve/
Cinetext)

**It's also a way to give a first opportunity to young actors?**
J-PD: Yes, of course. But we also enjoy very much discovering someone who walks, laughs, cries for the first time in front of a camera.

Luc Dardenne: Yes, as my brother said, when we make them walk, move for the first time, there are things in their behaviour that come from their body, that they don't act out, things which were there before. So you can catch moments you may not catch any more with an actor who has ten years of experience, who is able to control his body and work perfectly with it. A young actor doesn't have as much control over his body as an instrument, he just throws himself into it. What's extraordinary is that he's discovering himself in front of us.

And the more experienced actor playing with him has to adapt himself to it. It creates situations where something happens in front of the camera. And that's what we are interested in.

**One of the problems of European film is that films don't travel enough. Have you ever considered making a more international film, maybe filming elsewhere?**

LD: No. First of all, we do what we want to do. We've never thought of working with big international movie stars. It wouldn't be a problem to work with foreign actors, which we will do in our next movie. But that's because of the film itself, which requires foreign actors. We didn't start the film thinking we need foreign actors; it's not a matter of finding faces that will sell the film abroad. We cannot really complain about the export of our movies. We pretty much have a public everywhere.

**Is it harder for other European films to find an audience outside their borders?**

LD: Yes and no. Take for instance the film *12:08 East of Bucharest*. I don't know how the film is doing, but I'm under the impression that you can see it in a lot of countries.

**Of course there are exceptions. But if you compare it with the big American machinery?**

LD: Ah! (*laughs*). Of course, that's a different thing. But I think that has a lot to do with the actors' popularity, the budget of the film itself and the budget for promotion.

**How important is international co-operation if you come from a smaller country?**

LD: You cannot make a film in Belgium without [international] co-production. Not a single one! And our major partner is France. We always work – I say 'we' but it's a general thing, Belgian productions in French are made in co-operation with French partners like Canal Plus or ARTE, with advances on receipts [from the CNC], and with Eurimages. Sometimes we also work with Germany, but France is the main partner.

**And how does this influence your work?**

LD: When you work with partners, you have to give something in return. If you have money coming from France, normally it will mean that you may have to work with actors or technicians from France. This point does indeed have an influence. For instance, the sound in our movies is always done by Jean-Pierre Duret, a French sound engineer. When it comes to the actors, they respect our work. Our partners won't impose a French actor we don't want to take. If they suggest a French actor with a Parisian accent, that doesn't work! And they understand that. So for us, it hasn't been a problem. But it may be different for a young Belgian film-maker doing his first film with France. He may be inclined to take a French star to get money from Canal+. It does play a role because in order to get French funding it is of advantage to have a French actor or actress in the film. Take for instance Joachim Lafosse and his film *Nue propriété*. When Isabelle Huppert read the script and said 'I'm doing it', it unfroze everything immediately. For us, it would be easier to get more money if we worked with actresses like Isabelle Huppert or Juliette Binoche. But we don't need to. We have a very economic working method and this is important for the final production. It's all linked. Our films are like they are due to the fact that our budget never exceeds €3.5 million, and that's everything included. We normally find 1.2 or 1.3 million in our country, 1 million in France and the rest comes from Eurimages. This low budget is part of the way we see our cinema, the cinema we want to make. We don't negotiate with actors' agents because our budget is limited. We don't discuss. You know we refuse to pay an actor twice the amount another one gets just because he's famous.

**You started making documentaries. How do you think that has influenced your way of making films?**

LD: Actually, we started with theatre! My brother was the assistant of the Belgian director Armand Gatti. Theatre was our first contact with acting and performing, and then video. We made documentaries, but these are very different from our fictional films. The camera doesn't move, there are lots of interviews, archive footage. It's almost like a historian's job. However, there's one link between our documentaries and fiction films. When you shoot something for a documentary, people moving, something that happens in the street, anything, you can't predict what's going to happen. You can't, for instance, move the camera to a better position to catch something that was not foreseen. I think that we organise the *mise en scène* in a way to somehow give the camera this wrong place. That comes from our documentary experience, as if the object you're shooting could resist being captured. So there is this realistic feeling, which remains in the way we work. The idea of shooting Olivier Gourmet more from the back comes from this, I think. We don't especially like the kind of cinema where you've got the feeling that everything is set up to be shot by a camera, as in a big TV show. If you watch it, everything is organised, even the unexpected events are planned.

*Le Fils*
(Picture: Archipel 35/
Cinetext)

**Do you like the idea of randomness then?**
LD: Not randomness, but the question we asked ourselves was: how to film an actor to allow him to resist the fact that we're shooting him? This secret you give to the actor creates a strain and finally gives him some kind of existence as a character. The spectator is in a position where he's searching, trying to understand, trying to know what's going on.

**Is the documentary style also how you manage to stay so in touch with reality?**

LD: Not really. The result might have a documentary effect but every scene requires lots of rehearsing. The actors never improvise; on the contrary, they would probably say that we are meticulous, everything is minutely prepared.

**You told us about the TV shows that look unreal. Isn't this the exact opposite of your work?**

LD: Yes, as I said, there is this kind of cinema where everything is in the right place, ready to be shot. The scenery feels more and more 'plastic'. Also, movie stars become plastic, it gives you the feeling that they're here only to be filmed. You can store them in a closet, just like the scenery.

So yes, maybe we try to keep in touch with reality. This reality doesn't just come along, you have to look for it, take the time to wait for it.

**Where would you position yourself in the landscape of European cinema?**

LD: I believe there is a European cinema, but I don't know where our place in it would be. The way I perceive European cinema is that it is driven by languages, by a multiplicity of languages, even though it needs subtitles. American cinema speaks one language, Chinese cinema speaks one language, European cinema speaks various languages. I feel that European cinema likes reality better than illusion. It's not that I don't like illusion; illusion is just a different way to talk about reality, not worse or better. In Europe, someone filming in Bucharest, Sofia or Paris will try to give the city a role in the movie. In American movies – I wouldn't say that they could all be filmed at the same place, but the link to the reality of the place is secondary.

American cinema was born at a time when it was still necessary to unify. It has to speak to a number of people. Of course, you also have an American cinema that is very close to the European one. Scorsese's film *Taxi Driver* is very similar to European films – note that Scorsese has Italian origins (*laughs*)! There are definitely bridges between American and European cinema.

**In Belgium, are you especially confronted with this diversity of languages?**

LD: Yes, forty per cent of our Belgian audience comes from Flanders, from the Dutch-speaking part of Belgium. We don't feel like we're the centre of Europe, but, we are used to talking, to negotiating or making compromises with the other part. Politically, this is a good way to learn, but not artistically. In art, we're not into compromising, we don't do politics. If a Flemish investor wanted to impose a Flemish actor, we would decline his offer. We don't feel more European than others – Germans, Italians or Frenchmen. Well, maybe not the French, they rejected the European Constitution (*laughs*).

**As a final question we ask at the end of each interview: if you owned a cinema for one day, which films would you screen?**

LD: *Shoah* by Claude Lanzmann.

J-PD: *La Maison des Bois* by Maurice Pialat.

Telephone interview by Pascal Edelmann, translated by Philippe Dialo, on 7 February 2007.

The Belgian brothers **Jean-Pierre** (born 1951) and **Luc Dardenne** (born 1954) have been making films together since the 1970s. With a background in theatre, they started with documentaries on video and soon moved to film. Their international breakthrough came with *Rosetta* (1999) for which the received the Palme d'Or in Cannes. They returned to Cannes with *Le Fils* in 2002 and won another Palme d'Or with *L'Enfant* in 2005.

Florian Henckel von Donnersmarck (centre) with producers Max Wideman and Quirin Berg winning the European Film Award Best Film 2006 for *The Lives of Others* (Picture: Jaczek Turczyk/PAP)

# A World Without Red and Blue
## An interview with Florian Henckel von Donnersmarck

*A remarkably assured first feature from the maker of the award-winning shorts* Dobermann *and* The Templar, *writer-director Florian Henckel von Donnersmarck's* The Lives of Others *paints a dark picture of life under the Communist regime in East Germany. Eschewing a purely historical approach by creating fictional characters, the film is part thriller, and part love story and offers a compelling tale of individuals whose lives and search for dignity are shaped by the society in which they live. The film also shows with remarkable consistency that the mechanisms that upheld the GDR ultimately led to its demise. Von Donnersmarck spent four years conducting intensive research and writing his screenplay before beginning shooting. In addition to reading an abundance of specialised literature, the director also spent countless hours in conversation with eyewitnesses, former Stasi (State Police) employees and their victims. He was advised and supported on historical matters by a number of distinguished specialists, including Professor Manfred Wilke, head of the Research Committee on the SED (Sozialistische Einheitspartei Deutschlands – the Socialist Unity Party), Jörg Drieselmann, head of the Research Agency and Memorial*

*in Normannenstrasse and former Stasi Colonel Wolfgang Schmidt.*
*The film team also numbered several people who had been personally*
*involved with the GDR regime and whose experiences made the film*
*as authentic as possible. Further establishing time, place and texture*
*was von Donnersmarck's determination to shoot wherever possible on*
*original locations. These venues include the former Stasi headquarters*
*in Normannenstrasse, a feared address during the years of the SED*
*regime.* The Lives of Others *was also the first feature film that was*
*allowed to be shot in the original file-card archives of the former Stasi*
*headquarters. Awarded the grade 'particularly worthwhile' by the*
*German Film Evaluation Bureau,* The Lives of Others' *growing list*
*of accolades also includes the Best Foreign Language American*
*Film Academy Award, seven Lola German Film Awards and three*
*European Film Awards.*

**I was struck by the film's reference to Lenin and Beethoven's**
***Appassionata*. Was this a particular motivation?**
Florian Henckel von Donnersmarck: The quote from Lenin was really
the starting point. I remember very clearly the moment when I had the
idea of making the film. Listening to a Beethoven piano sonata I
remembered this quote I read in a book by Maxim Gorky, actually
a friend of Lenin's, and Lenin had said to him: 'Beethoven's *Appas-*
*sionata* is my favourite piece of music, but I don't want to listen to it
any more because it makes me go all soft, stroke people's heads and
tell them sweet, stupid things. But I have to smash in those heads.
Smash them in without mercy in order to finish my revolution.' And I
thought that perhaps I should find a film story or plot where I can force
Lenin to listen to the *Appassionata* just as he was getting ready to
smash in somebody's head. And would that change the course of
history? But I didn't want to make a surreal film, so I turned him into
this Stasi officer and the *Appassionata* turned into Gabriel Yared's film
music. When I thought about forcing Lenin to listen to the music I had
the story within a few minutes, the entire structure, and I sat down at
my computer and typed it within an hour. So that was a two-page
outline of the plot and that still is remarkably close to what I ended up
writing. It's just that it took another three years.

**Let's talk about those three years. What kind of processes did you go through?**

I knew all of the survivors of that period were still alive, so I knew if I got anything wrong I would be slaughtered. As a film-maker it is a matter of honour to get the setting for a film right. Even if most of the survivors of the Russian revolution were dead by then, I'm sure the makers of *Dr Zhivago* adopted exactly the same painstaking work to get the details right. There's something comically wrong with a film if you don't work on those details. Before writing the first line of dialogue, I spent one and a half years just researching. I didn't intend for it to take that long, but only after one and a half years did I reach a point where I really knew enough about it to tell the tale objectively. I'd heard both sides and so many contradictions in the ways that the stories were told that the point had come where I had enough to make up my own mind about how it was. I'd talked to Stasi victims and to Stasi officers. It was quite an emotional rollercoaster ride that year and a half. I'd be meeting one of the victims in the morning who would tell me about how they were tortured psychologically and in the afternoon I'd meet the person who did it. Of course I felt hypocritical sitting there, not telling someone what you think of them. You try and get information from them.

Jason, I know that you are interested in documentary and so you must have seen the great *Shoah*. Claude Lanzmann pulled himself back completely when talking to the Auschwitz camp guards, even going so far as to flatter them to get information. He, a Jew whose family had suffered greatly. That was because Lanzmann knew he would have the last word. And that last word would be the film. So I tried to remember that and extracted information from these people. I think they were pretty shocked when they saw the final film. I actually invited my main Stasi consultant to the film. Luckily, he didn't come in uniform but he did come with his wife who was also a Stasi officer; they were only allowed to marry amongst themselves. I was watching him out of the corner of my eye and he left immediately after the film was over. I thought that would be the last I ever heard from him, but then he wrote me a letter in which he said 'I'm glad at least you got the historical details right. But isn't it a sad state of things that the only way you can portray a Stasi officer as a hero is by making him a traitor.' I thought it was incredible that he could have seen the film and still be thinking 'What a traitor!' It was absurd, a bit like someone mocking Schindler in *Schindler's List* for being an asshole for saving the Jews.

But it was very important for me to hear that side too. I remember once talking to a Stasi officer about these odour samples; one of the most curious discoveries in the Stasi archives was these jars with little red pieces of cloth and names. It was like a primitive form of DNA sampling for the dogs. One of the theories was that the victim was given a piece of cloth with pliers and they would have to rub it between his or her legs so that they would know that the dogs would find them if they tried to flee to the other side. I had the man in charge of the section that did those things, but I restrained myself from saying 'Did you really do that?' or the conversation would have been over. So I asked 'You know these odour samples I read about . . . did they really work?' He would say, 'Yes! Yes!' and his eyes would be afire with pride and he would say, 'It worked incredibly well. The dogs were always able to identify so accurately. I don't know why they are not still continuing this system today.' But then he added, 'One time it didn't work. You know what the reason was? It was this girl and she had her period and there was just this one drop on this cloth and it completely confused the dogs.' Then he started laughing and said, 'I hadn't thought about that in twenty years.' I then needed a reality check, looking around at his wife serving tea, with pictures of his grand-children on the wall. And I thought that only twenty years ago this man was torturing a girl who didn't believe in his ideology, making her wipe between her legs with a cloth while she had her period, in order to save it in a jar for dogs to track her. My head was spinning and I considered that total barbarism and civilisation are that close to one another.

**Adding to the texture of the film and in line with your feeling that, though a work of fiction, the film be grounded in historical accuracy was your decision to shoot on location wherever possible. Given the amount of changes in so short a period in the former East Germany this must have been quite an undertaking.**

It was harder to shoot something in 1984 East Berlin than it would have been to make a film set in Renaissance Italy. At least if you go into other periods of history you have buildings that have been preserved. In Germany, since 1989 people have done nothing but try to destroy traces of that period. Fortunately, we got some very special authorisations to shoot in the real Stasi archives so what you see in the film are the real Stasi files and the real rooms with their revolving index card machines. I also found an apartment that had not been renovated, enabling me to get the texture of the walls. This always looks more authentic to me than if you try to build something in a studio.

What was really hard to find was the street outside Dreyman's apartment because I needed that as a 360 degrees location. Graffiti was everywhere and there was, of course, no graffiti in the GDR. Every morning we had to have a group of painters re-paint the walls of this entire street because every night the graffiti would reappear. Our producers even calculated to see if it would be cheaper to employ armed security guards to protect our clean walls overnight or to just have painters repaint from 4 a.m. to 7 a.m. every morning. We decided to do the latter.

**Your attention to colour is astonishing.**
I was very aware that the Eastern bloc had a very different palette of colours to the West. I even talked to a chemist who explained that the reason for this was that there were certain patents developed from the 1960s onwards that people in the East did not have access to. In the East the colours stayed similar to what they had been in the late 1950s: more subdued and less neon than those in the West. This also gave the East a more dignified and calm look; I was very aware of that from my trips to the East and the two years that I spent in the Soviet Union just as the Soviet Union collapsed.

I really tried to reconstruct that world and by looking at pictures I realised that red and blue, two colours that seem the most shocking to the eye and which have very extreme qualities to them were largely absent. It occurred to me that we could reconstruct the East by simply leaving out these two colours all together. That's what I did. I experimented through drawings and designs and when I showed these and shots from the film to my friends and relatives from the East, they remarked right away that it really reminded them of the GDR. I stuck to that principle and there is no red or blue in the film. Of course, there was red and blue in the GDR but eliminating them made it feel more like the GDR than it would if you reconstructed things exactly as they were. When the lead actors and I toured for several weeks in the East with the film, people just could not believe how they were able to re-enter their past. I decided not to tell them about my little trick with colour.

**I understand that there was interest in the film early on from financiers but they wanted you to write it as a comedy.**
Well, there had been a number of successful comedies treating this period in German history. *Good Bye Lenin!*, for example. So people felt that that was the recipe for success. They also read my screenplay and didn't know what to do with it and thought that as there were comedy elements in my short films, this was a route I should take again. What also happens is that when I start out writing a serious film, I end up writing more and more comedy because it is tempting to do that. It's a much more satisfying experience to be in a theatre and to hear people laugh at your film than to think you heard them sigh or sob. But I wanted to resist that temptation. Early drafts of *The Lives of Others* did also have more comic moments and people responded to that. Once I told them that this wasn't a route that I would go, I couldn't find a single German distributor. This, and the research, is why the film took so long to make.

I had offered it to every distributor in Germany for a ridiculously small sum. They could have had it for a relatively risk free minimum guarantee. For €25,000 they could have had the film but that was too much for them with their fears that it was going to be too dark, too intellectual and too uncommercial. A film that talks about Beethoven, Brecht and Lenin? There is a tendency the world over to underestimate audiences. I think it has been shown that, when someone presents something with challenging substance, if it is done well it will do well and make back its money. It is just so horrendously expensive to make films. No one wanted to take it, so we had to shoot without a distributor, but all the actors said they still believed in this project. Even if it doesn't get a distributor, they knew that they could still show their acting muscle and the department heads believed the same with their skill. That's the most important thing with actors. Sometimes the role may be good but they don't get the chance to show their ability. And I think that is what actors yearn for more than money and wide distribution. Take Sebastian Koch who plays Georg Dreyman. His curse is that he is so incredibly good looking, but he happens to be a better actor than he is good looking. He had never played a lead role in a movie before. He'd only done television. And now he has also made *Black Book* for Paul Verhoeven.

**Do you feel vindicated by your film's success? It has after all won just about every award going.**
Vindication has such a negative connotation. I try not to focus on the people who made it hard for me, but on those who fought with me. Everyone you saw in that long end credit. Those were people who were prepared to work for much less than they usually make and the actors even more so. I'm just grateful to those that stuck with me along this long path.

**One of the kernels of the film is the capacity for change.**
It is something I know to be true. I've seen people change and I've changed. I wonder why you hear so often from people that you can't change. People do hold that to be true although there are some spectacular examples in history; and I don't just mean half-documented cases like Saul turning into Paul. I mean like Gorbachev. A person who was a fierce Stalinist who cried hot tears at his death and yet ended up being the man who shut the gulags and who closed that chapter in history. I've seen change in the entire eastern population. This was a pretty socialist population. Let me put it this way, Chancellor Adenauer could have had unification at an earlier point. He didn't want it because he didn't want all those far-leftists joining his country and not voting for him. This was a country that believed in the ideals of Communism. Come 1989 and these people realised that the reality Communism had come to stand for was not something they

wanted to die for, not something they wanted to kill for any more. That's why I think the film struck such a chord with those in the East, they could identify with that character. They had taken part in that sort of passive heroism. If you can sin by omission then you can also be virtuous by omission as well. The Stasi did not use their arms to turn 1989 into a new Tiananmen Square, although they could have done.

**Let's talk about the moment where Wiesler [Ulrich Mühe] goes to Dreyman's apartment and discovers Brecht for the first time.**
He sees everything with different eyes. It's the first time he's not there to intimidate or to install wires and he sees that these people have lives. It's the scene that I'm most proud of in the film. It takes only one and a half minutes and it has no dialogue, but you can see how this person is searching for meaning and for feeling but has been repressed for so long that he doesn't know how to go about it. He thought that he could find feeling by hiring a prostitute but of course this is unable to satisfy him. Then he realises that these people are finding satisfaction through art so maybe this is something he should be doing; he thinks that maybe he should be reading Brecht.

**Do you think then that this is the moment where he decides his life should take a different direction?**
I don't think that there is a specific moment; I think that he is just gradually being pushed away from the path that he felt was the right path and that perhaps he was mistaken. He doesn't really know what he should do but he does know that what he has been doing so far isn't right. It's like a midlife crisis, only in a good way. It was always important to me that there not be one specific turning point. On the one hand, on the Stasi side he realises that his sacred mission to find enemies of the state is being used for personal motives and this central committee member just has the hots for this girl. He also realises that his friend Colonel Anton Grubitz [Ulrich Tukur], who was always a little less intelligent and a little less party loyal than he is, is making a better career and that people actually distrust him for being religious in his support of the party. On the other hand, as he is monitoring the so-called enemies of the state, he has to ask himself are these really the

people I've been fighting against all my life? They seem so normal to him, especially as he experiences them in moments of greatness and moments of weakness. These moments always seemed easier to ignore in an interrogation scenario. There is also a third level that leads to change and that is art. He experiences that it is possible to live with music and to live with poetry and he realises that it is possible for him to live with these things too. All these things together make him change. And the change is gradual, he is almost a reluctant hero at first, letting things go and falsifying reports; it is only right at the end that he decides to do something to help Dreyman. People often don't feel they are that heroic when they are doing heroic acts, it is often only in retrospect that they recognise their heroism.

**You show people resisting whilst also trying to live their lives.**
I think it's important to realise that oppression under a dictatorship doesn't feel like something out of a comic book where you have people in leather coats with scars on their faces beating to death all those that express a dissenting opinion. While it's happening, it feels so much more normal and it's only in certain moments that you can detect that dictatorship. You have to pay close attention in order to sense whether people are interfering with your freedom. The most dangerous form of dictatorship, I feel, is one where you feel that there is nobody curtailing your freedom. A lot of artists in the GDR felt completely free, they didn't realise that they were censoring themselves. This was because there were a few people that were being censored so heavily that they served as a deterrent.

One thing many artists in the GDR don't realise is how influenced they were by the Stasi. The Stasi targeted young artists before they became famous and destroyed their will to write or to paint, weeding them out before they could exert any influence and thereby become untouchable. Those that rose to prominence felt that they had done so freely, not realising that they were considered politically correct artists. The Stasi was monitoring art schools and colleges and if somebody wrote even a few lines that showed promise but which did not configure politically then that person would go to jail for five or six years. The majority of the population rallied behind the famous artists, believing that they were being daring when really they had been selected, and were not being daring at all.

*The Lives of Others*
(Picture: © Wiedemann Berg
Productions)

**Mühe is phenomenal as Wiesler.**
Ulrich Mühe was probably the most formidable actor of the former GDR. At a very young age, he became incredibly famous and was at the Deutsches Theater in East Berlin. He received all the main roles and Heiner Müller even constructed entire theatre evenings around him and considered him the greatest actor ever. But for this film he didn't prepare at all. He told me his only preparation was to remember. He knew all that. And he came to know more than he did at the time. Afterwards, he claimed his Stasi files. Every victim has the right to do so, although fewer than ten per cent have chosen to do that. He was one of the people who did that. He found out that four members of his theatre group, which for an actor is like his family, were actually placed there by the Stasi to monitor him, to write reports on him. He found out the name of two of the traitors, but the other two remain anonymous. Some had codenames and some of the cards are lost or destroyed. And he also found out, perhaps the most painful discovery, that his wife of six years had been listed as an informer and had been reporting on him. He's a very sensitive man. In the interview I did with him to accompany the published screenplay, I told him that these are things the tabloid press will find out, it'll be grossly misrepresented, so why don't you tell me the story from your perspective.

And he did. And we took twenty pages to properly cover the subject. Most people thought we had gone too far, washing dirty laundry in public. And he was attacked very severely. In some parts he was hailed as the person who finally crossed that bridge and talked about these things. But it was really a very painful thing for him. He really couldn't enjoy the success of this film because of the vicious attacks. Every day the answering machine would be full of the most awful venom. And all he was saying was 'I want to be able to talk about my past when people ask me. I have nothing to be ashamed of.' He said something interesting in that in dictatorships they force their victims to be silent out of a sense of shame. Often Jews who experienced something similar in the concentration camps talk about not talking about it out of a sense of shame, some weird malfunction in the brain that makes you ashamed of injustices that you have suffered. Many victims of child abuse know about that. And he said he didn't want that to happen to him, he wanted to talk about these things. But he was attacked so viciously. He really suffered for that. I think you get to know Ulrich Mühe very well through this film. Part of his genius is that when you look into his eyes you look into his soul.

Interviewed by Jason Wood, 2 June 2007.

**Florian Henckel von Donnersmarck** (born 1973, in Cologne, Germany) grew up in New York, Berlin, Frankfurt and Brussels. Following his Russian Studies at the National IS Institute in Leningrad (now St. Petersburg), he enrolled at Oxford University to study Political Science, Philosophy and Economics. He then went on to study directing at the Hochschule für Fernsehen und Film München and wrote and directed various award winning short films. His debut feature *The Lives of Others* his also his official graduation film, a film which shot to international success winning virtually every award there is to win.

[Ulrich Mühe died in July 2007]

*Ressources Humaines* (Picture: Gilles Marchand)    *Vers le Sud* (Picture: Haut et Court)

## France Isn't Paris
### An interview with Laurent Cantet

*Laurent Cantet has established himself as one of France's most intriguing talents, directing pictures with a strong social undercurrent, and revealing a natural gift for directing actors.*

**Your films are removed from everyday surroundings. Is that deliberate?**
Laurent Cantet: There are several reasons for that. First off, I'm from the provinces, although I've lived in Paris for twenty years. I come from a very rural area, Niort, between Poitiers and La Rochelle. It's important to decentralise films, socially as well as geographically. Paris is not the centre of the world. The point of view of a Parisian is perhaps somewhat narrower than that of someone from outside. Besides, the cinema is often a very Parisian practice – it's easier to shoot in places you know well, even within the Paris area. I always like going off the beaten track. Surprise and misunderstanding are stimulating.

In *Les Sanguinaires*, a man retreats to a remote island in order to escape the madness of the Millennium celebrations.

Yes, it's to emphasise that life doesn't just occur in Paris. Moreover, I'm curious about landscapes and towns and the people that I don't know. My desire to shoot in Haiti stemmed from that. A film is also a human adventure, and the adventure arises more easily in a place that's not my everyday location.

**Is it easier to shoot in a place like that?**

For *Heading South*, it was extremely complicated to set everything up for shooting on the other side of the world, in a country as unstable as Haiti, with actors coming from all over the place, as well as a crew coming from Canada, France, the Dominican Republic, and Haiti itself. Getting all these actors together is complicated, but for me that's also part of the pleasure of making a film. It's all about bringing together different people, and plunging them into a context that's unfamiliar to them. That I find interesting, something exciting.

Sometimes I'll make portions of my films in Paris, or my shorts, and I always have the impression that everyone goes home at night, and so suddenly one loses something I enjoy very much during shooting which is this team, which comes together little by little and which lives together throughout the 'adventure'. It creates a sense of camaraderie that I don't find in Paris. I believe that a film shows something of the circumstances in which it's made. You feel that in the finished movie. There's this sense of being united for a particular project.

*Heading South* **takes place during the 1970s. Would it have been different had it been set in 2005?**

I could not have set it in Haiti because it's now totally abandoned by tourists. There are no more hotels, no infrastructure, nothing. So I could not have made it a contemporary story, or I would have had to film it elsewhere, in say the Dominican Republic, but to be historically authentic, I couldn't have set it in the 2000s. In fact, we didn't work hard on reconstitution, but it was important for me that it was during the period of Duvalier's dictatorship. It's true that the situation in Haiti is not exactly paradise right now. One can't say, that socially and

politically, things have improved much, but there was an institutional-
ised violence at the time that one encounters less nowadays.

### Were the 1970s more liberal from a sexual point of view?

Absolutely, and that corresponds to a part of the history of Western
sexuality that's changed a lot in the interim. I think that we're certainly
more open about these things than we were at the time and, of
course, there has been the scourge of AIDS which has altered things
enormously. I also wanted to be faithful in spirit to Dany Laferrière's
novel.

### Did you come across the book by chance?

Yes. I went to Port-au-Prince four years ago without knowing that I'd
go back to make a film there. I went there to work, and I was very
struck by the country, at once impressed by many of the things I discovered, and revolted by so many other aspects of the place. While I
was there, I began to think about a tourist-type film without knowing
exactly what form it could take, and by chance I bought Dany
Laferrière's novel in a bookshop, and read it on the plane back to
Paris. I felt he was a writer who touched me profoundly and who
communicated things I might have been able to feel myself during my
short stay in Port-au-Prince.

### Was it difficult to find the funding for a film that takes place abroad like that?

It certainly wasn't very easy. First off, there was a very risky element
to the film. We had to delay the shoot by a year after having planned to
film the story in 2003; but then President Aristide was ousted and
every day there were demonstrations, leaving people dead each time.
So the shoot was postponed and for film financiers that's not very
reassuring. So it was all rather complicated. Besides, although the film
was not excessively expensive, it cost more than a movie one would
make at home. We made it in co-production with Canada, and we
needed that. Dany Laferrière is rather well known in French-speaking
Canada, and that, along with Louise Portal [who played Sue], helped
facilitate the co-production deal.

**In *Time Out*, a man loses his job and hides away in the countryside. How did that film originate?**

At the outset, it was my memories of an affair that we'd followed closely in France, the story of Jean-Claude Romand who wasn't working and convinced everyone that he was working because of course he needed the social status that a job brings with it. I didn't do any research into the man's character nor his story, leaving out all the sordid details, the murders of his family, the way his secret had been uncovered and so on. Instead, I just built a character around him himself. Like Romand, Vincent is not an ordinary unemployed guy; he is a man who chooses not to work and tries to invent his life as though he was writing a script. Even if he is trapped in his story, he finds it really exciting and that is something a lot of spectators refuse to see in the film. What interested me was to see a man of this kind alone in a landscape.

We shot a lot of it in the Alps, in Grenoble and the surrounding area, and then on the motorways and a little in Switzerland, in Geneva.

**In *Human Resources*, one has a strong sense of location. Was the film shot in a real factory?**

It was indeed shot in real surroundings while the factory continued to function normally. It was at Gaillon in the Eure area of Normandy, the part closest to Paris. I was interested in evoking the atmosphere of my youth, at a time when I had pals who were somewhat confronted with this problem vis-à-vis their parents, and then also because Paris is not really a workers' city. It's a milieu that would be difficult to identify in Paris. Also, I wanted to show that this young man coming from the capital has a kind of Parisian status among his friends, and vis-à-vis his parents; he's no longer part of the same world because he's been to Paris. In French, the expression, 'monter à Paris' has a kind of status, and also something fatalistic.

**A little like Claude Goretta's film *La provinciale* on the same theme?**

Yes. In France it's something very powerful because it's a very central-ised country and everything is supposed to happen in Paris. Most of my high-school friends now live in Paris.

**It's one of the rare films since 2000 to address the contemporary political situation with the thirty-five-hour week and so on.**
I really like topical issues. The reality of our world is so complex that it's worth studying very carefully, and we often leave that task just to journalists. But our view of current affairs is always spontaneous, there's little distance between the journalists and the topics they're addressing. There's something unrefined in their analysis.

**Where would you place yourself in the current French cinema? Is there a tradition in France that's different to that in other countries?**
The great privilege that we enjoyed, and still enjoy – although to my mind it's the thing most under threat – is the French tradition of making marginal films, and we need that to continue.

It's less easy now than it was during the 1990s to raise money. It's true that there's a concentration on financing big projects that the financiers know will recover their budget at the end of the day. But I have the impression that we're moving towards a two-speed cinema: on the one hand very expensive movies and on the other, very cheap ones that are made more and more quickly, in economic conditions so tight that it's only the goodwill of all concerned in the production that makes them possible at all. And between these two extremes there's a middle layer in which my films lie and, of course, they are more and more difficult to set up because they involve an initial investment and they are by no means sure of recovering their outlay.

**Do you feel that there's a gulf between the big American studios and the European films that struggle for a share of the market?**
Where the situation seems to me to be the most dangerous is in the exhibition sector. The fact is that some French films are released with 1,000 prints, and the smaller films with 10 prints, which have neither the room nor the time to exist. The gap is growing between movies that do well at the box-office, and films that I like – films like my own in fact – that don't do so well because they need time to develop an audience. People don't rush to see them in the first week, because they are not 'must-see' movies. You don't have the option when a film stays in the cinemas for just one week.

**How would you compare European films to those from elsewhere?**
The distinction is not necessarily a geographical one in my opinion. I find myself more absorbed by certain American or Asian films than I am by a French film. I feel closer to Edward Yang or Abbas Kiarostami than to Luc Besson, for example.

**And your next project?**
I'm working on a film that somewhat resembles *Human Resources*. It'll be made in much the same way, exclusively with non-professional actors, and it will take place in a junior high school, among kids of fourteen to fifteen years of age – a 'difficult' school, with all kinds of different communities and social classes in Paris rubbing side by side.

The links between apprenticeship, work, and language will form the real gist of the film. I'm going to improvise a lot with the pupils. I know them already because I've been working with them since September [2006] in a kind of makeshift studio in a high school. I'd like to capture the fragments of life, and the reflections of each youngster on the essential issues that France and perhaps countries beyond France have to confront today. It's also adapted from a book written by François Bégaudeau, published last year. He's both a critic for *Cahiers du Cinéma* and a teacher of French in a junior high school in Paris, and his book charts a year in the life of his class. So we are building the film around this concept, even if it will not be so much an adaptation as an extension of the book. It's called *Between the Walls* (*Entre les murs*). We'll shoot this coming July and August, for release in early 2008.

Telephone interview by Peter Cowie on 18 December 2006.

**Laurent Cantet** (born 1961, in Melle, France) made his debut with two shorts: *Tous à la manif* (1994) and *Jeux de plage* (1995). His maiden feature, *Human Resources* (*Ressources humaines*, 1999) won the César for Best First Film, the same prize at the San Sebastian Festival and the EFA's European Discovery 2000. *Time Out* (*L'emploi du temps*) followed in 2001, winning an award at Venice, and in 2005 Cantet attracted widespread attention for *Heading South* (*Vers le sud*), which again earned prizes at the Biennale in Venice.

Javier Bardem
(Picture: Reposado)

## Hard Work

An interview with
Javier Bardem and
Fernando León de Aranoa

*Winner of the European Actor 2004 award for his role in* Mar Adentro
*(The Sea Inside) and various Goya awards, Javier Bardem is one of
Spain's most known and established actors. One of the many successful collaborations he has entered was with director Fernando León
de Aranoa on* Los Lunes al sol *(Mondays in the Sun) for which both
received a Goya. We met up with them during the Berlinale where
they were presenting* Invisibles, *a tandem project which Javier Bardem
produced and of which Fernando León directed one of the episodes.*

**Javier, you come from a family of actors but say you never wanted to
be an actor yourself. So how did you end up becoming one?**
Javier Bardem: Well, I studied painting and then I had to make some
money so I started to work as an extra in movies. Little by little they
gave me more chances, little roles to play. I did that just to get some
money and keep painting. And then, one day when I did this part for
Bigas Luna in *The Ages of Lulu* I realised that that was what I wanted
to do. I wanted to express myself and I was able to do that through the

acting rather than through painting. So, even though I had tried to avoid being an actor because of my roots, in the end it was impossible, it was in my blood. So I surrendered. I said, okay, this is what I am, this is what I feel, I have to be responsible about it. I have to work on it, to improve, go to an acting school, take it seriously. Because the one thing I knew for sure from my mum and all my family, was that if you're going do it, go for it, don't play.

**Fernando, you started as a scriptwriter and still write your own scripts. Where do you find your stories?**

Fernando León: I started working as a scriptwriter for other film-makers so sometimes the stories came from the producer or from film-makers who wanted me to write something. And then after writing six or seven scripts for other film-makers, I had a story that I wanted to keep for myself.

I think that stories are a bit like cats, you can't run after them, you can't chase them. It's just the opposite, you have to wait and then they come to you. And it's not like a complete story suddenly unfolds. Sometimes you have just an idea and then, two or three months later, another one comes from a completely different environment, from a newspaper or from something a friend tells you, and then these two or three ideas form a coalition and a story comes out of that. Usually, the stories don't have only one source and it's very difficult to determine exactly when a story was born.

**Do you normally have a story first and then try to find a setting for it or do you find a place that inspires a story?**

FL: For sure I first have the story. Sometimes I don't even care so much about the location. Of course, it's important but I think all four films I have done aren't very specifically located, even if I shoot in Madrid or in Vigo in the north of Spain. I try to tell stories that can work in any place of the world. For me, the place where *Mondays in the Sun* takes place is just an industrial town and it could as well be in the north of France or in Britain. I don't want very specific places to shoot my films. I even avoid showing the places; sometimes this drives my DoP crazy because I never want the name of the town or any famous sights to appear in the movie. I always look for very normal neighbourhoods that you could find anywhere.

**Javier, what influence do you think a location has on your acting and on the film?**

JB: A lot. As an actor it's different from a director. He might choose not to make the identity of the town part of the story but as an actor, even if you're playing somebody who could exist in that place as much as he could exist in any other place, there is no way you can't be influenced by your surroundings. I think this is even more so outside of Spain. What I mean is that when I went to shoot in Texas with the Coen brothers, there was a moment when I could not avoid taking that culture in and putting it into my character. My character wasn't supposed to live there but he was going through Texas, so something of the character of the place had to be there. So, for an actor, I think it's different.

FL: So, when we work together, we have a problem! (*laughs*)

JB: Actually, it's not a problem, but I remember a moment when we were shooting *Mondays in the Sun*. Those guys have an accent and he didn't want to locate it and I wanted to. We met in the middle with a very soft accent so that Spaniards would be able to identify it from somewhere in the north, but they wouldn't know exactly where.

**At a time when Spain is looked at internationally as a booming place with a developing economy, you describe people on the edge of society. Has this portraying of a different Spain ever played a role for you?**

FL: Yes, when I was presenting my film outside Spain. I remember a couple of times in Mexico and in Cuba, in Latin America, people were surprised, they asked, 'Is Spain really like that?' For some of them Spain is a place where you go to have a better life, not to have a difficult life.

But, again, I think that my films are telling stories about landscapes and people that you can find in Italy, in France, in Germany. For example, when we released *Mondays in the Sun* in Germany, it was at a time when unemployment was really high. So, I'm not interested in portraying Spain. I'm just interested in telling stories and, of course, they represent a bit of reality. Maybe in ten or twenty years, somebody will get a taste of what our life in Spain is like today. But this is not my main aim.

JB: Thank God, we have more than just one film-maker; it would be ridiculous if people saw a country only through the eyes of one person. Almodóvar's Spain exists, or if it doesn't exist, it's funny to think that it does, but *Mondays in the Sun* and *Princesas* are also Spain and that's the good thing about having even a small film industry: you have the chance to see the place through different eyes.

FL: Probably all of us together – the twenty, thirty, forty film-makers whose movies are shown beyond Spain – all of us together give a proper view of what Spain is like today – not only mine, and not only Almodóvar's movies, because they all display specific issues.

Fernando León on the set
for *Princesas*
(Picture: Teresa Isasi)

**Javier, you have played everything from a paralysed ex-cop to a gay poet and a quadriplegic. What does a role need to get you interested?**
JB: I think some human nature – which is what any actor would ask for. Some people think that they need to portray something they are not, some kind of hero. But most of us actors need to be *emotionally* touched by what we do. And the only way to be emotionally touched by a role is if I can figure him out, if I can really believe that this man could exist and if he existed I'd be interested in getting to know him because he's human, he's contradictory, he has fears, victories and

weaknesses. So in the end, if it's well written and the character develops over the course of the film, I'll do it. But if it is a straight line towards nothing, it doesn't make any sense to play the part.

**And how do you prepare to get into a character?**
JB: I try to understand him and to put myself aside as much as I can. I am not interesting to watch or hear, Javier Bardem is not interesting at all. What is interesting is to see that guy, so you have to find that particular voice, that walk, that behaviour. But you have to make it *real*. What I mean is you have to find a way from here to there, so you have to take yourself out of it and embody this character. How you do it? I don't know, pray, man! (*laughs*)

**Fernando, have you ever thought about doing a more commercially oriented film, maybe with an international cast?**
FL: At least until today, no, I don't think so. From the beginning, when I start writing a story, and then when I start thinking about who is going to play the roles in the movies, I've never stopped to think how I could make this more commercial or more international. I don't think that's the kind of thing that a writer or film-maker has on his mind when starting to write. Maybe someone else will ask you why you don't shoot it in English. But I really think that the story is the boss in a movie, the story gives the direction and tells you the language in which you have to tell it. Maybe one day I'll have a story that takes place in England or in North America so that it has to be in English. If the characters speak English I will feel comfortable shooting in this language. But if the story takes place in the north of Spain, the natural thing is to shoot it in Spanish.

And when it comes to the characters, I just try to look for the best actor who can do it. And when I look at a film with some distance I see that there are very different people in it. For example, in *Mondays in the Sun* there is Javier who has done a lot of work before and is a well-known, great actor. And there are people for whom it is their first role. There are actors from theatre, some from television, very different backgrounds. When I was working with them, they were right for these characters, so that's the main thing.

**So what's it like to work with him?**

JB: With Fernando? Hard, it's not easy.

FL: Oh, come on! (*laughs*)

JB: What? (*laughs*) No, he really works very hard himself. He goes on and on, through the text, through the dialogue. I wouldn't say he's a perfectionist because I don't think that's a good thing. But he really gets to a point where he lets the story go, but until he reaches that point, he has looked at it from every possible kind of angle. So when you do these dialogues, there is a guy there who knows everything about those scenes. And he really wants to go all the way, to squeeze the last out of it. And he's right. I mean, I prefer that to the people who say 'Action!' and then 'Okay, that's fine, let's move on.' 'No,' he says, 'wait, let's look at that again.' And he does that even under pressure. And what happens when you see the movie, and I've seen all four of them, is that there is not a single actor who isn't good in these movies. And every actor in Spain that I talk to wants to work with him because you know that you are safe.

**Where do you see the strengths of European cinema?**

JB: It's funny because I have a problem with this thing, *European cinema*. Of course, there is European cinema if you look at Europe and America, two big continents that produce a lot of movies. But it is so different because we don't share as much as they do, in language, in culture. So that's why it is so difficult for me to see European cinema as something united. I can see it, and that's what I think is great about the [European Film] Academy, as something that we share and we can take the opportunity to see what's going on in other countries and to understand the way they do things. But that doesn't mean that we have a united language. That's why we, the actors, don't work in Europe. For me, to work in Italy, Germany, France is impossible as long as I don't speak the language perfectly and there is a role about a Spaniard who lives there. They will never call me. In the States, I'm a foreigner. I can play German, Italian, everything. If I work on the accent, I'm a foreigner. That's why we usually work more over there than in Europe. It's a pity because I'd love to work with Bertrand Tavernier, for example. But it's impossible because I don't speak French. For the same reason French actors don't work in Spain, because they don't speak Spanish. So that's the problem I see.

FL: I agree with that; also, I think that in Europe the different national cinemas have always been very strong. For example, if you look at Italian films, they can be very different from British movies and from Spanish movies. So, we are very strong cultures with very strong characters and you realise that when you see the best movies of each country. That's why it's difficult to see one European way of making movies. I think that's what makes it very interesting.

JB: Exactly!

FL: If all of us were doing the same, it wouldn't be so interesting. I have always loved Italian movies and now, when people see my movies and say that they are a bit like British movies, I think I've failed because I wanted them to look like Italian movies. I always loved the kind of relationships that Italian film-makers create with their characters, and the same with French film-makers. I think that the relationships directors create with their characters are very different in France than in Italy or Spain. That depends on the different character of people in the different countries.

JB: That's why I think the [European Film] Academy is so powerful and important because it draws attention to the films in the selection. Of course, it can never be fair because there are so many movies, but at the end of the day you have to choose a few movies that the members want to lay emphasis on. That's a good thing because it draws attention to every country, to see what is going on there. Otherwise, we would never have the chance to see these movies. Like *Mondays in the Sun*, which came to Italy and France, and if there is the success of getting a nomination, you can see how much it helps to make people think, 'Ah, that was nominated, I want to see that!'

FL: In a way, you could say that the EFA does the work that the market itself doesn't do because sometimes it is very difficult for us to see German movies in Spain, and only few Spanish movies come to Germany. So the EFA can make this work – of course, not in distribution – but just to make people aware of the work that comes from other European countries. Sometimes the distribution market doesn't allow us to see that.

**It is often said that one of the problems of European films is the lack of real stars . . .**

JB: Come on, man, look at me! (*laughs*) Don't write that! If you write that, say that I was laughing [*which he was*]. I don't want people to think that I'm that kind of guy!

FL: (*laughs*) Well, I don't think of that as a bad thing, I'm sorry to say.

JB: Yes, that's what I was going to say.

FL: I don't think that's a problem for European movies. Of course, in France, in Italy, everywhere, there have always been big actors who can play as stars in American movies and in big European movies, like Catherine Deneuve or Gérard Depardieu, a lot of very good actors. There are very big actors who can sometimes help you to do a movie, in terms of funding.

So, maybe there is no real star system, but I don't think that's a bad thing because it can pervert the way movies are made. I think there is room for that, but limited room. Not everything is about that.

JB: I think it's a cultural thing. In order to be a well-known actor in Europe, you have to go to the American market. Of course, there are exceptions, like Mastroianni, and all those people who were gods. But for us humans it's more difficult to spread your work throughout Europe than from the States to Europe. Why is that? We don't have stars because an actor who wants to be a star has to play a star, has to present himself as a star. And you see that much more in the States than here – I don't know why, but it's like that. Here, it is much more difficult to see somebody who really feels like they want to put themselves in that place. I think that's cultural. I'm not saying it's better or worse, I'm just saying that it's a fact. You don't see people behaving in the way that some American actors do. In my humble opinion that has to do with the surroundings, with how important the idea of success is in the States. It's about always trying to be number one. Being number two is not enough. And here you can maybe be number ten – and that's fine!

**And according to that logic, are you a star?**

JB: No, I'm not. I think it is a role that you put yourself into. I mean, today I'm wearing this jacket because we have a press conference and I want to look good and respectful but it isn't a statement by which I say 'Listen guys, I'm untouchable, I'm flying an inch above the floor.' You need that to be a star. And the funny thing is when you see a star and they actually play the star, you feel it, you feel like 'Wow! They are untouchables.' I'm not because it is completely against my job. My job is to portray those guys in the street. If I'm flying, I cannot reach them. It's not easy though, because in Spain the media push me up into a place where I don't want to be and it's my decision to get out of there.

**As a final question, if you owned a cinema for one day what films would you show?**

JB: Porn! (*laughs*)

FL: (*laughs*) That's because you're a businessman. Not a star, a business-man.

JB: Okay, that was my answer.

FL: I don't know. That's a dream, to have a theatre. But it's so difficult! I would love to screen European movies because they don't have a lot of room on the Spanish screens. There are a lot of American movies, and then Spanish movies. But there is not a lot of room for the European or Latin American movies I like. So I would try to show a few of the movies from the 1960s and 1970s in Italy. Maybe I would show the first film I saw, *Maccaroni* by Ettore Scola, as a sentimental screening for myself. When I saw that film I thought if one day I can do something that's even a little bit close to this, I will be happy and it was like a guide for me when I was young. Maybe it isn't the most famous of Ettore Scola's movies but it was an important one for me.

Interviewed by Pascal Edelmann in Berlin on 16 February 2007.

Born in 1969 in Madrid, **Fernando León de Aranoa** started working as a screenwriter. His first film as a director, *Familia* (1996), instantly won the Spanish Film Academy's Goya for Best New Director. His next film, *Barrio* (1998), received the Goya for Best Director and Best Original Screenplay and *Los Lunes al Sol* (2002) again won the Goya for Best Director and was also nominated for the European Film Academy's People's Choice Award. His latest film, *Princesas*, won three Goya awards and was in the Selection for the European Film Awards 2006.

**Javier Bardem** (born in 1969 in Las Palmas de Gran Canaria) comes from a family of actors. He studied painting but eventually found his way into film where he acquired instant popularity for his impersonation of the sexy stud in Bigas Luna's *Jamón, jamón* (1992). In 1994 he received the first of what would become a series of Goya awards for *Días contados* by Imanol Uribe. He worked with Pedro Almodóvar in *Carne trémula* (1997) and won the European Film Academy's People's Choice Award for Best Actor. These were followed by striking performances in Fernando León's *Los lunes al sol* (2002), as the gay poet Reinaldo Arenas in Julian Schnabel's *Before Night Falls* (2000) and the quadriplegic Ramón Sampedro in *Mar adentro* by Alejandro Amenábar (2004) which won him another Goya and a European Film Award.

# 9   Independent and Successful?

*The power of the Hollywood studios is legendary, and an abiding fact of life. But the European 'majors' such as Gaumont in France, Constantin Film in Germany, or Svensk Filmindustri in Sweden, have also exerted considerable sway over their national cinemas. With each passing decade, too, the financial influence of television entities such as the RAI in Italy, or Canal Plus in France, has been indispensable to film-makers, while funding bodies such as Eurimages or Filmstiftung Nordrhein-Westfalen have also played a vital role in supporting production. But the true independent spirits of European cinema are a breed apart. They battle with the censors as much as with budgetary problems. They seek out unusual stories, and film them in offbeat locations. They tackle political and sexual taboos. Above all, they cherish a sense of Europe as a whole, a complex gathering of nations that can, if everything gels, give birth to the most exciting films on the planet.*

Dušan Makavejev and
Jeremy Thomas at the EFA
General Assembly 1994 in
Berlin
(Picture: gerhardkassner.de)

# Catching the Moment

## An interview with Dušan Makavejev

*Dušan Makavejev symbolised the idiosyncratic spirit of the 1960s
more than any single director. Working until his forties in the 'multi-
culti' atmosphere of Tito's Yugoslavia, he blended politics, agit-prop,
aesthetic experiment, and caustic humour with the devastating aplomb
of a Cubist. Films like* Man is Not a Bird, Switchboard Operator, *and*
WR: Mysteries of the Organism *emerged from Makavejev's imagination to delight or chastise a public far beyond the Balkans.*

**How would you contrast film-making in the wild 1960s with
conditions today in Europe?**
Dušan Makavejev: The 1960s were a period of open eyes – 'Cinema
direct', 'Cinéma vérité'! Our hand-held cameras were curious and
critical. Instead of performing, our actors were asked just to be alive.
Our stories on film became unpredictable, as life.

The power of photography is in catching the moment. Everybody
looks at the world in front of him or her, few people really *see*. The
miraculous quality of the photographic image is derived from the
fact that the world on the photograph is *seen*. The world caught by our

cameras being seen by us became alive and accessible. We felt responsible for it.

With moving images produced now by pocket telephones, security cameras everywhere and cameras looking at us from the computers, where does it all leave classical film images? Film images, we must not forget, were not continuous moving images, they were imaginary – produced inside the viewer – from a sequence of stills projected on the screen!

There is something idiotic in the non-stop digital image; it has no more responsibility than a piss, it just flows. There is no heart-beat in it, no personality.

**How has the film-making landscape in Europe changed during the twenty years since the EFA was established (with you as one of the founder members)?**
Almost as mirroring the domination of the American majors, films you could call 'European Films' were for a long time produced only by France and Italy. In the meantime almost all countries developed film productions of their own as part of their national cultures. Still it seems that in Europe no more than a tiny proportion of national films reach even the closest neighbours.

**You have often suffered from censorship and the rejection by the authorities – in former Yugoslavia – of your work. What effect has this had on your creative work? Does it make you want to be even more provocative?**
Well, these experiences certainly were not at all inspiring. They were funny remnants of the religious fear of images.

The funniest exchange with a censor I've had was in the UK, with John Trevelyan, who was secretary of the British Board of Film Censors. In the late 1960s, the UK distributor of *Switchboard Operator*, Connoisseur Films, could not get the film passed by the censors. The scene in the morgue with a naked female corpse rolled out of the elevator was analysed pedantically: a few seconds of nipples here, a few seconds of pubic hair there, etc. So it was arranged for the censor, John Trevelyan, to meet me. It was on Soho Square. He was a nice old gentleman, he offered me tea with milk, telling me how sorry he was, how well made he thought my film was, '... interesting; unfortunately, however . . . there are rules.'

I tried to explain that what we see in the film is not a woman, 'it is a corpse, to be dissected'. 'Don't tell me that, please!' he responded. 'We see the pubic hair very clearly.' Another scene regarded as offensive by the BBFC was a funny clip from a silent movie in which two naked 'models' pose for the imaginary photographer, while the camera circles around them. Trevelyan wanted the scene completely excised.

I proposed the French censor's solution: stretch through the middle of the shot a black strip covering the sexual parts of the models. 'Oh, no!' exclaimed Trevelyan. 'We tried it once, and I'll show you what happened.' He grabbed a cigarette box from the table, and drew on it, in pencil, a naked woman – a nice little drawing, with nipples, pubic triangle, a face too, arms and legs . . . Then he drew over the pubis of his imaginary woman a black square. 'Look here, the people in the first rows, did this . . . And holding the cigarette box with a 'naked woman' with a tiny black square in her middle in front of his eyes, he ducked his head, eyes up, slightly bent the lower part of the cigarette box forward . . . Eyes wide open, he tried intensely to see what was beneath the 'square'. He was not interested in the content of the film. In the name of the UK government he was pursuing the spectacle of a few pubic hairs. As I watched this elderly man, I could not believe my eyes and ears.

The irony is that schoolchildren in Belgrade were free to see the film exactly as it was made.

The best censors were the Norwegians. They would negotiate with Tore Erlandsen, my distributor, and each time he protested or pleaded, they would give him back odd clips of fifty or a hundred metres, in instalments as it were! Finally they cut from the wild, ugly lunch sequence in *Sweet Movie* the more unpleasant moments and left in all sexy parts and the music. Actually, the scene was all the better for it!

**Can a film-maker work anywhere in Europe, or is it vital to let your work flow from your national roots, the culture that you know?**
I think it depends on the individual film-maker. Sure, the most

important part of the 'work' comes from the dark corners – from the guts, the soul, the intestines.

And what *is* 'the culture that I know'? Well . . . as a kid I listened to Hitler's speeches over the radio. I thought this screaming guy was about to die. Was it 'my culture'?

The happiest day in my high school town (Novi Sad) was when a war criminal was hanged in public. We were let out of school at the age of twelve, to join our relatives and watch the spectacle . . . That was a massive release of joy, the celebration of the end of the war and all the suffering. Of course, I can't judge the usefulness of this experience.

When the American General Short bombed three beautiful bridges in Novi Sad, in 1999, he got his two minutes of fame and boasting on CNN. This sight was quite disgusting. The general, the river, the bridges and CNN, beauty, excitement, information and concern – all of it I keep in the folder 'The culture that I know'.

**How would you distinguish the work you made outside the former Yugoslavia (*The Coca-Cola Kid*, for example, or *Montenegro*) from the films that made your reputation like *Man is Not a Bird*, *Switchboard Operator*, or *Innocence Unprotected*?**

Commercial films have to attract a much wider audience than just a director's fans. Accordingly, they are obliged to go the extra mile with well-crafted ingredients, wonderful colours, aerial shots, and expensive actors. It was great having Dean Semler or Tomislav Pinter as cinematographers on my international productions.

It was fun, too, to shoot over Niagara Falls, or in the Blue Mountains in New South Wales, Woolomooloo, Sältsjöbaden and Skofja Loka.

**Can you describe the circumstances that made you leave the former Yugoslavia?**

At the end of 1972, the liberal leadership in Serbia was forced to resign. An ideological/fundamentalist tsunami threw the media into a kind of psychotic vertigo. Already printed books were chopped up into old paper, theatre plays were removed from the repertory, and a campaign against the 'black wave' in films treated us as foreign agents.

Only in the late 1990s did the 'Mitrokhin Papers' reveal that we were the targets of a special invisible multi-purpose task force. Nine under-cover KGB operatives acted in Yugoslavia under the Code Name 'Operation Progress'. So Aleksandar Petrović and myself left for France, Žilnik and Sajtinać left for Germany. Many were silenced for years. Lazar Stojanović was sentenced to three years in jail for a student film he had made and that was seen by no one. [An article in *The New York Times* on 4 February 1973 noted that Makavejev had been indicted on a criminal charge of derision 'of the state, its agencies and representatives'.]

**What compromises did you have to make in order to get some of your 'Western' films off the ground?**
You go through a process of trial and error all the time. Everything negative is dressed up as a question of personal like or dislike. It's like learning a new language constantly. In movies you have to suffer a lot of fools regardless of political geography. What makes the difference is the mimicry you have to apply.

**Can you sum up, in a witty way, the fundamental differences between film-making under Communist rule, and film-making under capitalist pressures**
During the sixties, the former Yugoslavia was changing from 'Communist-ruled' if you wish, to more like 'Communist controlled'. We had personal freedom to move and choose where to live. Open frontiers and foreign co-financing in films, was okay. Only, from time to time, the system, having stupidly (and unfortunately) no feedback in place, would fall into spasmodic convulsions. Otherwise it was like everywhere, Kodak or Fuji.

In the 'West' I was lucky with producers who wanted my films, but life is not so simple. Anatole Dauman wanted me to direct *Farewell Waltz*. But Milan Kundera, the author, was raising the price for the rights to his book every second week, so the wonderful Dauman just got fed up, and I lost six months. The film was never made. Philip Roth flirted with us with his novel, *The Professor of Desire*. He proposed David Mercer as the writer and six months later angrily rejected

Mercer's screenplay. The producer was afraid to go with my version, which Roth also did not want. Again, the film was never made. Mel Gibson wanted to do *The Coca-Cola Kid*, had we been willing to stand in line after the three films that he had already signed to make.

Yet, in a way, this stop-go routine could be exhilarating. After many years I found that no less than seven scripts that had been offered to me, and which I found stupid or unpromising, were actually produced, none of them really interesting. We had a great Jerusalem story post-poned for ever because of a sudden war against Lebanon. All these examples – and excuses – do not make me proud. Directors should know how to direct, or ambush, or seduce, financiers too.

**You have spent a lot of time in the United States. How would you define the differences between European film-making and American independent film-making?**
Europe has a strong supportive mix of government and private financing. In between rare great successes and horrible failures, they produce a lot of local films that just do not travel. All governments and politicians like to be seen as patrons of movies, extracting at the same time concessions, which does not help.

The best European productions share with the true American independents the film-maker's personal engagement, the beauty of the risk that's so fundamental to real art, and the freedom to deal with the unknown. I do not see any fundamental differences.

E-mail interview by Peter Cowie in early 2007.

**Dušan Makavejev** (born 1932, in Belgrade) took a degree in psychology from the University of Belgrade, then enrolled in film school. He made various documentaries in Zagreb Film and Dunav Film, before gaining a place at the Critics Week at the Cannes Film Festival with *Man is Not a Bird*, in 1966. The following year he made the mordant *Switchboard Operator*, and then *Innocence Unprotected* (1968). His most success-ful, and indeed notorious, film is *WR: Mysteries of the Organism* (1971), which established his reputation in the United States with its witty and yet poignant image of Wilhelm Reich's liberated approach to sex. His subsequent work included *Sweet Movie* (1974), *Montenegro* (made in Sweden in 1981), *The Coca-Cola Kid* (shot in Australia in 1985), *Manifesto* (1988), *Gorilla Bathes at Noon* (1993), and *Hole in the Soul* (1994). Makavejev has frequently taught film classes at Harvard and other universities.

Jeremy Thomas
(Picture: Angus Forbes)

## An Almighty Task

An interview with
Jeremy Thomas

*London-based Jeremy Thomas is a true citizen of world cinema, a maverick producer who has retained his independence for more than three decades, and continues to foster the careers of young directors from Europe and elsewhere.*

**Could you say something about the passion of being an independent producer, as opposed to the image so many people have of the producer with a cigar interested only in money?**

Jeremy Thomas: I grew up in a cinema household, I had cinema in my veins. My father was a film-maker, as was my uncle. I love the movies. It's a hobby of mine, but also a passion.

**Is there an example of a film where you believed in it completely, but it required some years to get it off the ground?**

Oh, definitely *The Last Emperor*. I believed in Bernardo Bertolucci, and Bernardo's a director who believes in the big idea, also Nagisa Oshima, with *Merry Christmas Mr Lawrence*. You need to share that passion, to bring everyone along with you, in order to make these films, which are unusual and outside the mainstream of ideas.

## Do you see yourself as a European, or an international producer?

I see myself as working in the global arena. I like making films in any language, or working with subtitles. I'm willing to work on any continent, with any director. I don't think of myself as a British producer. Rather as an adventurer, a producer who likes moving and working around the globe, and after years of doing so I know I really like it, and find it very stimulating. Therefore the prize given to me in 2006 by the European Film Academy for 'World Cinema' is correct. I like the scent of the exotic. I find it attractive in design, in literature, art, and in places in which to situate films. I've just been drawn to it, subconsciously: *The Sheltering Sky* in Morocco, *Rabbit-Proof Fence* in Australia, *The Cup* in the Himalayas, *Little Buddha* in Bhutan, and *Eureka* with Nic Roeg in Jamaica.

## Your first triumph was Jerzy Skolimowski's *The Shout*, which won the Special Jury Prize at Cannes in 1978. Can you recall how you managed to get that off the ground?

Sandy Lieberson had produced *Brother, Can You Spare a Dime?*, which I edited, and we worked on it for a year until it was time to show it in Cannes, where it was selected for the Critics Week. So I got a taste for Cannes, and thought I would bring my own first film as a producer to the festival. It was *Mad Dog Morgan*, directed by Philippe Mora (who had done *Brother, Can You Spare a Dime?*) and although we only screened it in a sidebar section I learned about selling a picture and setting it up.

*The Shout* came about when I was at work on *Brother, Can You Spare a Dime?* in a cutting-room in Kensal Rise. Next door was Michael Austin, the writer and documentarist, and I became friendly with him. He was writing the script of *The Shout*, from a short story by Robert Graves. I took the script on, and I'd seen *Deep End*, directed by Jerzy Skolimowski, so I gave him Michael's script and persuaded him to come aboard the project. The National Film Finance

Corporation and the Rank Organisation gave us support, and we put together a fantastic stellar cast – Alan Bates, John Hurt, Susannah York, Robert Stephens, Tim Curry and others. *The Shout* turned out to be a very good film, and I was inducted into all that, which is an area I'm still grazing on today.

**How would you compare conditions for an independent producer in Europe before and since the introduction of Eurimages and the MEDIA Programme's subsidies? Has there been a dramatic change?**

It's hard to know if it was easier or more difficult to raise financing in the early days. You always think it was easier, but I don't know that it was. It's always pretty tricky to make movies.

I'm optimistic by nature. That's my spirit and that's why I make movies, and get movies made. But putting the money together, and getting a movie off the ground, is an almighty task.

There have been dramatic changes. But the thing pulling independent production down is the lessening of specialised cinema. And now it's *really* specialised, the repertory cinema has been replaced with something else, and the independent film mogul is a very, very rare item. In the 1960s, there were many, many large-sized independent producers striding across the European cinema scene. They're like dinosaurs. They've gone. It's been replaced by a TV-driven cinema, driven by the need for rights. If you examine the funding of these films, you'll see how important TV backing is, in every country in Europe. In the States, TV companies like HBO and Showtime are also in the cinema business.

**How important a part of your work is the sales operation – and how difficult is it to sell films in Europe?**

If you've got the right movie, it's always easy to sell. It's the 'big idea' that sells well. I have been involved with the sales of my films from the very beginning. Foreign sales are an integral part of the work of an independent producer. HanWay Films has an operating sales team that works not just for myself, but for other film-makers like Saul Zaentz and Woody Allen (*Match Point* and *Scoop* were sold by us, for example) – about a dozen titles each year. So Recorded Picture Company is a sister operation.

## Could you say something about Bernardo Bertolucci and why you two have formed such a successful partnership?

I knew Bernardo's brother-in-law, the screenwriter Mark Peploe, very well, and Bernardo suggested a meeting. He gave me the two copies of the autobiography of Pu Yi. He said, 'I see you've done a film in Asia with Oshima [*Merry Christmas Mr Lawrence*], and I wonder if you'd like to do one with me.' That was *The Last Emperor*. I jumped at the opportunity, although little did I know what a rollercoaster it was going to be! If I look back now, I don't know how we did it! After all, it covered sixty years of history, in all its detail – 'Son of Heaven', 'Ruler of the World', and so on. Altogether we spent four years on the project and just took it one day at a time.

## Did the nine Academy Awards won by *The Last Emperor* change your career?

I didn't go with the flow as perhaps I should have done. There were some very lucrative offers. But I stuck in my mould and continued my independent ways. But of course the Oscar for Best Film will always be the two Michelin stars on my restaurant! You don't make the film with that in mind, and *The Last Emperor* was not positioned as an Oscar film, but it does give you credibility.

## How many films do you have in development and/or in production at the same time? Is there a ceiling beyond which Recorded Picture would become just overcrowded and you would lose that 'small is beautiful' feeling?

I do one or two films each year, but at any one time I might have around ten films in various stages of development and pre-production. I don't have a desire to become bigger. I executive-produce films, and use my skills and contacts to help other people to get their films made. That's a side I want to build, because it helps to oil the wheels of this business. At the end of the day, it's a business like any other, and you have to cover the bottom line. It's because of what happened in my life as a producer in terms of the rights – the idea at the back of my mind to have a piece of each film, and that has worked in my favour over the long term. I'm one of the few producers who has a catalogue, and I use that catalogue as a cushion to support my business. I have no share-holders, and no debt, no investors – which gives me independence. It looks ideal from the outside, but of course there are always very difficult moments – moments of gambling and risk-taking beyond the point you should go – and then something you've been developing for years disintegrates, with big numbers involved. Perhaps I should be more risk-averse than I am!

**Do you think there's something that makes European film special?**
Talent. Take a film like *13 Tzameti*, directed by Géla Babluani [which won the European Film Academy's European Discovery 2006 award]. It's talented, and it also *feels* European. And there are film-makers who can travel anywhere and make good cinema, who don't need to rely on their own country's culture and subject matter. But there are cycles, just as you had the European films to the fore in the 1960s, American independent film in the 1970s, Asian films in the 1990s – and now you can see the Latin-American cinema coming up.

Telephone interview by Peter Cowie on 31 January 2007.

**Jeremy Thomas** (born 1949, in London) is the son of Ralph Thomas, who directed *Doctor in the House* and its sequels, and nephew of Gerald Thomas, who did equally well with the farcical *Carry On . . .* series during the 1950s and 1960s. He began his career as an editor, and produced his first film in his twenties (*Mad Dog Morgan*). Since 1978 he has produced a stream of award-winning movies by directors from various countries, including Jerzy Skolimowski (*The Shout*), David Cronenberg (*Naked Lunch, Crash*), Nagisa Oshima (*Merry Christmas Mr Lawrence*), Nicolas Roeg (*Bad Timing, Eureka*), Bob Rafelson (*Blood and Wine*), Phillip Noyce (*Rabbit-Proof Fence*), and Richard Linklater (*Fast Food Nation*). His richest collaboration has been with Bernardo Bertolucci, six of whose films he has produced. In

1987 he won the Academy Award for Best Film for *The Last Emperor*, and in 2006 he was honoured by the European Film Academy with the award for European Achievement in World Cinema.

*In This World*
(Picture: Marcel Zyskind)

## Making Political Films

An interview with
Michael Winterbottom

*Michael Winterbottom has directed a rich, diverse, and often provoca-*
*tive body of work since beginning his career in the late 1980s with two*
*excellent documentaries on Ingmar Bergman.*

**Has the advent of digital technology made it easier to make political**
**films? Could you give an example, perhaps, from *In This World*, or**
***The Road to Guantanamo*?**
Michael Winterbottom: Digital [technology] obviously enables you to
work with very small crews, and allows you to film in smaller places,
and places where if you were surrounded with a big crew, you'd be
attracting too much attention. In the case of both *In This World* and
*The Road to Guantanamo*, both road movies, it was advantageous to
be with a crew that looked like a bunch of amateurs on holiday, and in
areas where we could not get permission to work, we could do so
because it wasn't clear that we were making a professional film.

More generally speaking, and more importantly in fact, digital
allows you to film at a very low cost. Anyone in theory can go out with

a DV camera and shoot whatever they want. You don't *have* to have the finance. (Both *In This World* and *Guantanamo* were financed up-front, but we financed 9 *Songs* ourselves.)

But although you can shoot on digital for very little money, once you want to exhibit the film at the end of it all, there are a lot of costs you incur these days because you are dependent on traditional methods of distribution, and that's where the restrictions lie. If all the talk about screening films via the Internet comes to fruition, then obviously that would affect the way your films are shown as well as made, and you could end up with an entirely new kind of audience.

**Was *Welcome to Sarajevo* done digitally, and, if not, would you have made it differently today?**
No, it was shot on 35mm. Whenever we consider the format, whether it be on DV, 16mm, 35mm, or HD, we review all the options and choose what's right for that particular film. Quite a while back, I did *Wonderland*, which we shot with available light, in real locations, hand-held camera, on 16mm, and at the end of the day there isn't an enormous difference in the way you shoot a film in 16mm or DV, but there's a cost difference. *Welcome to Sarajevo* had a different approach to a political subject, and maybe would have been better on DV. Maybe . . . After all, we were weaving archive footage, elements of real stories, but also fictional stories, so we felt at the time that the mixture of 35mm, Beta newsreel stuff, and archive material was appropriate for what we were trying to do. Another film, *24 Hour Party People*, was a blend of 35mm, 16mm, 8mm, DV, archive footage . . .

**Has digital technology enabled you to accelerate your production pace, both on a particular film, and in terms of how many films you can do in (say) a two year spell?**
Not at all – in fact, almost the opposite. If you are working in real locations, with a very small crew, you don't necessarily have the traditional structure of pre-production, followed by a very tense six to eight week production period, and then post-production. What we can do is sometimes do two or three weeks' filming, have a look at what

we've got, then do some more preparation, film again, do some more preparation, and so on. Now you can do that with a very small crew and a very small cast, and you can spread the process out – but it does not necessarily speed it up. One thing that DV encourages you to do, if you're making road movies, is that you tend to shoot a lot more material, so the post-production period can be longer than usual.

**Do you think your political films reach a wider audience because of digital projection entering the exhibition domain nowadays?**
It's hard to know, because digital projection hasn't made such an impact yet. Again, whether you reach an audience or not is not entirely down to the technology, it's more to do with the context. For example, putting digital projection into a multiplex will not in itself create the audience for my kind of film. If you think about going to a multiplex on the edge of a town, in some suburban shopping centre, a kind of British version of suburban America, it's not conducive to our kind of British films. You want to screen your work in places that are appropriate for it. Just changing the projection system, but keeping the traditional box-like cinema on the edge of town, is not the best way of reaching a different audience. So I think that using Internet distribution is a much more optimistic way of reaching an audience, but then of course you're not watching in a cinema, you're sitting at home in front of a computer screen.

**Is it difficult to be a committed film-maker in today's rather complacent world?**
Well, it's difficult to be any sort of film-maker! But certainly the films from the 1960s were the ones I started watching as a teenager, and they seemed incredibly romantic. But I'm sure that although it seems in retrospect like some kind of golden era, it must have been equally difficult to make movies at that time. After all, the French New Wave emerged from a huge frustration with the *cinéma du papa* that those young directors were watching. I think every generation suffers from this kind of exasperation, and you hope that you'll get the opportunity to rebel against it.

The three guys from *The Road to Guantanamo* went all over the world with the film, and had a great reception, but they were too nervous to go to the United States! I did do some TV interviews over there, with the three men in a TV studio in Britain at the same time. And it was frightening to find that the Americans presented them as terrorists, despite the fact that there was no evidence to suggest that aside from their having been wrongfully imprisoned for several years in Guantanamo, deprived of any access to justice. Yet here were people saying that, basically, if you were in Afghanistan you must be terrorists.

So from that point of view it was very shocking, and very depressing. But I don't think that reflects what people overall in America think about Guantanamo, and it's become an unpopular place even over there, and George Bush has said that he thinks it should be closed. I screened the film for audiences in America where people came up afterwards and said they thought it was important that a picture like that was being made. The thing about doing independent films is that you may only reach a small audience, but it's a small audience in lots of different countries, and you hope that the numbers accumulate sufficiently for you to be able to make your next film. I remember that when I first started going to the cinema, I loved watching films from Japan, or Germany, or wherever, because they were about other cultures, and that's the great thing about the medium.

**Can politics be expressed in a metaphorical sense, using literary models such as *Jude the Obscure* or *Tristram Shandy*?**
Thomas Hardy's *Jude the Obscure* is a very radical book, and Hardy was writing it at a time when society was undergoing major economic and cultural change, and he was trying to deal with those political issues – very hostile to the church, very hostile to the institution of marriage, critical of the way in which the education establishment was excluding people, describing the way in which rural populations were moving to the cities, describing the ways in which Britain as a society was becoming more mobile *physically* and had the appearance of being more mobile in terms of class – but in practice the institutions were still restricting them. So you hope that there is a contemporary resonance in these issues (for example, the rural–urban situation in

China) and in a character like Jude, who is cheated by society. At the end of the day, you have to feel strongly about your story, and if that particular story happens to have a connection to social issues, or political issues, or cultural issues, then fine. But I never start from the basis that there is something that's terribly unjust, and what kind of story can I find that would embody that.

**Two of your earliest films, made just at the time the EFA was being launched, were two documentaries devoted to Ingmar Bergman. Bergman is hardly the most political of film-makers, but what is it about his genius that you feel most attracted to?**
Bergman is a genius, and he made a great number of brilliant films across a huge range of subjects and genres. I devoted six months to seeing his films and to talking to people who had worked with him; I had just come from being a researcher on a Lindsay Anderson documentary about British films, and although I admired Lindsay, I could understand why he'd had difficulty in producing many films. Whereas Bergman was incredibly prolific, writing at least one film each year and sometimes directing two films in a single summer, and I think the lesson of his career for me was this productivity, this single-minded energy and discipline. Bergman could put aside all the distracting paraphernalia usually associated with film-making – stars, publicity etc. – and concentrate on expressing something meaningful within his work.

I also admired his sense of 'family' – the fact that he had worked with the same team of people over some forty years. When I started making films in Britain, I found it difficult to come to terms with the fact that you are working with a bunch of people who come together for such a brief period of time, and they don't know you, and you don't know them. Gradually, over a period of years, you make friends and when you are working together, a lot of the practical problems become simpler, you're more at ease with one another. So instead of the atmosphere being incredibly tense and artificial, things are more relaxed, and to some extent the distinction between pre-production, production, and post-production tends to disappear. And individuals like the line producer or the first assistant director become as integral a part of the creative process as more obvious people like the cinematographer or the production designer.

## How important is sound in your films, and how do you record your sound when on location?

We try to use as much sound as possible recorded while on location, and since *Wonderland* (1999) we've had radio mikes to record eight or more channels at the same time. We wanted to be discreet, so we didn't want to use clapperboards, or have a boom-mike out, and so on. We also wanted the actors to be able to improvise, and to talk whenever they want. So if you want to have overlapping dialogue, it's best to record the actors separately, which means having eight, or twelve, or even sixteen channels of sound open simultaneously.

I'm working now on another film [*A Mighty Heart*] set in Pakistan, about the death in 2002 of Daniel Pearl, the American journalist. We were actually out there filming *In This World* at the time of his kidnapping.

Telephone interview by Peter Cowie on 20 September 2006.

**Michael Winterbottom** (born 1961, in Blackburn, England) began his career with two outstanding documentaries on Ingmar Bergman, made for British television. He began a fruitful partnership with the screenwriter Frank Cottrell Boyce with *Forget About Me* (1990), and then *Butterfly Kiss* (1995). Winterbottom directed prolifically for the large and the small screen during the 1990s, and showed his versatility with *Jude* (1996, based on the Thomas Hardy novel), *Welcome to Sarajevo* (filmed on location in 1997), and *Wonderland* (1999, a study of loneliness in London). In recent years Winterbottom's pace has not slackened, and he has experimented with form in *24 Hour Party People* (2002), *In This World* (Golden Bear at the Berlinale and nominee for the European Film Awards 2003), *A Cock and Bull Story* (2004), and *The Road to Guantanamo* (Silver Bear at the Berlinale and nominee for the European Film Awards 2006).

# Understanding Different Cultures
## An interview with Marco Müller

*Marco Müller has forged a remarkable career as both independent producer – working with some of the most distinctive European and Asian directors – and festival director: Pesaro, Locarno, Rotterdam, and now Venice.*

**From your vantage point as programme director of the Venice Film Festival, how do you see the development of European cinema during the twenty years since the European Film Academy was founded?**
Marco Müller: To me one of the major changes has been that now everyone's talking about 'centre-range' films as the only viable option for a film that will travel outside one's own national borders. And I find it very dangerous: twenty years ago you would talk about independent films, i.e. smaller films that would travel in a very special way. They would be personally handled by the director and the producer in connection with the world sales, but it wouldn't really be a totally new marketing concept entirely handled by the sales organisation. What we are losing now is the multiplicity of the aesthetic experience. And the variety of modes of production is giving way to a

polarisation between what is now called the 'centre-range film' (which in most territories means a film made on a budget of over €5 million), and the really low-budget films which are always made for less than €1.5 million. In the middle lies a grey zone which, in fact, does correspond to what we used to call European independent films.

**What about the increase in funding since 1988 – Eurimages, the MEDIA Programme, sources of finance that did not exist before. Has that helped or hindered the cause of good European cinema?**
Eurimages helps finding an intelligent strategy so that a film can be co-produced by various European countries, and the MEDIA Programme, for me, has been instrumental in making it possible for projects to be developed with much more care, attention, and time compared with what had been possible in the past. I honestly feel this, not just as a producer who has made use of all the MEDIA funds and Eurimages, but also as a festival director because I can see the results. So in that respect, I think, the limitations of the low-budget film have been removed.

**As an independent producer, do you find that it's difficult to set up productions without the help of subsidy systems?**
If I look back over my experiences, I must say that it forced me to try to understand how I could work with producers from other nations without having to sacrifice anything in terms of the authenticity of the screenwriting process. At the same time it helped me to tell a director, 'You know what, although you will be co-writing this film, at some point we will have to discuss the script with our French, or Swiss, or Eastern European partners. We must get their agreement to the final script.' It's good in that it allows you to check already on the feedback the film will receive, at the script stage. Of course, it did not influence choices on a casting level too much, although we might always say, we'll get a couple of foreign actors involved. But now, thanks to all this, I have a detailed knowledge of cinematographers, costume designers, production designers, special effects supervisors throughout the whole of Europe. In that sense, I tried to grasp the specific potential existing in several territories. To give you an example, I'm currently

producing a Swiss 'Alpine horror' film, co-produced with Hungary and Italy. So we have some Italian actors, but we also managed to single out a great legend of the Hungarian cinema, the actress Mari Törocsik. We needed a mature actress, but still with an enormous screen presence. At the same time, I realised that Hungary is now an excellent testing-ground for new visual strategies, so our DoP is Hungarian and we are considering using digital cinema and a digital intermediate, so that the picture quality will be even stronger – and enhanced by special effects designers who have not lost a certain 'artisanal' touch.

**What made you go further afield, to Turkey (Dervis Zaim), Russia (Aleksandr Sokurov) or Iran (Samira Makhmalbaf) etc.? Most of your productions have been made outside the traditional core block of European cinema (France, Germany, Italy, Spain, the UK).**
I was genuinely interested in understanding different cultures. For example, one of the recent films I've produced, *Little Red Flowers*, directed by Yuan Zhang, premiered at Sundance and was then shown in the Berlin Panorama, and went on to receive many awards all over Europe. As with one of his previous films, *Seventeen Years*, the contribution of the Italian editor Jacopo Quadri was significant. And already at the scriptwriting stage, I said to Yuan Zhang, although you don't want to make a screenplay aimed totally at the American market, you cannot take it for granted that foreign viewers will understand. We shot the film in the army studios in China, which meant that we could get wonderful production design at one-third the cost of elsewhere. But most of the post-production was done in Europe, so the composer, Carlo Crivelli, worked with the director from the very beginning, as did Jacopo Quadri (who had cut for Bertolucci). So for the first time we have a small, independent Chinese movie which is doing well at the box office in Italy.

Sokurov came to me with his early short films, which had been banned and which, in my capacity during the early 1980s as head of the Pesaro Festival, I'd screened. So later, as a producer, I told him that I wanted to do a project with him, but something that would have to appeal to our part of Europe. So I started with *Moloch*, which is a film nobody wanted to touch, and then *The Sun*. He's a totally original artist. The third part of his trilogy, *Faust*, will again be a Russian-Italian production, shot in Italy. Thus the situation slowly evolved, with me starting by bringing Italian help to an entirely Russian project, to the point that we now have a Russian project being made entirely in Italy yet by no means a 'Europudding'.

With the Benetton Group I created Fabrica Cinema because Luciano Benetton agreed to gamble on the new creative experience afforded by young directors, and to be associated with the directors I love. But I have had to form my own company, Downtown Pictures in Italy, and Riforma Film in Switzerland.

**You have promoted the cause of Asian cinema in Europe and at the Venice festival. What lessons can be drawn by European film-makers from the success of Asian cinema in recent years?**
American cinema's only worthy opponent today is indeed the Asian cinema. I'm really talking about the very small group of artistic yet commercial directors who have been able to impose their own vision, even when they are working on a budget tailored to meet the marketing needs of the various Asian territories. They have successfully inverted the genre picture to suit a global audience: the Japanese did so in the 1950s and 1960s, Hong Kong cinema did so in the 1970s and 1980s, and in recent years many Asian nations have done so too.

**Why do you think that Italian cinema lacks the high-quality image it once had, despite the fact that so many features are produced each year in Italy?**
I think we are missing good stories. In the golden age of Italian cinema, we had the 'soggettisti', really unique writers like Ennio Flaiano, who would only be involved at the story and treatment stage. They came up with a considerable number of original, important ideas.

**Venice is a glamorous event, where the celebrity factor is significant, and media interest is intense. Do you ever feel that this is at odds with the 'art-house' image of European cinema, or independent films?**
I don't think the Mostra should ever become a mixed bag of elements.

I tend to divide films into two categories: films that need a festival, and films that the festival needs. So for films that need the festival, we try not just to enhance their visibility, but to create a different impact. If I consider my first three festivals, and the three Golden Lions (*Vera Drake, Brokeback Mountain,* and *Still Life*), then it's clear that the festival has been instrumental in order to impose a special profile for the films. It's interesting that in 2006 the producer Harvey Weinstein wanted us to bill *Bobby* as 'A Work in Progress', which means he was using Venice as a testing-ground.

**If you could programme an art-house for just one day, what film or films would you like most to screen?**
A film that brought together many of the best European qualities, directed by Roberto Rossellini: *Europa '51*, starring Ingrid Bergman.

Interviewed by Peter Cowie in Berlin, 12 February 2007.

**Marco Müller** (born 1953, in Rome, Italy) is renowned both as a festival director and an independent producer. He studied sinology and anthropology, and contributed to numerous film periodicals before becoming involved in festival programming – first in Turin, then in Pesaro. In 1989 he became director of the Rotterdam Film Festival, and from 1991 to 2000 was director of the Locarno event. Since 2004 he has been head of programming at the Venice Film Festival. In his other capacity, Müller has co-produced some 200 films in Europe, Asia, Africa, and Latin America, and from 1998 to 2002 was head of the Film and Video Department of Benetton's Fabrica Cinema. He is also widely respected for his writings on Asian cinema.

## An Uphill Battle

An interview with
Jean-Marc Barr

*Jean-Marc Barr became an international star at the age of twenty-seven, as one of the deep-sea divers in* Le Grand Bleu. *His fluency in several languages has enabled him to find roles throughout Europe and in the United States, but since the late 1990s he has turned his attention to producing and directing independent films in France.*

**How difficult is it to get a film off the ground in the French system?**
Jean-Marc Barr: Over a period of twenty to thirty years a system had developed whereby most of the films were getting money from the national, terrestrial television channels, TF1, France 2, and France 3 and, of course, from the even bigger source, Canal Plus. Along with international sales and a minimum distribution guarantee, a majority of French films were produced with help from regular television as well as cable television. That's how things used to be done, when times were good. But when Pascal Arnold and I did our first three movies, we went to see Pierre Lescure [at Canal Plus] and over three years we got around €1.5 million for those three films.

Then came the Millennium, and Canal Plus imploded. All of a sudden, at the start of the century, we found ourselves faced with the reality that the only projects in which the terrestrial television or cable channels were willing to invest had to be prime-time material. That meant very light comedies, and films that are aimed at a young audience. So during the past four or five years, many *auteurs* have not been able to make a film because their work does not fall into those categories. The problem is that the minimum budget for most films in France today is €3 to €4 million, where they should be costing €500,000 to €1 million. People are being paid at the same level as they were during the 1980s and 1990s, but the films aren't recouping that much because they are aimed at a French TV audience, and they can't be sold internationally, so all of a sudden the system is collapsing. This makes life rough for the *auteurs* and some of the independent film-makers. Take Lars von Trier, for example. For his latest film, Lars got €100,000 from Canal Plus; we got €150,000 for our project. So we are obliged to make films for €500,000 to €1 million. Instead of using thirty people on a crew, we are getting by with four or five, paying them at normal rates. We are shooting in digital, and Pascal Arnold and I have been able to maintain some economical coherence in the production, so we can stay tuned to what we want to communicate.

But it remains an uphill battle. We have released *Chacun sa nuit*, and the film is faring not too badly, but you've only got about sixty to seventy screens, and you're up against four or six hundred cinemas that are constantly evaluating who can stay the course and who can't. The system is fixed in such a way as it's almost impossible for independent film-makers to exist. So they are seeking other media, other venues, in which to show their material.

It's often said that too many films are made in France, but those films are made to keep the system running. They need to keep the industry going, and they are in a horrible panic because they know that individuals will have to be sacrificed because too many people are competing for too few jobs.

**What happens when a film in France cannot recover its budget from a domestic release? Does the production company go into liquidation?**

Well, in their heyday Canal Plus was buying such companies, as they went bankrupt. So during a twenty year period, Canal Plus created a whole group of dependent producers and distributors who were attached to them. That is no longer so, and thus many people are simply going out of business. Pascal Arnold and I have to take risks, not huge risks, but significant risks, and cut our costs, in order to survive.

**You have worked with Lars von Trier as an actor on many occasions. How would you compare the Danish with the French system of production and distribution?**
The Danes work on a much smaller scale, but I think the philosophy is pretty much the same. There's the Danish Film Institute, of course, and Zentropa, Lars's company, has quite a few resources. Peter Aalbæk Jensen, Lars's producer and co-owner of Zentropa, is some-one who invests in other films, in America, and so Zentropa does not exist just on Lars's output. Now, the advantage Lars enjoys stems from when he started shooting his films in English, so all of a sudden he had a large potential audience. Zentropa has been able to assimi-late what's happening in America and use it in a European and worldwide cycle – just as Luc Besson has used the American phil-osophy in France with such success. Luc, incidentally, is someone who knows how to make his sales internationally, cover his costs that way, and so he's not dependent on the French subsidy system and things like that.

On the whole, however, neither the French nor the Danes will pro-duce films in English, because it's against their domestic policy. We found ourselves completely out of fashion when we were shooting in English. Pascal and I had two projects – one was a €700,000 to €800,000 film with Kathleen Turner and Geraldine Chaplin for shoot-ing in Savannah, Georgia. Ten years ago, you could have financed such a budget in half a day with those names attached. But we never got the money together – Canal Plus wouldn't contribute. Then we had another picture, with Charlotte Rampling, Rosanna Arquette and myself in the cast, for about €800,000. It was the same problem. We were going to shoot in English, so we never found the money in

France. That's why we had to write a new film immediately – and shoot in French!

As I've said, in France when you try to finance a film, first you go to terrestrial as well as cable television, and then you go to an international sales agent, as we did, such as François Yon from Films Distribution. The minimum guarantee from a distributor and an advance from international sales generally amount to no more than twenty per cent of a film's budget. Very minimal, unless you're Luc Besson! But they do form part of the financing budget. Then you go to the region where you intend to shoot the film, and they contribute money, often from €100,000 to €200,000.

In France the situation resembles Hollywood and the big studios, in that you have four or five huge conglomerates or companies that have been dominating the market for the past thirty to forty years. They don't want to relinquish their power, and they are confronted by an immense revolution involving where kids are going to go to see their movies in the future, and how people are going to be consuming images. What Pascal Arnold and I are forced to do now is to shoot a film for somewhere between €500,000 and €1 million – or even less; so we are approaching private investors and giving them twenty to thirty per cent of the film, and taking maybe €200,000 to €300,000, which is not a huge investment for them. Because television is no longer a viable source of production finance. People are not watching TV so much, especially movies on TV. In late summer 2006, TF1 cancelled their last remaining 'Movie of the Week' slot.

**How do you manage to juggle your career as an actor with your career as a producer and maker of films?**
I'm learning day by day! When I appeared in *The Big Blue*, all of a sudden the figures became very big, and I began talking about money. But Pascal Arnold and I, we have to take huge risks, not necessarily financial risks, but risks in terms of the choices we're making instead of participating in the system that exists today. We don't pay each other much on these films, because we are the ones organising the production; if the films do well, then perhaps we can pay ourselves. Of course,

you take some roles you don't really think highly of, because once you play against the system, the system will not help you. They are not going to give you interesting roles within the system, because they know perfectly well what you're doing.

Another thing that Pascal and I are doing is trying to use the new technology to focus on the humanity *behind* the camera, concentrating on why we are doing these films. That's something I admire about Lars von Trier, and I love this concept of using a smaller crew, young actors, and a compressed shooting schedule, so that all of a sudden you realise you're doing something that could be important.

Telephone interview by Peter Cowie on 22 September 2006.

**Jean-Marc Barr** (born 1960 in Germany, of a French mother and an American father) enjoyed small parts in the TV adaptation of Anita Brookner's *Hotel du Lac* (1986), and John Boorman's *Hope and Glory* (1987), before becoming an overnight sensation as Jacques Mayol in Luc Besson's *Le Grand Bleu* (1988). Three years later he appeared in Lars von Trier's *Europa*, and has since featured in five of the Danish director's features. In 1999, he made his directorial debut with a Dogma film, *Lovers*, and has made three further features, *Too Much Flesh, Being Light*, and *Chacun sa nuit*. A versatile talent, Barr has also worked on the screenplays of his own films, as well as serving as cinematographer on *Searching for Debra Winger* and *Chacun sa nuit*.

Baltasar Kormákur
(Picture: EFA/Andreas Böhmig)

## A Ray of Sunshine in a Cold Country

An interview with
Baltasar Kormákur

*Baltasar Kormákur is one of the Nordic region's most exciting talents, both as an actor and director. He was nominated for European Discovery 2000 for* 101 Reykjavík, *and his latest feature film,* Jar City, *swept all the major national film awards in 2006, while his stage version of* Peer Gynt *was invited to the Barbican Centre in London in February 2007, and then to Poland, Russia, and Lithuania.*

**Icelandic cinema is really only about a quarter century old, since Ágúst Gudmundsson's and Hrafn Gunnlaugsson's first features appeared. Did they have an impact on you when you were a teenager?**
Baltasar Kormákur: I was especially impressed by Ágúst Gudmundsson's *Outlaw* (1982), because it was about something that related to us, and we didn't see many films of that kind at that period. The Icelandic cinema seems to work best when it is based on literature, and it reaches a large audience. People often think that's only so because the audience knows the original material, but that's a short-sighted conclusion. I think that in some way the richness of the

storytelling in those sagas and novels is what comes through on the screen in the final analysis. Maybe we film-makers are not so strong storytellers as our writers are! In the case of *101 Reykjavík*, the novel was badly reviewed and did not really sell in Iceland. But when the film came out, and worked well with audiences here and abroad, the novel started to sell, too. The screen adaptation is quite far removed from the structure of the book, the tone of the book is in some degree harsher, even pornographic compared to the film. Hallgrimur Halgason is a wild writer, and I like his work immensely; I also adapted his previous novel, *Everything's On the Up*, for the stage.

### Are there any professional screenwriters in Iceland?

Not really, although there are some who would like to do that. It's not the fault of the writers, it's because the directors are almost always involved in their own work. It also means that screen versions of novels have proved more successful than original scripts. It's such a small market, dominated by a few individuals.

I read Arnaldur Indriðason's *Jar City* when it was published, around Christmas 2000, and bought it right away. Its sales gathered momentum, and perhaps no novel since Halldór Laxness had enjoyed such popularity in Iceland. I liked it because of the issue – genetic research – and its development as a kind of mystery drama. The book is based on a company that persuaded the Icelandic government to give it access to the medical records of all Icelanders, so that individual genes could be isolated and then studied as to where they come from, how they travel from generation to generation and so on. But this is a highly sensitive matter because you are also gaining access to personal information about individual human beings. So insurance companies and employers might want to get hold of that information.

I can see both sides of the issue, so I went to the head of the company, which is quoted on NASDAQ, and to my surprise he rather liked the novel and felt that it addressed the dilemma involved in this tracking of private information. He allowed us to shoot the whole film on the company premises. So I arranged for a journalist to ask him some very probing questions about the invasion of privacy, and gave him the opportunity to answer them.

You first made your mark as an actor, in films like *Wallpaper* and
*Agnes*. Did you gravitate towards production and direction because
it's such a small film-making community in Iceland?
It might have speeded up the process, but I think I would have gravi-
tated towards directing in any event. I was still only twenty-six or
twenty-seven years old when I started directing in the theatre. I wasn't
a film buff obsessed with the cinema, but then I started acting in films
and from there I moved into directing.

Victoria Abril plays the Spanish flamenco teacher in *101 Reykjavík*.
You had presumably seen her in Almodóvar's movies, but was the
production easier to set up because of her being in the cast?
It actually made it more difficult, because we had to shoot the film in
two parts, as Victoria was not going to come to Iceland in mid-winter.
So I had to 'create' winter conditions during the middle of summer for
her role. It was hard because it was my first feature film, and I had
to shoot some scenes from one angle in summer, and from another
direction altogether in winter! And at that stage I did not have any
studio experience.

Having a foreign star doesn't bring you money immediately. It
may help with foreign sales at a later stage. But I chose Victoria Abril
primarily because I felt she was right for the part. I'd been in love with
her as an actress ever since I had been a kid. She had impressed me not
so much in Almodóvar's films as in Vicente Aranda's *Amantes* (1991).
Of course I changed the character to suit her – the original character in
the novel was a psychotherapist from Akureyri in northern Iceland!
My idea was to bring a ray of sunshine into this cold country! Everyone would fall in love with her, and she would make everything and
everyone go crazy around her. I also liked this kitsch idea of Icelandic
housewives dancing flamenco in the depths of winter.

The same applies, presumably, to Peter Coyote and Forest Whitaker in
*A Little Trip to Heaven*? How did you persuade them to come to
Iceland?
That was more an issue of money. Forest, however, really liked Iceland
and its people and culture, and wanted to come. He stayed for the whole

shooting period, two months and really seemed to enjoy it. Peter Coyote was only here for a couple of days, so it wasn't such a huge experience. But in one scene, showing an accident, he was so cold, he was almost crying, and he could barely speak because his lips were frozen.

**When Icelandic feature films first began appearing, wasn't there a period when people willingly paid more to see an Icelandic film than they would for a regular movie?**
And we still do! I think the habit started because at the outset it was difficult to recoup the budget of any film, and the Icelandic Film Fund did not exist in the form that it does today. At first, Icelandic films were very popular indeed, but it remains an extremely small market. Compared to Denmark, for example, with its 5 to 6 million people, we are a mere 300,000 – and it costs exactly the same to make a film here as it does in Denmark. And the fact that our films have to be sold in subtitled versions restricts the outlook for foreign sales.

The average budget of an Icelandic feature film is between €1.1 and €1.5 million. The only way of working less expensively is by shooting with digital, and it's certainly easier to make a first film thanks to digital equipment. But, of course, the more such films are made, the more the audience will be diminished for each title, and the harder it may be to gain attention. And the equipment represents only a fraction of what it costs to make a film. That said, it is probably somewhat cheaper to do a feature now than it was a couple of years ago.

We now have quite generous funding through the Icelandic Film Fund, and then you can also apply to the Nordic Film and TV Fund, especially if you have a good script.

**How many theatres are there in the country?**
About fifty to sixty at present. The top foreign-language film this year was *Pirates of the Caribbean II*, with about 65,000 admissions (out of a population of 300,000). *Jar City* beat those figures, and we are very proud of that. In fact we are now up to 85,000 admissions which makes *Jar City* the all time box-office record holder. The average Icelandic production attracts about 17,000 spectators here at home, and some can reach only 10,000.

**The music in Icelandic films is often extremely subtle, extremely sophisticated. What's the explanation for that?**
In *Jar City*, for example, the music is sung by male choirs, of which we have a great many in Iceland. We have a lot of Russian tradition in our folk songs. I start thinking about the music at an early stage, while writing the script. And with the pop scene so vibrant here, you don't have to look very far to find talent in music. Mugison, who wrote the score for *Jar City* and my previous film, comes from the west of the country, and is recognised on the world scene (just like Hilmar Örn Hilmarsson, who's done the music for so many Icelandic feature films). Mugison's album of the music from *A Little Trip to Heaven* was at the top of the charts for a long time, but that's not always the case.

**Is there a temptation to work abroad? What keeps you working in Iceland?**
Well, I'm very torn at the moment, because on the one hand I'd like to reach a larger audience, and tell stories that don't necessarily happen in this country, but on the other hand I have to admit that it's a great place to work in. You have good crews, who work hard, and you have control over your material. You benefit from terrific locations, and everything is just five minutes away, or so it seems. You need something, so you call someone, and it's fixed.

I may be tempted to make a film abroad, but I suspect that at the end of the day most of my work will be shot here on Iceland. The downside is that many excellent film-makers do not reach a great many people, because they remain at home, working in the surroundings they know best. Iceland is drifting in the sea between America and Europe. Right around the time of the Second World War and afterwards, we were under the American influence, and in recent years we've been drifting somewhat more towards Europe.

Telephone interview by Peter Cowie on 23 November 2006.

**Baltasar Kormákur** (born 1966, in Reykjavík, Iceland) trained at the Drama Academy of Iceland. He made a stunning debut as Lass in Julius Kemp's *Wallpaper* (1992), and impressed as Natan in Egill

Edvardsson's *Agnes* (1995). He appeared in two films by Fridrik Thór Fridriksson – *Devil's Island* (1996) and *Angels of the Universe* (2000) before moving behind the camera to direct Victoria Abril and an Icelandic cast in the hilarious comedy *101 Reykjavík* (2000). His second work, *The Sea* (2002), swept the local Edda film awards, and *A Little Trip to Heaven*, three years later, won the FIPRESCI prize at the Gothenburg Film Festival. His latest film as a director, *Jar City* (2006), has performed remarkably at the Icelandic box-office and won five Edda awards.

# 10   My Own Cinema
Films That European Film-makers Would Screen

*We have asked almost all people interviewed for this book which films they would screen if they owned a cinema for one day. Some of them have answered during the interview and you can read their full response in the respective chapter, some of them have sent us a list. Below you will find a compilation of all the films that were mentioned:*

**Javier Bardem**
Porn

**Jean-Marc Barr**
*Some Like It Hot / The Apartment* by Billy Wilder
*Horse Feathers* by The Marx Brothers
*Stalker* by Andrei Tarkovski
*Ice Cold in Alex* by J. Lee Thompson
*L'Idiot* with Gérard Philipe [by Georges Lampin]

**Bernardo Bertolucci**
*La Règle du jeu* by Jean Renoir

**Daniel Brühl**
*Rocco and his Brothers* by Luchino Visconti
*El angel exterminador* by Luis Buñuel
*Max et les ferrailleurs* by Claude Sautet
*High and Low* by Akira Kurosawa
*The Shining* by Stanley Kubrick
*The Wild Bunch* by Sam Peckinpah
*Garde à vue* by Claude Miller
*Platoon* by Oliver Stone
*Les 400 coups* by François Truffaut
*Nosferatu* by F.W. Murnau

**Laurent Cantet**
A film by Bergman
*Voyage en Italie* or *Stromboli* by Roberto Rossellini
A film by John Ford
*La Maison des bois* by Maurice Pialat
*Love Streams* by John Cassavetes
*Ten* or *The Taste of Cherry* by Abbas Kiarostami

**Jean-Pierre & Luc Dardenne**
*Shoah* by Claude Lanzmann
*La Maison des bois* by Maurice Pialat

**Olivier Ducastel**
*La Règle du jeu* by Jean Renoir.
*La Chambre verte* by François Truffaut
*La Geule ouverte* by Maurice Pialat
*Le Petit prince a dit* by Christine Pascale
*Les Parapluies de Cherbourg* by Jacques Demy
*Playtime* by Jacques Tati

**Constantine Giannaris**
*The Gospel According to St Matthew* by Pier Paolo Pasolini

**Agnieszka Holland**
*Daisies* by Vera Chytilová
*Diamonds of the Night* by Jan Němec
*The Mirror* by Andrei Tarkovski
*Barry Lyndon* by Stanley Kubrick
*Throne of Blood* by Akira Kurosawa
*8½* by Federico Fellini
*Oedipus Rex* by Pier Paolo Pasolini
*Persona* by Ingmar Bergman
(without subtitles)

**Fernando León**
*Maccaroni* by Ettore Scola

**Jalil Lespert**
*La Dolce Vita* by Federico Fellini

**Dušan Makavejev**
*The Brig* by Jonas Mekas
*Ashes and Diamonds* by Andrzej Wajda
*You're a Big Boy Now* by Francis Ford Coppola
*Valeri Chkalov* by Mikhail Kalatozov
*Viva Zapata!* by Elia Kazan
*A Place in the Sun* by George Stevens
*Healthy People for a Good Time* by Karpo Acimović Godina (short)
*Angel* by Andrei Smirnov
Plus any film by Ivan Passer and John Boorman,
    and a few thousand more

**Jacques Martineau**
*Une chambre en ville* by Jacques Demy
*Nosferatu* by F.W. Murnau (in the original version)
*My Own Private Idaho* by Gus van Sant

**Jeanne Moreau**
*Route One USA* by Robert Kramer
*The Great Dictator* by Charles Chaplin
*The Sun* by Alexandr Sokourov
*Chimes at Midnight (Falstaff)* by Orson Welles
*De battre mon cœur s'est arrêté* by Jacques Audiard
*Mademoiselle* by Tony Richardson
*Oedipus Rex* and *Teorema* by Pier Paolo Pasolini
*Voyage en Italie* by Roberto Rossellini
*La femme d'à côté* by François Truffaut
*Die Sehnsucht der Veronika Voss* by Rainer Werner Fassbinder
*Le Boucher* by Claude Chabrol
*Sous le sable* by François Ozon
*Cet amour-là* by Josée Dayan
*The River* by Jean Renoir
*The 39 Steps* by Alfred Hitchcock

**Marco Müller**
*Europa '51* by Roberto Rossellini

**György Palfi**
In the morning, from 10 to 12, for the children, some very good
Hungarian animation films.
12–4, for retired people, a Hungarian romantic film from the 1930s
   (*Fatal Spring*, for example) and a Chaplin movie (maybe *City
   Lights*).
4–6 *Quest for Fire* by Jean-Jacques Annaud
6–8 *Paths of Glory* by Stanley Kubrick
8–10 Terry Gilliam's *Brazil*
10–midnight Miklós Jancsó's *Szegénylegények (The Round-Up)*
midnight–6am party with DJs, VJs, cocktails and food

## Ventura Pons

*Rocco e i suoi fratelli* or *Il Gattopardo* by Luchino Visconti
*All about Eve* and *A Letter to Three Wives* by Joseph L. Mankiewicz
*Annie Hall* and *Husbands and Wives* by Woody Allen
*Summer with Monika* or *Fanny and Alexander* by Ingmar Bergman
*Viridiana, Simon of the Desert* by Luis Buñuel

## Cristi Puiu

*La Maman et la putain* by Jean Eustache
*A Woman Under the Influence* by John Cassavetes
*Ma Nuit chez Maud* by Eric Rohmer
*Fear Eats the Soul* by Rainer Werner Fassbinder
*The Son* by the Dardennes
*Urgences* by Depardon
*Suspicion* by Alfred Hitchcock
*Mouchette* by Bresson
*Trash* by Paul Morrissey

## Wieland Speck

11:00 *Ludwig* by Luchino Visconti (the long cut)
13:00 *From Here to Eternity* by Fred Zinnemann
16:00 *Im Himmel ist die Hölle los* by Helmer von Lützelburg
18:00 *Ich kenn keinen – Allen unter Heteros* by Jochen Hicks
20:30 *Nicht der Homosexuelle ist pervers, sondern die Situation, in der er lebt* by Rosa von Praunheim.
23:30 *Myra Breckenridge* by Michael Sarne

## Paprika Steen

*The Dictator* by Charlie Chaplin
*Nashville* by Robert Altmann
*The Conversation* by Francis Ford Coppola
*Jaws* by Steven Spielberg
*Roma* by Roberto Rossellini
*Love Streams* by John Cassavetes
*This is Spinal Tab* by Rob Reiner
*Raging Bull* by Martin Scorsese
*Manhattan* by Woody Allen

**Vittorio Storaro**
*2001: A Space Odyssey* by Stanley Kubrick

**István Szabó**
*Ivan the Terrible* by Sergei Eisenstein
*Ladri di biciclette* by Vittorio De Sica
*Wild Strawberries* by Ingmar Bergman
*Ashes and Diamonds* by Andrzej Wajda
*8½* by Federico Fellini
*Les Quatre cents coups* by François Truffaut
And to close the programme: *The Red and the White* by Miklós Jancsó

**Jeremy Thomas**
*A Matter of Life and Death* by Michael Powell & Emeric Pressburger
*The Music Room* by Satyajit Ray
*The Conformist* by Bernardo Bertolucci
*A Taste of Cherry* by Abbas Kiarostami
*Walkabout* by Nicolas Roeg
*The Rise of Louis XIV* by Roberto Rossellini

**Michael Winterbottom**
Ingmar Bergman's *Through a Glass Darkly*
Ingmar Bergman's *Winter Light*
Ingmar Bergman's *The Silence*

# 11   The Audience: Who Watches What?

Voices From the Cinema-Loving Public Across Europe

*Very often, when people get together to discuss European cinema, it is emphasised that there is a fantastic diversity of witty, well-made, story-driven films with a message, which are great to watch but, alas, there still aren't enough possibilities to see these films (although the situation is improving). While a better distribution of European films across the continent remains one of the major tasks for both the industry and its support schemes, not only to give the films better exposure but also to increase their chance of becoming economically profitable, it is often surprising to learn where exactly in Europe audiences have had the chance to see a particular movie and been impressed by it. It might not always be in the most crucial window after a film's initial release, and maybe it isn't in a big cinema. It might be at night on public television, on DVD or in a special programme at a local art-house cinema, years later. Wherever and whenever it is, the fact remains that at least some European films manage to reach people far from where they were made.*

NOTE: all images in this chapter appear courtesy of the individuals interviewed

## An escape to a saner world in London

Although I love films from Germany, Italy and Spain (I'll never forget my first Almodóvar), I have to pick a French one because of the extra pleasure I get from being at home in the language.

And although I'm an austere and ferocious intellectual, I'm going to pick *Gazon Maudit* directed by Josiane Balasco. I found it sexy, charming, funny and self-confident at a time when I felt in need of all four of those qualities.

The film is really brilliant on the hypocrisies of men about adultery.

I also had great pleasure from explaining to my monoglot companion the precise inadequacies of the subtitling.

Sometimes a film doesn't have to be a great work of art to secure a permanent place in your memory. This one took me into a different and saner world than the one I was then inhabiting.

There's a line I'm reminded of frequently: a businessman in a restaurant with his secretary is approached by one of those flower sellers – 'Non merci,' he says, 'on a déjà baisé.' One day I'm going to say that.

Christopher Campbell (46 years old)
*Assistant Literary Manager*
*Royal National Theatre*
*London, UK*

## Almodóvar at the Illusion in Prague

It is hard to select one favourite film from the diverse multitude of European cinematography. But it is always Pedro Almódovar's films that stir my emotions and stay with me long after the film ends.

What appeals to me is the humanity and playful lightness with which Almódovar brings across some of the toughest realities. I like the way he plays with exaggeration and humour so that the images he creates are not absurd but magical.

I also love Almódovar's sense of beauty. The individual shots show a photographic perfection and, together with his charismatic cast and beautiful music, create the unique atmosphere of his films.

One of Almódovar's strongest films is in my opinion *Hable con ella*. I remember the first time I saw it very well. It was in Prague, in an old cinema with wooden seats and chandeliers, called conveniently 'Illusion'. I went with my boyfriend and another friend and got one of the last tickets that night. Without any doubt, the special atmosphere of the cinema intensified the whole experience and I still remember the goose bumps we had when we were leaving the cinema.

Zuzana Partlova (29 years old)
*English teacher/translator*
*Prague, Czech Republic*

## *Amélie* in Gran Canaria

The European film I first think of is *Le fabuleux destin d'Amélie Poulain* [by Jean-Pierre Jeunet]. I watched it during my stay abroad in Berlin, where I lived for about a year. I watched it because I read many good reviews about it, and many friends said it was a wonderful film. I went to the movies with my best friend, and I really enjoyed this movie. It is like a modern fairytale how Amélie tries to help everyone else, almost forgets about herself, and in the end still finds happiness. The images and the lighting are what I remember as being very touching. I have seen this movie three times by now, and if you asked me, I would watch it again – immediately.

Joana Pérez Stribel (24 years old)
*Student*
*Las Palmas de Gran Canaria, Spain*

## A box of letters in Lisbon

My parents really like *Amor de Perdição* by Manoel de Oliveira. They saw the film about thirty years ago, on my mum's birthday, in a cinema that is now known as a theatre called 'Politeama'. Dad knew the tragic love story from the book by Camilo Castelo Branco which one of his sisters had given to him before he went to the army. He read it a dozen times while he was doing his military service in the city of Porto. Later, when he came to live in Lisbon, he lent it to a colleague at work, who never returned it. He still talks of it with a bit of sadness because the book had such great sentimental value to him. The film tells the unhappy love between Simão Botelho and Teresa de Albuquerque who are from two rival families. Mum and dad both found the story very moving, how the lovers have to meet in secret and, once found out, are separated. Teresa is put into a convent and the only way to communicate is by writing letters to each other. This is something my parents used to do when they were dating and they still keep the letters in a wooden box on top of their closet.

My mum also remembers one of the songs of the film, and even sang a bit for me as I was writing down their words. It goes something like this: 'Simão has killed for love. He never got forgiveness for his deed, and wept his pain near the bars of a prison cell.'

Both of my parents say that the film moved them so much because the love between Simão and Teresa was really tragic, and because of all that they went through only to be together – something that they couldn't have because of their families' selfishness.

Maria Emília Marinho de Oliveira (68 years old) *Housewife/seamstress*

Gonçalo de Freitas (71 years old) *Driver*

Lisbon, Portugal, recorded by their daughter, Patricia.

## Head-on from Slovenia

One of my favourite European films is *Gegen die Wand* [by Fatih
Akin]. I saw the film for the first time in Karlovy Vary at the film
festival. I like it because it shows love, passion, pain and other feelings
in a way that touches you and doesn't leave you cold-blooded. The
scenes and especially the music create a perfect background for sharing
the characters' feelings. The love story of two desperate characters
who find each other and start a relationship which leads them through
happiness, joy, jealousy and frustration is shown realistically and
rudely without embellishment. It reveals also the dark side of the characters and their collision with tradition which gives the film an additional social dimension. Although the story is quite heavy and bitter, it
isn't pathetic but makes one eager to live and love.

Mitja Janza (36 years old)
*Hydrogeologist*
Ljubljana, Slovenia

## A Danish passion for *Burnt by the Sun*

My favourite movie is *Utomljonnye solncem* (*Burnt by the Sun*) [by
Nikita Mikhalkov]. The brilliant actor Oleg Menshikov plays the leading role. The first time I saw it was in a small cinema with my students.
Why do I love it? It shows the history of the early Stalin period in a
terrifying way – the scene where the huge Stalin-flag is rising in the sky
stays with you for ever. The nerve of the film is very intense – the
beautiful dacha, the happy family and the sneaking terror. Moreover, it
is full of humour. I think it shows the dilemmas that politics can put

you into and in that way, it is not only historical but terribly relevant for society even today.

Lisa Bendsen (57 years old)
*Teacher*
*Skoerping, Denmark*

# A view from Jerusalem

Mike Leigh's *Secrets and Lies* is a masterpiece. I really love it. It is a very human film that deals with naked, basic emotions in a wonderful way. The subject is very human, and so is the director.

I also really love *Landscape in the Mist* by Theo Angelopoulos – a

Moshe Brandwine (57 years old)
*Advocate and notary*
*Jerusalem, Israel*

very strong film. It is the complete opposite of light entertainment and a genial mixture of music, picture and story. And it has such wonderful symbolism!

## Watching films in your father's bed in Athens

One of the first European films I can remember that thrilled me was *L'Important c'est d'aimer* (*That Most Important Thing: Love*) directed by Andrzej Zulawski which was filmed in Paris. I saw it when I was fourteen with my father in his comfortable double bed on TV. I was really moved by this film and began to realise that Europe has the soul and touch and America has the money and the studios. I always enjoy, especially after a difficult day, a film which is easy and full of special effects but nothing compares to the taste left after a good European film. Another film which I also saw when I was very young is *Time of the Gypsies* directed by Emir Kusturica in 1989. I saw it in the same comfy bed but alone on a video tape that I had earlier bought at the local video store. I was amazed by Kusturica's direction and the story was strong with a balance between laughter and feeling so it gained a very quick entrance to my heart and is among my all-time favourites. To tell you the truth, I couldn't sleep that night, maybe because I felt so fulfilled by this film and couldn't stop my thoughts from running to it. I love stories so I enjoy all the movies I see. I feel I am there, inside the film playing my part in the story. Sometimes we all need a good story to keep us going . . .

Lefteris Laskaridis (28 years old)
*Dentist*
*Athens, Greece*

## Volver in Warszawa

The last European movie I saw was *Volver* by Pedro Almodóvar. I went to see it with my fiancée, of course hoping that an Almodóvar movie MUST be something she will adore. It happened to be a good guess, and she did enjoy it very much.

Moreover, we've been discussing it a lot, outlining for each other the differences between the man's and the woman's points of view. I don't feel like an expert concerning the female world of emotions and feelings but maybe I just understood something?

It doesn't happen very often that you have a lot to discuss and to think about after seeing a movie. This one was a good piece of art for both of us.

Piotr Prasula (35 years old)
*Chef Concierge*
*Warsaw, Poland*

## The *Science of Sleep* in St Petersburg

The most remarkable film for me recently was *La Science des rêves* by Michel Gondry. We knew him from his video clips for Björk, and *Bachelorette* is the best clip I've ever seen. Someone said this is an entire world in five minutes and I think it's exactly true.

I haven't seen the first film by Gondry [*Eternal Sunshine of the Spotless Mind*] although many friends of mine used to say it was Jim Carrey's only first-class role, but I'd heard about *La Science des rêves* long before it was on screens in Russia. The presentation took place during the International Moscow Film Festival, in July 2006, in a voice-over version, and I remember after the very first screening our Moscow friends called us in St Petersburg saying: 'Look! Soon you will see the best European film!' But it appeared in St Petersburg only several months later. There is a cinema in our city that prior to perestroika belonged to the Syndicate of Film-makers and the screenings there used to be free. Now all the film-makers' unions have collapsed but nevertheless the film programme there is more varied than in other cinemas that usually show blockbusters and the same films that are shown everywhere. People go there to see European and Russian films, even if film buffs say the sound is not quite good. But you see the picture! And it's there that I went to see *La Science des rêves* with some friends from my last class in school. I remember we cried so much that we couldn't speak! But the other guys were just laughing. I think if you have memorised only two or three jokes from a film, you surely have missed something. This film is more like real life but is also an absolute fairy tale: Charlotte Gainsbourg is both the Princess and the Frog, and Gael García Bernal is very like a character of the Fool from Russian folklore, plus the genial Alain Chabat and the Teddy Bears and the sea made of candy wrappers! I think this film is not estranged from reality, but magnifies it and allows us to see the magic places where everything moves according to boring and irritating rules. It offers a very simple truth: Hey, people, the magic is close to you, you only have to take a step . . . It's like the *Little Prince* of Saint-Exupéry, something that adults have forgotten.

Alexandra Khazine (17 years old)
*Student*
*St Petersburg, Russia*

## A Dutch passion for film

From my student years (during the 1980s) in Groningen I have great memories of watching Monty Python movies with a bunch of friends, beers and crisps. Up to three a night, using a rental video recorder. The hilarious moments, absurd situations, like the fat man who literally eats till he bursts, or the crucified guys happily singing, are so extremely funny that millions of people can still remember them.

From my Amsterdam days (since the 1990s) a couple of movies pop into my mind, especially the documentary about André Hazes, I believe it was called *Zij gelooft in mij* [*André Hazes, zij gelooft in mij*]. It was shocking to see that this singer, who was extremely popular in the 1980s, had fallen so far, getting drunk every day and being nervous before every single performance. The people around him, real people, seemed like cartoon characters. We (my wife Suzanne and I) saw it in 'het Ketelhuis' a theatre in an old gas factory close to where I live (Jordaan), where you can see unusual, often non-commercial productions.

One of the most impressive movies I recently saw was *Der Untergang* [*Downfall*]. I watched it alone, at home, on DVD. Completely different from what I've seen in World War II movies. The perspective of 'the enemy'. How big decisions were made, how Hitler even seems human, on occasions. I think every European should see this movie, so as never to forget.

Marcel Orie (42 years old)
*Key account manager for
the world's largest flower
auction*
Amsterdam

## *Pan's Labyrinth* in Oslo

*El laberinto del Fauno* – an utterly beautiful film! I saw it three weeks ago in one of the main cinemas in Oslo.

The change between reality and fantasy, and how in moments we wonder in which of them we are, is wonderful and pulls me into the story and the fantasies. Its description of both bad and nice monsters is fantastic; it is able to display brutality in a beautiful and artistic way.

I also love what to me seems quite Spanish (I might be wrong) in the way that it makes me accept completely unlikely situations (which I hate in typical Hollywood movies). Most concrete and easiest for me to mention is the final sequence where Ofelia pours sleeping medicine in the captain's drink, he gets unsteady in seconds, and then just stays like that for a long time. A medicine can hardly work that way. Some other sequences, like some of the battles, and the horses running after Mercedes, also appear to me a bit in the same way. But – the point is that what appears on the screen is not necessarily exactly what happens, but the *essence* of what happens. It allows the bad guys to be bad right through and the good ones be purely good. Time is unimportant, facts are unimportant. It's the essence and the aesthetics that count.

Henning Hoyer (43 years old)
*Paediatrician*
*Oslo, Norway*

## *Daens*, a Belgian saga

My favourite European film is actually a Flemish film: *Daens* by Stijn Coninx. It is a film which both in cinematographic terms and in terms of content extends far beyond the boundaries of Belgium. 'Daens' is the name of a priest who dedicated himself to the cause of workers in the area of Aalst (near Brussels) at the end of the nineteenth century. He became so popular that he founded his own political party. After being elected as a Member of Parliament, he came into conflict with the established Catholic party . . . and even with the Vatican. In fact, when the film was shown at the Venice festival, there was once again a clash with the Vatican.

So I was looking forward to seeing it when it was shown a couple of weeks later in 1992 as the opening film of the Flanders International Film Festival in Ghent. Not only because of the commotion around it, but above all because of its realistic subject matter. Of course I was also curious to see how director Stijn Coninx had set about filming *Daens*, the epic book by Louis Paul Boon.

My wife and I were both deeply impressed. It was as though we had travelled back in a time machine to the previous century. Thanks to the talent of the first-class actor Jan Decleir, we felt as if Daens, the priest, had risen again.

Later, while we were discussing *Daens* at home, not only did our admiration for Jan Decleir increase further, but the film became even more personal for us. We realised that what we had seen in the film was what our mothers had experienced as children and young women, about which they had told us so much: about exploitation, about lack of respect, about their dreams and how social circumstances stood in the way of the realisation of those dreams. And how, nevertheless, they did not give up hope.

Wim Velghe (80 years old)
*Pensioner*
*Jochristi, Belgium*

## The tears of an Italian carpenter

I saw *Amore mio aiutami* (*Help Me My Love*) by Alberto Sordi on a summer night when there was nothing interesting on TV.

I was really fascinated by the dedication Giovanni Macchiavelli (Sordi) has for his wife (Monica Vitti); he's so tormented by his passion that only at the end can he really acknowledge and accept her. Blinded by love, he is so determined to save their marriage that he is unable to see how cruel and selfish his wife is.

I think there is no escape from the problems in their relationship and the sad ending points at the great difficulties that the couple had in a time of change – the unique character of Sordi's tragicomedy.

I enjoyed this movie a lot and it remains one of the few European films that can make me cry and laugh at the same time.

Alessandro 'Diccio' Della
Corte (23 years old)
*Carpenter*
*Figline Valdarno, Italy*

## Cinema zapping in Paris

I live in Paris, in the 6th Arrondissement, not far away from the Montparnasse area, which is lined with the big multiplexes that are swarmed over by a never-ending flow of people during weekends.

With utter astonishment, I watch these youngsters who cram themselves into American blockbusters which are not even subtitled but are dubbed in French. I believe multiplexes have invented the 'zapping cinema'. With the help of their unlimited passes, these young people can go from theatre to theatre and gulp a piece of each film. Listening to their conversations, I am alarmed to find out that some of them have had a small glimpse of each of the programmed films but have not managed to see one film entirely . . .

Luckily, apart from these multiplexes, in my neighbourhood, there are still two cinemas, Les Sept Parnassiens and L'Arlequin, which pro-gramme a majority of European films. Several times a week, having calculated that I need to walk fifteen minutes to reach one of these so as not to miss the ten o'clock evening screening, I get out after dinner, sometimes in the cold, knowing that at the end of this walk, I will be offered another universe – made up of works by a confirmed European master or by a young author. I like particularly the Arlequin cinema because each year, in October, they organise a festival of German films. It is a small, friendly festival during which I have the opportunnity of discovering each evening a new face of German cinema.

Silver Simphor
*Photographer*
*Paris, France*

## Connected to Israeli reality from Berlin

I was deeply impressed by *The Bubble* [by Eytan Fox], really very impressed. I've never been to Israel or Palestine but the film makes you feel as if you're there. Maybe I could have done without the ending . . . But it's full of beautiful people, beautiful aesthetics – the movie manages to bring across the lightness and also the deep problems of daily life, the reality between people, the little world you live in. It's a love story between a Palestinian and an Israeli soldier and eventually they come to realise that it isn't that easy, even on a private level. The constellations are very fascinating, it's not just about two men in a relationship. It's also about the relations between the flatmates, the gays who aren't 'typical', the queer and his butch lover. And all of this is connected to reality!

Dirk Walsh (28 years old)
*Barkeeper*
*Berlin, Germany*

## Taking your nieces to a cinema in Austria

Sometime in 2006, I took my nieces, thirteen and fifteen years old, to watch *Grenzverkehr* [by Stefan Betz]. My favourite scene is when one of the characters, Hunter, sings 'Herr, deine Liebe ist wie Gras und Ufer . . .' [a church song] and sways back and forth deliriously trying to ignore the fact that a young girl is giving birth in a stolen Volkswagen van. That kind of thing brings joy to the heart of someone who was in the Catholic Jungschar [Catholic youth organisation] and makes me smile and hum even days afterwards.

Also refreshing was the adolescent distress, mainly of boys, because of 'the first time'. Men are cool, know the ways of the world and, even when still young, are already experienced – that's what we girls think, at least when you look at those largely stupid teenager comedies and TV series. Now, as a mature thirty-one-year-old woman I almost wanted to take action and show the poor lads what real love is.

I was thankfully held back by my nieces. As the cool aunt, I had wanted to finally prove that I take the staggering advances in their growing up very seriously and didn't choose a classic children's film. And – what a surprise! – there I was, sitting in my comfortable cinema seat feeling a bit uncomfortable and only half able to enjoy the movie. 'You just want to fuck,' (pregnant) Alicia says to the boys – and I flinch. These are regular boys, they speak in our dialect, those are our meadows that they drive along, up to the Czech border and into adventures. I have corrupted my girls for good.

Michaela Luger (31 years old)
*Student*
*Linz, Austria*

## A Corsican discovery

When *Train of Life* (*Train de vie*) was released in September 1998, I discovered the director Radu Mihaileanu. I loved the strokes of inspiration in the screenplay (a fake deportation train), the directing of the actors (with a special mention for Rufus) that this Romanian-born French director showed and his way of bathing in Jewish humour the fate of a Central European shtetl during the Second World War through to Shlomo, the village fool (though he isn't so foolish . . . ). So much so that a communicative solidarity spread through the audience already converted to this likeable Jewish community fleeing its own contradictions.

Roberto Benigni – whose *Life Is Beautiful* came out the following month – was criticised for dealing with such a serious subject in such a light way. Nevertheless, the enormous success of Benigni's film quickly eclipsed Radu's.

More recently, I had the opportunity to be present when the director was presenting his third film, *Live and Become* (*Va, vis et deviens*), which deals with the story of Ethiopian Jews settling in Israel in 1980. Here again, with a tone which is more serious but not totally without humour, we can see the mark of this exile fascinated by human destiny.

Père Vincensini
*Catholic priest*
Corsica

## A crazy atmosphere in Vilnius

It's absolutely impossible to pick just one of all the European films I saw, and to say that's the one I prefer. Thus I will talk about a film I recently saw in a small cinema in Vilnius called Skalvija. The film is *Transylvania* by Tony Gatlif. I went to see it with my mother – who rarely goes to the cinema except when it's a movie by Tony Gatlif,

Emir Kusturica – whom I also appreciate very much – or by Tarkovskij for instance.

I enjoyed this movie for many reasons, of course the gipsy music contributed a lot, and the performance of the actors and this crazy atmosphere that I love. I also felt a kind of uneasiness, an uncertainty because Tony Gatlif asks a lot of questions and he does not always give you the answers. I noticed how much people feel the need to criticise a movie, to argue about what was good or bad. I always try to watch a film with a certain tolerance, questioning myself, because maybe it was on purpose that the director left some scenes so that they may seem too long or eluded others or left things unexplained.

At the end, this movie made me think, I smiled a lot and I shed some tears.

To conclude I just want to say: Long live European cinema!

Elzbieta Noemi Josadaite (16 years old)
*Student*
*Vilnius, Lithuania*

# 12   European Networks
by Martin Blaney


## The MEDIA Programme of the EU

Launched at this year's Berlinale in February, the European Union's new MEDIA 2007 programme is providing a €755 million boost to Europe's film industry over the next seven years, with almost 65 per cent of the total budget being deployed to facilitate a wider circulation of European works to other countries in Europe and worldwide.

The MEDIA 2007 funding is focused on the phases before and after film production, with a budget spread over five action lines:

- Training (scriptwriting techniques; economic, financial management; digital technologies) (7 per cent);

- Development (single projects, catalogues, new talent, co-productions, other financing) (20 per cent);

- Distribution (distributors, sales agents, broadcasters, cinema exhibitors, digitising works) (55 per cent);

- Promotion (market access, festivals, common events, heritage) (9 per cent);

- Horizontal actions (to make it easier for small and medium-size enterprises (SMEs) to access funding, and to encourage the presence of European films on digital platforms) (5 per cent), and Pilot Projects (embracing new technologies such as digital ones for film development, production and distribution) (4 per cent).

The successor to three previous programmes MEDIA I, MEDIA II and MEDIA Plus which had been supporting the European audiovisual sector since 1990, MEDIA 2007 simplifies the programme's administration, but upholds its key objectives:

- a stronger European audiovisual sector, reflecting Europe's cultural identity and heritage;

- increased circulation of European audiovisual works inside the European Union and beyond;

- a more competitive European audiovisual sector through easier access to finance, in particular for SMEs and the use of digital technologies.

Although the MEDIA 2007 budget is limited in absolute terms – it will increase year-by-year as the programme gathers momentum, starting with €75 million in 2007 and culminating with €107 million in 2013 – it nevertheless has a strong knock-on effect in terms of investments in the audiovisual sector. During the programmes preceding MEDIA 2007, each €1 of Community funding generated about €6 in private investment from industry. Thus, according to the programme's architects MEDIA 'meets the challenges of a rapidly growing and changing sector shaped by new technologies, new players and participating countries, market fragmentation and lack of private investment.'

By increasing the investment in distribution, MEDIA aims to raise the market share of non-national European films from 10 per cent to 20 per cent over the next seven years.

Among the films made possible over the years thanks to MEDIA support are: Pedro Almodóvar's *Volver*, Roberto Benigni's *La Vita è bella*, Wolfgang Becker's *Good Bye Lenin!*, Jean-Pierre Jeunet's *Le fabuleux destin d'Amélie Poulain*, Michael Winterbottom's *In This*

*World*, Lars von Trier's *Dogville* and Florian Henckel von Donnersmarck's *The Lives of Others*.

European professionals can benefit from MEDIA not only by applying for funding. There are over fifty training initiatives and a wide variety of festivals, markets and other events which are also supported by MEDIA.

The training schemes include Arista, Moonstone, and Sources 2 (scriptwriting); ACE, Berlinale Talent Campus, EAVE, Film Business School, NIPKOW, and Strategics (management); and European Animation Masterclass and SAGAS Writing Interactive Fiction (new technologies).

The promotion initiatives focus on supporting European film festivals (Clermont-Ferrand, Oberhausen, Tampere, etc.) and European films at festivals outside Europe (Pusan, Rio de Janeiro, Shanghai, Toronto, etc.) as well as backing such specialised markets such as CineMart, Cartoon Forum, and Amsterdam FORUM for co-financing of documentaries. MEDIA is also supporting the European Film Awards, the annual showcase promoting the outstanding film performances and artistic achievements in European film production.

As part of the MEDIA Programme, Europa Cinemas set up an initiative in the film exhibition sector and created the first international film theatre network for the circulation of European films, giving support to theatre exhibitors in order to encourage the programming of European films and particularly European non-national films, and to foster initiatives towards Young Audiences.

Meanwhile, the development and promotion of Europe's up-and-coming acting and film-making talent is fostered by supporting projects developed by European Film Promotion.

On 1 January, Romania became the thirty-first member of the MEDIA programme, joining the other twenty-six members of the European Union, Iceland, Liechtenstein, Norway and Switzerland.

MEDIA 2007 is jointly run by the Information Society & Media Directorate General under the authority of Commissioner Viviane Reding and the Education, Audiovisual and Culture Executive Agency (EACEA).

Contact:
European Commission,
BU 33 02/10
1049 Brussels
BELGIUM

Media Programme (Head of Unit: Aviva Silver)
phone: ++32 2 298 50 17
fax: ++32 2 299 22 90
email: infso-media@ec.europa.eu
http://ec.europa.eu/media

Education, Audiovisual & Culture
Executive Agency
Head of Media Unit:
Constantin Daskalakis
Avenue de Bourget 1
BOUR
1140 Brussels
BELGIUM
email: eacea-info@ec.europa.eu
http://eacea.ec.europa.eu

# Eurimages

Established in 1988 as a Partial Agreement by the Council of Europe in Strasbourg, the Eurimages fund for the co-production, distribution and exhibition of European cinematographic and audiovisual works currently has thirty-two member states (see below).

Eurimages aims to promote the European film industry by encouraging the production and distribution of films and fostering cooperation between professionals.

The fund has two objectives:

cultural – endeavouring to support works which reflect the multiple facets of a European society whose common roots are evidence of a single culture.

economic – investing in an industry which, while concerned with commercial success, is interested in demonstrating that cinema is one of the arts and should be treated as such.

Bearing this in mind, Eurimages has developed three funding programmes:

Assistance for co-production;
Assistance for distribution;
Assistance to cinemas.

Almost 90 per cent of the fund's resources – which originate from contributions paid by the member states – goes to supporting co-production. All projects submitted must have at least two co-producers from two different member states of the fund. The participation of the majority co-producer must not exceed 80 per cent of the total co-production budget, and the participation of the minority co-producer must not be less than 10 per cent. In the case of bilateral co-productions with a budget over €5 million, the participation of the majority co-producer must not exceed 90 per cent of the total budget of the co-production.

Eurimages also commits more than €760,000 annually to support distribution measures complementary to those offered by the MEDIA

Programme of the European Union. The support is open to distributors of member states who are not able to benefit from the MEDIA support, i.e. Bosnia-Herzegovina, Turkey, Croatia, and allows them to apply for distribution support for films originating from any of the Eurimages member states.

Moreover, distributors from any member state can apply for assistance for films originating from these non-MEDIA countries – as happened last year with the granting of support for the distribution of Bosnian film-maker Jasmila Žbanić's Golden Bear winner *Grbavica* and Romanian Cornel Porumboiu's *12:08 East of Bucharest*.

In addition, Eurimages, in partnership with Europa Cinemas, supports thirty-two cinemas in five different countries. Around €616,000 is awarded year as assistance to cinemas.

Eurimages is managed by a board of management where each member state is represented and the fund's policy as well as the conditions on which it awards financial support are determined. Usually meeting five times a year, the board's sessions together are primarily devoted to considering the applications for support and then also selecting which projects should be supported.

The board of management elects its president – currently, France's Jacques Toubon – from among the personalities proposed by the member states. The president's role is 'to represent the fund on audiovisual policy matters, to conduct the debates and to engage in an active dialogue with professionals of the cinema sector'.

The board's meetings and the implementation of its decisions are administered by the Eurimages Secretariat which is headed in Strasbourg by Jan Vandierendonck (since 2006), under the responsibility of the Secretary General of the Council of Europe.

Eurimages has the following member states: Austria, Belgium, Bosnia-Herzegovina, Bulgaria, Croatia, Cyprus, Czech Republic, Denmark, Estonia, Finland, France, Germany, Greece, Hungary, Iceland, Ireland, Italy, Latvia, Lithuania, Luxembourg, Netherlands, Norway, Poland, Portugal, Romania, Serbia, Slovak Republic, Slovenia, Spain, Sweden, Switzerland, the 'Former Yugoslav Republic of Macedonia', and Turkey.

To date, Eurimages has been involved in the co-production of more than 1,119 full-length feature films and documentaries with funding of €326 million. A number of these received prestigious awards such as Oscars, Golden Palms, Golden Bears and Golden Lions.

Backed projects range from Lars von Trier's *Europa* and Xavier Koller's *Journey of Hope* through Gerardo Herrero's *Territorio Comanche* and Alain Berliner's *Ma Vie en Rose* to the latest projects by Nana Djordjadze (*The Rainbow-Maker*) and Andrzej Wajda (*Post Mortem*).

Contact:
Eurimages
Conseil de l'Europe
Av. de l'Europe
67075 CEDEX Strasbourg
FRANCE
Executive Secretary: Jan Vandierendonck
phone: ++33 3 88 41 26 40
fax: ++33 3 88 41 27 60
eurimages@coe.int
www.coe.int/eurimages

## European Film Promotion

During the 1997 Berlinale, a pan-European promotion agency for European films – European Film Promotion (EFP) – was established to give a higher profile to films and film-makers from Europe and support their international marketing.

EFP's ten founding members were Belgium (Flanders Image, Wallonie Bruxelles Images), Germany (German Films, previously Export Union), France (Unifrance), Greece (Greek Film Centre), Great Britain (British Screen Finance), Netherlands (Holland Film), Austria (Austrian Film Commission), Switzerland (Swiss Films, previously Swiss Film Centre), as well as Denmark, Finland, Iceland, Norway and Sweden as a country grouping (Scandinavian Films; represented since 1998 as individual institutes: Danish Film Institute, Finnish Film Foundation, Icelandic Film Centre, Norwegian Film Institute and Swedish Film Institute).

In the following years, the network with its headquarters in Hamburg has grown to include twenty-seven promotion and export organisations from twenty-eight countries in Europe with the addition of Ireland (Irish Film Board), Portugal (ICA) Spain (ICAA), Luxembourg (Film Fund Luxembourg), Italy (Filmitalia, previously Italia Cinema), Czech Republic (Czech Film Centre, previously APA), Hungary (Magyar Filmunió), Estonia, Latvia and Lithuania (Baltic Films), Slovenia (Slovenian Film Fund), Bulgaria (National Film Centre), Poland (Polish Film Institute), Slovakia (Slovak Film Institute) and Romania (Romanian Film Promotion).

EFP's annual budget of €2.2 million is provided by contributions from the MEDIA Programme of the EU, the BKM (the German State Minister of Culture and the Media), the Cultural Authority of the City of Hamburg, the French film fund CNC, EFP's members and private sponsors.

In its efforts to increase the interest of the industry, press and audience in European cinema, EFP assumes clear-cut duties. At selected international film festivals and film markets, EFP on behalf of the members organises projects to put their actors, directors and producers into the international spotlight, get them talking with one another and support them in their efforts to work across borders. As a group, the EFP members generate much more attention and build up contacts that they would hardly be able to reach as a single country. The founding members profit just as much here from Europe's growing diversity as the new accession states from Central and Eastern Europe do: while one group contributes the marketing know-how and contacts, the others bring fresh ideas and a rapidly growing market to the group.

EFP's programme of activities for 2007 includes:

- The 10th anniversary of the 'Shooting Stars' initiative during the Berlinale which presents Europe's latest wave of acting talent to the press, industry and public. A 'Touring Shooting Stars Film Programme' presents some of the actors with their films at three festivals in Europe.

- A new pilot project 'Picture Europe! The Best of European Cinema' features a selection of European films in cinemas in Berlin, Madrid and London to cultivate new audiences for successful European films which have not yet had an opportunity for wider distribution outside of their home territories.

- The annual showcase of young creative producers in 'Producers on the Move' during the Cannes Film Festival.

- The *Variety* Critics' Choice, a special sidebar at the Karlovy Vary International Film Festival, spotlighting ten young European directors and their films.

- Platform for European films at the Toronto International Film Festival.

- Platform for European films at the Pusan International Film Festival.

- Industry screenings of new European films with commercial potential in New York twice a year.

- Film Sales Support available to world sales agents with European films screening at festivals in Sundance, Mar del Plata, Guadalajara, Shanghai, Toronto, Rio de Janeiro and Pusan.

Contact:
European Film Promotion e.V.
Friedensallee 14–16
22765 Hamburg
GERMANY
Managing Director: Renate Rose
phone +49 40 3 90 62 52
fax +49 40 3 90 62 49
email: info@efp-online.com
www.efp-online.com

# The European Film Academy

The creation of the European Film Academy (EFA) was the initiative of a group of Europe's finest film-makers brought together on the occasion of the first European Film Awards ceremony held in November 1988 in Berlin. The EFA was finally founded in 1989 as the European Cinema Society by its first president Ingmar Bergman and forty film-makers to advance the interests of the European film industry. Wim Wenders was elected as first chairman of the association which two years later was renamed the European Film Academy. In 1996, he followed Ingmar Bergman as president of the EFA.

In 2007, the European Film Academy unites 1,800 European film professionals – directors, producers, actors and actresses, cinematographers, screenwriters, editors, production designers, sales agents, distributors, composers, etc. – with the common aim of promoting European film culture.

Throughout the year, the EFA initiates and participates in a series of activities dealing with film politics as well as economic, artistic, and training aspects. The programme includes:

**EFA Master Classes:** courses on continuous training held by highly acclaimed and internationally successful film-makers who dedicate one week of intensive training to young talents from all over Europe, passing on their individual knowledge and personal experience. The content is especially tailored each time in cooperation with the master according to his/her special interests. The courses concentrate more on the practical side of learning than on bare lecturing; at least half of the time is spent with hands-on training like shooting, live-rehearsals, (post-) production and the creation of visual effects. The high-profile list of renowned film-makers includes Jean-Jacques Annaud, Henning Carlsen, Bernd Eichinger, Krzysztof Kieślowski, Jiří Menzel, Tilda Swinton, István Szabó, Mike Newell, Tsui Hark, Allan Starski and Anthony Dod Mantle.

**A Sunday in the Country:** special weekend encounters between approximately ten young European film-makers and some established EFA members. The private atmosphere of these gatherings guarantees an exchange of ideas and experience which goes far beyond the results of usual workshops.

**EFA Conference:** every year, as part of the Awards Weekend programme, the European Film Academy presents a conference to enhance a European debate on film, create platforms for a vivid exchange among film professionals and ensure that the discussion of what European film is, how it is changing and where it is going never expires.

In addition to the above, the European Film Academy participates in and initiates various other conferences, seminars and workshops, and a common goal is to build a bridge between creativity and the industry.

## The European Film Awards

The activities of the European Film Academy culminate in the annual presentation of the European Film Awards. Produced together with EFA Productions, the Awards are presented in fifteen categories including film, director, actor, actress, screenwriter, cinematographer, composer, discovery, documentary and short film. Special prizes include the European Film Academy Lifetime Achievement award and Achievement in World Cinema award.

Broadcast to over sixty territories, the European Film Awards are presented in Berlin, the European Film Academy's home, every second year. In the other years, supported by the local film industry and international partners, the event travels to different European cities to highlight the achievements in cinema from the different regions of Europe and to involve the EFA members from across the continent. The European Film Awards are supported by the MEDIA Programme of the EU.

Contact:
European Film Academy e.V.
Kurfürstendamm 225
10719 Berlin
GERMANY
Director: Marion Döring
Tel: +49 30 887 167 0
Fax: +49 30 887 167 77
efa@europeanfilmacademy.org
www.europeanfilmacademy.org

# Appendix 1:   The European Film Awards
## All Winners 1988–2006

## 2006

EUROPEAN FILM 2006
*Das Leben der Anderen* (*The Lives of Others*), Germany
directed by Florian Henckel von Donnersmarck
produced by Wiedemann & Berg Filmproduktion/Bayerischer Rundfunk/ARTE/
Creado Film

EUROPEAN DIRECTOR 2006
Pedro Almodóvar for *Volver*

EUROPEAN ACTRESS 2006
Penelope Cruz in *Volver*

EUROPEAN ACTOR 2006
Ulrich Mühe in *Das Leben der Anderen* (*The Lives of Others*)

EUROPEAN SCREENWRITER 2006
Florian Henckel von Donnersmarck for *Das Leben der Anderen* (*The Lives of Others*)

EUROPEAN CINEMATOGRAPHER 2006 (ex aequo)
Barry Ackroyd for *The Wind that Shakes the Barley*
José Luis Alcaine for *Volver*

EUROPEAN COMPOSER 2006
Alberto Iglesias for *Volver*

EUROPEAN DISCOVERY 2006
*13 Tzameti* by Gela Babluani, France

EUROPEAN FILM ACADEMY AWARD FOR AN ARTISTIC CONTRIBUTION 2006
Pierre Pell & Stéphane Rozenbaum
for the production design in *La Science de rêves*

EUROPEAN FILM ACADEMY SHORT FILM 2006 – Prix UIP
*Before Dawn* by Bálint Kenyeres, Hungary

EUROPEAN FILM ACADEMY LIFETIME ACHIEVEMENT AWARD
Roman Polanski

EUROPEAN ACHIEVEMENT IN WORLD CINEMA 2006 – Prix Screen International
Jeremy Thomas

EUROPEAN FILM ACADEMY CRITICS AWARD 2006 – Prix FIPRESCI
*Les Amants réguliers* by Philippe Garrel, France

EUROPEAN FILM ACADEMY DOCUMENTARY 2006 – Prix ARTE
*Die Grosse Stille* (Into Great Silence) by Philip Gröning, Germany/Switzerland

THE PEOPLE'S CHOICE AWARD 2006
for Best European Film
*Volver* by Pedro Almodóvar, Spain


## 2005

EUROPEAN FILM 2005
*Caché* (*Hidden*), France/Austria/Germany/Italy
directed by Michael Haneke
produced by Les Films du Losange, Wega Film, Bavaria Film, BIM Distribuzione

EUROPEAN DIRECTOR 2005
Michael Haneke for *Caché* (*Hidden*)

EUROPEAN ACTRESS 2005
Julia Jentsch in *Sophie Scholl, die letzten Tage* (*Sophie Scholl, the Final Days*)

EUROPEAN ACTOR 2005
Daniel Auteuil in *Caché* (*Hidden*)

EUROPEAN SCREENWRITER 2005
Hany Abu-Assad & Bero Beyer for *Paradise Now*

EUROPEAN CINEMATOGRAPHER 2005
Franz Lustig for *Don't Come Knocking*

EUROPEAN COMPOSER 2005
Rupert Gregson-Williams & Andrea Guerra for *Hotel Rwanda*

EUROPEAN EDITOR 2005
Michael Hudecek & Nadine Muse for *Caché* (*Hidden*)

EUROPEAN PRODUCTION DESIGNER 2005
Aline Bonetto for *Un long Dimanche de fiançailles* (*A Very Long Engagement*)

EUROPEAN FILM ACADEMY LIFETIME ACHIEVEMENT AWARD
Sir Sean Connery, UK

EUROPEAN ACHIEVEMENT IN WORLD CINEMA 2005
Maurice Jarre, France

EUROPEAN FILM ACADEMY DISCOVERY 2005 – Prix Fassbinder
*Anklaget* (*Accused*), by Jacob Thuesen, Denmark

EUROPEAN FILM ACADEMY CRITICS AWARD 2005 – Prix FIPRESCI
*Caché* (*Hidden*) by Michael Haneke, France/Austria/Germany/Italy

EUROPEAN FILM ACADEMY DOCUMENTARY 2005 – Prix ARTE
*Un Dragon dans les eaux pures du Caucase* (*The Pipeline Next Door*)
by Nino Kirtadzé, France

EUROPEAN FILM ACADEMY SHORT FILM 2005 – Prix UIP
*Undressing My Mother* by Ken Wardrop, Ireland

EUROPEAN FILM ACADEMY NON-EUROPEAN FILM 2005 –
Prix Screen International
*Good Night, And Good Luck*, by George Clooney, USA

THE JAMESON PEOPLE'S CHOICE AWARDS 2005
Chosen by Europe's film fans –
Best European Director
Marc Rothemund for *Sophie Scholl, die letzten Tage* (*Sophie Scholl, the Final Days*)
Best European Actor
Orlando Bloom in *Kingdom of Heaven*
Best European Actress
Julia Jentsch in *Sophie Scholl, die letzten Tage* (*Sophie Scholl, the Final Days*)

## 2004

EUROPEAN FILM 2004
*Gegen die Wand* (*Head-On*), Germany
directed by Fatih Akin
produced by Wüste Filmproduktion/ Corazon International/ NDR/ Arte

EUROPEAN DIRECTOR 2004
Alejandro Amenábar for *Mar adentro* (*The Sea Inside*)

EUROPEAN ACTRESS 2004
Imelda Staunton in *Vera Drake*

EUROPEAN ACTOR 2004
Javier Bardem in *Mar adentro* (*The Sea Inside*)

EUROPEAN SCREENWRITER 2004
Agnès Jaoui & Jean-Pierre Bacri for *Comme une image* (*Look At Me*)

EUROPEAN CINEMATOGRAPHER 2004
Eduardo Serra for *Girl With a Pearl Earring*

EUROPEAN COMPOSER 2004
Bruno Coulais for *Les Choristes* (*The Chorus*)

EUROPEAN FILM ACADEMY LIFETIME ACHIEVEMENT AWARD
Carlos Saura, Spain

EUROPEAN ACHIEVEMENT IN WORLD CINEMA 2004
Liv Ullmann, Norway

EUROPEAN FILM ACADEMY DISCOVERY 2004 – Prix Fassbinder
*Certi Bambini* (*Stolen Childhood*) by Andrea & Antonio Frazzi, Italy

EUROPEAN FILM ACADEMY CRITICS AWARD 2004 – Prix FIPRESCI
*Trilogia – To Livadi pou dakrizi* (*Trilogy – The Weeping Meadow*)
by Theo Angelopoulos, Greece

EUROPEAN FILM ACADEMY DOCUMENTARY 2004 – Prix ARTE
*Darwin's Nightmare*, by Hubert Sauper, France/Austria/Belgium

EUROPEAN FILM ACADEMY SHORT FILM 2004 – Prix UIP
*J'attendrai le suivant*, by Philippe Orreindy, France

EUROPEAN FILM ACADEMY NON-EUROPEAN FILM 2004 –
Prix Screen International
*2046*, by Wong Kar-Wai, France/China

THE JAMESON PEOPLE'S CHOICE AWARDS 2004
Chosen by Europe's film fans –
Best European Director
Fatih Akin for *Gegen die Wand* (*Head-On*)
Best European Actor
Daniel Brühl in *Was nützt die Liebe in Gedanken* (*Love in Thoughts*)
Best European Actress
Penelope Cruz in *Non ti muovere* (*Don't Move*)

# 2003

EUROPEAN FILM 2003
*Good Bye Lenin!*, Germany
directed by Wolfgang Becker
produced by X Filme Creative Pool GmbH

EUROPEAN DIRECTOR 2003
Lars von Trier for *Dogville*

EUROPEAN ACTRESS 2003
Charlotte Rampling in *Swimming Pool*

EUROPEAN ACTOR 2003
Daniel Brühl in *Good Bye Lenin!*

EUROPEAN SCREENWRITER 2003
Bernd Lichtenberg for *Good Bye Lenin!*

EUROPEAN CINEMATOGRAPHER 2003
Anthony Dod Mantle for *28 Days Later* and *Dogville*

EUROPEAN FILM ACADEMY LIFETIME ACHIEVEMENT AWARD
Claude Chabrol, France

EUROPEAN ACHIEVEMENT IN WORLD CINEMA 2003
Carlo di Palma, Italy

EUROPEAN FILM ACADEMY DISCOVERY 2003 – Prix Fassbinder
ВОЗВРАЩЕНИЕ *Vozvraschenie (The Return)* by Andrei Zvyagintsev, Russia

SPECIAL MENTION
*Gori Vatra (Fuse)* by Pjer Zalica, Bosnia and Herzegovina

EUROPEAN FILM ACADEMY CRITICS' AWARD 2003 – Prix FIPRESCI
*Buongiorno, notte (Goodmorning, Night)* by Marco Bellocchio, Italy

EUROPEAN FILM ACADEMY DOCUMENTARY 2003 – Prix ARTE
*S21, la Machine de mort Khmere Rouge (S21: The Khmer Rouge Killing Machine)*
by Rithy Panh, France

EUROPEAN FILM ACADEMY SHORT FILM 2003 – Prix UIP
*(A) Torzija* by Stefan Arsenijević, Slovenia

EUROPEAN FILM ACADEMY NON-EUROPEAN FILM 2003 –
Prix Screen International
*Les Invasions Barbares* by Denys Arcand, Canada

THE JAMESON PEOPLE'S CHOICE AWARDS 2003
Chosen by Europe's film fans –
Best European Director
Wolfgang Becker for *Good Bye Lenin!*
Best European Actor
Daniel Brühl in *Good Bye Lenin!*
Best European Actress
Katrin Sass in *Good Bye Lenin!*


## 2002

EUROPEAN FILM 2002
*Hable con ella (Talk to Her)*, Spain
directed by Pedro Almodóvar
produced by El Deséo

EUROPEAN DIRECTOR 2002
Pedro Almodóvar for *Hable con ella (Talk to Her)*

EUROPEAN ACTOR 2002
Sergio Castellitto in *Bella Martha (Mostly Martha)* and *L'Ora di religione (My Mother's Smile)*

EUROPEAN ACTRESS 2002
The ensemble cast of *8 Femmes*:
Catherine Deneuve
Isabelle Huppert
Emmanuelle Béart
Fanny Ardant
Virginie Ledoyen
Danielle Darrieux
Ludivine Sagnier
Firmine Richard

EUROPEAN SCREENWRITER 2002
Pedro Almodóvar for *Hable con ella* (*Talk to Her*)

EUROPEAN CINEMATOGRAPHER 2002
Pawel Edelman for *The Pianist*

SCREEN INTERNATIONAL AWARD 2002 FOR A NON-EUROPEAN FILM
*Divine Intervention* by Elia Suleiman, Palestine

EUROPEAN DISCOVERY 2002 – Fassbinder Award
*Hukkle* by György Palfi, Hungary

EUROPEAN SHORT FILM AWARD 2002 – Prix UIP
*10 Minuta* (*10 Minutes*) by Ahmed Imamović, Bosnia and Herzegovina

EUROPEAN DOCUMENTARY AWARD 2002 – Prix ARTE
*Etre et avoir* (*To Be and To Have*), France
directed by Nicolas Philibert
produced by Maia Films

EUROPEAN ACHIEVEMENT IN WORLD CINEMA 2002
Victoria Abril, Spain

EUROPEAN FILM ACADEMY LIFETIME ACHIEVEMENT AWARD
Tonino Guerra, Italy

EUROPEAN CRITICS' AWARD 2002 – Prix FIPRESCI
*Sweet Sixteen* by Ken Loach, UK

PEOPLE'S CHOICE AWARDS 2002
Best European Director
Pedro Almodóvar for *Hable con ella* (*Talk to Her*)
Best European Actor
Javier Cámara in *Hable con ella* (*Talk to Her*)
Best European Actress
Kate Winslet in *Iris*


## 2001

EUROPEAN FILM 2001
*Le fabuleux destin d'Amélie Poulain* (*Amélie*), France
directed by Jean-Pierre Jeunet
produced by UGC Images, Victoire Productions, Tapioca Films, France 3 Cinéma,
MMCI

EUROPEAN DIRECTOR 2001
Jean-Pierre Jeunet for *Le fabuleux destin d'Amélie Poulain* (*Amélie*)

EUROPEAN ACTOR 2001
Ben Kingsley in *Sexy Beast*

EUROPEAN ACTRESS 2001
Isabelle Huppert in *La Pianiste* (*The Piano Teacher*)

EUROPEAN SCREENWRITER 2001
Danis Tanović for *No Man's Land*

EUROPEAN CINEMATOGRAPHER 2001
Bruno Delbonnel for *Le fabuleux destin d'Amélie Poulain* (*Amélie*)

EUROPEAN DISCOVERY 2001 – Fassbinder Award
*El bola* (*Pellet*) by Achero Mañas, Spain

EUROPEAN SHORT FILM AWARD 2001 – Prix UIP
*Je t'aime John Wayne* by Toby MacDonald, UK

EUROPEAN DOCUMENTARY AWARD 2001 – Prix ARTE
*Black Box BRD* (*Black Box Germany*), Germany
directed by Andres Veiel
produced by Zero Film

EUROPEAN CRITICS' AWARD 2001 – Prix FIPRESCI
*La Ville est tranquille* (*The Town is Quiet*) by Robert Guédiguian, France

SCREEN INTERNATIONAL EUROPEAN FILM AWARD 2001
(Non-European)
*Moulin Rouge* by Baz Luhrmann, Australia/US

EUROPEAN ACHIEVEMENT IN WORLD CINEMA 2001
Ewan McGregor, UK

EUROPEAN FILM ACADEMY LIFETIME ACHIEVEMENT AWARD
Monty Python, UK

PEOPLE'S CHOICE AWARDS 2001
Best European Director
Jean-Pierre Jeunet for *Le fabuleux destin d'Amélie Poulain* (*Amélie*)
Best European Actor
Colin Firth in *Bridget Jones's Diary*
Best European Actress
Juliette Binoche in *Chocolat*


## 2000

EUROPEAN FILM 2000
*Dancer in the Dark*, Denmark
directed by Lars von Trier
produced by Zentropa Entertainments4, Trust Film Svenska, Film i Väst,
Liberator Productions

EUROPEAN ACTRESS 2000
Björk in *Dancer in the Dark*

EUROPEAN ACTOR 2000
Sergi Lopez in *Harry, Un Ami qui vous veut du bien* (*Harry, He is Here to Help*)

EUROPEAN SCREENWRITER 2000
Agnès Jaoui & Jean-Pierre Bacri for *Le Gout des Autres* (*It Takes all Kinds*)

EUROPEAN CINEMATOGRAPHER 2000
Vittorio Storaro for *Goya en Burdeos* (*Goya in Bordeaux*)

SCREEN INTERNATIONAL EUROPEAN FILM AWARD 2000
*In the Mood for Love* by Wong Kar-Wai, France/Hong Kong

EUROPEAN CRITICS' AWARD 2000 – Prix FIPRESCI
*Mayis Sikintisi* (*Clouds of May*) by Nuri Bilge Ceylan, Turkey

EUROPEAN DOCUMENTARY AWARD 2000 – Prix ARTE
*Les Glaneurs et la Glaneuse (The Gleaners and I)*, France
directed by Agnès Varda
produced by Ciné Tamaris

SPECIAL MENTION
*Heimspiel (Home Game)*, Germany
directed by Pepe Danquart
produced by Quinte Film, ARTE, Goethe Institut

EUROPEAN SHORT FILM 2000 – Prix UIP
*A mi Gólyánk (Our Stork)* by Livia Gyarmathy, Hungary

EUROPEAN DISCOVERY 2000 – Fassbinder Award
*Ressources humaines (Human Resources)* by Laurent Cantet, France

EUROPEAN ACHIEVEMENT IN WORLD CINEMA 2000
Jean Reno, France
Roberto Benigni, Italy

EUROPEAN FILM ACADEMY LIFETIME ACHIEVEMENT AWARD
Richard Harris, UK

PEOPLE'S CHOICE AWARDS 2000
Best European Director
Lars von Trier for *Dancer in the Dark*
Best European Actor
Ingvar E. Sigurdsson in *Englar Alheimsins (Angels of the Universe)*
Best European Actress
Björk in *Dancer in the Dark*

# 1999

EUROPEAN FILM 1999
*Todo sobre mi madre (All About My Mother)*, Spain
directed by Pedro Almodóvar
produced by El Deséo, Renn Productions, France 2 Cinema

EUROPEAN ACTRESS 1999
Cecilia Roth in *Todo sobre mi madre (All About My Mother)*

EUROPEAN ACTOR 1999
Ralph Fiennes in *Sunshine*

EUROPEAN SCREENWRITER 1999
István Szabó & Israel Horovitz for *Sunshine*

EUROPEAN CINEMATOGRAPHER 1999
Lajos Koltai
for *La Leggenda dell Pianista Sull'Oceano* (*The Legend of 1900*) and *Sunshine*

SCREEN INTERNATIONAL AWARD 1999 (for a non-European film)
*The Straight Story* by David Lynch, US

EUROPEAN CRITICS' AWARD 1999 – Prix FIPRESCI
*Adieu Plancher des Vaches* (*Farewell Home Sweet Home*)
by Otar Iosseliani, France

EUROPEAN DOCUMENTARY AWARD 1999 – Prix ARTE
*Buena Vista Social Club*, Germany
directed by Wim Wenders
produced by Road Movies

EUROPEAN SHORT FILM 1999
*Benvenuto in San Salvario* (*Welcome to San Salvario*) by Enrico Verra, Italy

EUROPEAN DISCOVERY 1999 – Fassbinder Award
*The War Zone* by Tim Roth, UK

EUROPEAN ACHIEVEMENT IN WORLD CINEMA 1999
Antonio Banderas, Spain
Roman Polanski, Poland

EUROPEAN FILM ACADEMY LIFETIME ACHIEVEMENT AWARD
Ennio Morricone, Italy

PEOPLE'S CHOICE AWARDS 1999
Best European Director
Pedro Almodóvar for *Todo sobre mi madre* (*All About My Mother*)
Best European Actor
Sean Connery in *Entrapment*
Best European Actress
Catherine Zeta Jones in *Entrapment*

# 1998

EUROPEAN FILM 1998
*La Vita è bella* (*Life Is Beautiful*), Italy
directed by Roberto Benigni
produced by Cecchi Gori Group, Melampo Cinematografica

EUROPEAN ACTRESS 1998
Elodie Bouchez and Natacha Regnier in *La Vie Revée des Anges* (*The Dream Life of Angels*)

EUROPEAN ACTOR 1998
Roberto Benigni in *La Vita è bella* (*Life Is Beautiful*)

EUROPEAN SCREENWRITER 1998
Peter Howitt for *Sliding Doors*

EUROPEAN CINEMATOGRAPHER 1998
Adrian Biddle for *The Butcher Boy*

SCREEN INTERNATIONAL AWARD 1998 (for a non-European film)
*The Truman Show* by Peter Weir, US

EUROPEAN CRITICS' AWARD 1998 – Prix FIPRESCI
*Bure Baruta* (*The Powder Keg*) by Goran Paskaljevic, Yugoslavia

EUROPEAN DOCUMENTARY AWARD 1998 – Prix ARTE
to Claudio Pazienza, Belgium

EUROPEAN SHORT FILM 1998
*Un Jour* by Marie Paccou, France

EUROPEAN DISCOVERY – Fassbinder Award 1998
ex aequo for *Festen* (*The Celebration*) by Thomas Vinterberg, Denmark
and *La Vie Rêvée des Anges* (*The Dream Life of Angels*) by Erick Zonca, France

EUROPEAN FILM ACADEMY SPECIAL ACHIEVEMENT AWARD 1998
Jeremy Irons, UK

EUROPEAN ACHIEVEMENT IN WORLD CINEMA 1998
Stellan Skårsgard, Sweden

PEOPLE'S CHOICE AWARDS 1998
Best European Director
Roland Emmerich for *Godzilla*
Best European Actor
Antonio Banderas in *The Mask of Zorro*
Best European Actress
Kate Winslet in *Titanic*

# 1997

EUROPEAN FILM OF THE YEAR
*The Full Monty*, UK
directed by Peter Cattaneo
produced by Redwave Films, Uberto Pasolini

EUROPEAN ACTOR OF THE YEAR
Bob Hoskins in *Twenty Four Seven*

EUROPEAN ACTRESS OF THE YEAR
Juliette Binoche in *The English Patient*

EUROPEAN SCREENWRITER OF THE YEAR
Alain Berliner and Chris Vander Stappen for *Ma Vie en Rose* (*My Life in Pink*)

EUROPEAN CINEMATOGRAPHER OF THE YEAR
John Seale for *The English Patient*

EUROPEAN ACHIEVEMENT IN WORLD CINEMA
Milos Forman, Czech Republic

EUROPEAN DISCOVERY OF THE YEAR – Fassbinder Award
*La Vie de Jésus* (*The Life of Jesus*) by Bruno Dumont, France

EUROPEAN DOCUMENTARY OF THE YEAR – Prix ARTE
Benoit Dervaux, Jean Pierre and Luc Dardenne for *Gigi, Monica . . . et Bianca*, Belgium

EUROPEAN FIPRESCI AWARD
*Viagem ao Princípio do Mundo* (*Journey to the Beginning of the World*) by Manoel de Oliveira, Portugal

SCREEN INTERNATIONAL FIVE CONTINENTS AWARD
*Hana-Bi* (*Fireworks*) by Takeshi Kitano, Japan

EUROPEAN FILM ACADEMY LIFETIME ACHIEVEMENT AWARD
Jeanne Moreau, France

PEOPLE'S CHOICE AWARDS 1997
Best Film
*The Full Monty* by Peter Cattaneo, UK
Best Actor
Javier Bardem
Best Actress
Jodie Foster

# 1996

EUROPEAN FILM OF THE YEAR
*Breaking the Waves*, Denmark
by Lars von Trier
produced by Zentropa Entertainments

YOUNG EUROPEAN FILM OF THE YEAR
*Some Mother's Son*, Ireland
directed by Terry George
produced by Hell's Kitchen

FELIX OF THE CRITICS – FIPRESCI AWARD
*Breaking the Waves* by Lars von Trier, Denmark

EUROPEAN ACTRESS OF THE YEAR
Emily Watson in *Breaking the Waves*

EUROPEAN ACTOR OF THE YEAR
Ian McKellen in *Richard III*

EUROPEAN SCREENWRITER OF THE YEAR
Arif Aliyev, Sergei Bodrov and Boris Giller for *Kavkazskij Plennik* (*Prisoner of the Mountains*)

EUROPEAN FILM ACADEMY LIFETIME ACHIEVEMENT AWARD
Sir Alec Guinness, UK

SCREEN INTERNATIONAL FIVE CONTINENTS AWARD
*Dead Man* by Jim Jarmusch, US

EUROPEAN DOCUMENTARY OF THE YEAR – Prix ARTE
Jerzy Sladkowski, Sweden
Stanislav Krzeminski, Poland

# 1995

EUROPEAN FILM OF THE YEAR
*Land And Freedom*, UK
directed by Ken Loach
produced by Parallax Pictures, Messidor Films and Road Movies Dritte

YOUNG EUROPEAN FILM OF THE YEAR
*La Haine* (*Hate*), France
directed by Mathieu Kassovitz,
produced by Les Productions Lazennec, Le Studio Canal Plus and La Sept Cinema

EUROPEAN DOCUMENTARY AWARD OF THE YEAR
Jens Meurer, Germany

EUROPEAN FILM ACADEMY LIFETIME ACHIEVEMENT AWARD
Marcel Carné, France

FELIX OF THE CRITICS (FIPRESCI AWARD)
*To Vlemma tou Odyssea* (*Ulysses' Gaze*) by Theo Angelopoulos, Greece

## 1994

EUROPEAN FILM OF THE YEAR – ARTE AWARD
*Lamerica*, Italy
by Gianni Amelio
produced by Cecchi Gori Group Tiger

YOUNG EUROPEAN FILM OF THE YEAR
*Le Fils du Requin* (*The Son of the Shark*), France
directed by Agnés Merlet
produced by François Fries
*Woyzeck*, Hungary
directed by János Szász
produced by Peter Barbalics

EUROPEAN DOCUMENTARY FILM OF THE YEAR (ARTE – AWARD)
Saga-Group Sarajevo

EUROPEAN FILM ACADEMY LIFETIME ACHIEVEMENT AWARD
Robert Bresson, France

FELIX OF THE CRITICS (FIPRESCI AWARD)
*Caro Diario* (*Dear Diary*) by Nanni Moretti, Italy

## 1993

EUROPEAN FILM OF THE YEAR
*Urga – Territoria Liubvi* (*Urga – The Territory of Love*), Russia
directed by Nikita Mikhalkov
produced by Michel Seydoux

YOUNG EUROPEAN FILM OF THE YEAR
*Orlando*, UK
directed by Sally Potter
produced by Christopher Sheppard

EUROPEAN ACTRESS OF THE YEAR
Maia Morgenstern in *Balanta* (*The Oak*)

EUROPEAN ACTOR OF THE YEAR
Daniel Auteuil in *Un Coeur en hiver* (*A Heart in Winter*)

EUROPEAN ACHIEVEMENT OF THE YEAR
Nik Powell and Stephen Woolley as producers of *The Crying Game*, UK

EUROPEAN FILM ACADEMY LIFETIME ACHIEVEMENT AWARD
Michelangelo Antonioni, Italy

EUROPEAN FILM ACADEMY AWARD OF MERIT
Erika and Ulrich Gregor and Naum Kleiman, The Berlin-Moscow-Connection

FELIX OF THE CRITICS (FIPRESCI AWARD)
*Benny's Video* by Michael Haneke, Austria

EUROPEAN DOCUMENTARY OF THE YEAR (ARTE – AWARD)
*Det Sociala Arvet* (*Misfits to Yuppies*) by Stefan Jarl, Sweden

SPECIAL MENTION
*The Man Who Loves Gary Lineker*, UK
directed by Ylli Hasani and Steve Sklair
produced by BBC Video Diaries
*89 mm od Europy* (*89 mm of Europe*), Poland
directed by Marcel Lozinski
produced by Studio Filmowe Kalejdoskop

## 1992

EUROPEAN FILM OF THE YEAR
*Il Ladro di bambini* (*The Stolen Children*), Italy
directed by Gianni Amelio
produced by Angelo Rizzoli, Erre Produzioni/Alia Film

YOUNG EUROPEAN FILM OF THE YEAR
*De Noorderlingen* (*The Northerners*), the Netherlands
by Alex van Warmerdam
produced by Laurens Geels & Dick Maas, First Floor Features

EUROPEAN ACTRESS OF THE YEAR
Juliette Binoche in *Les Amants du Pont-Neuf* (*The Lovers on the Bridge*)

EUROPEAN ACTOR OF THE YEAR
Matti Pellonpäa in *La Vie de Bohème* (*Bohemian Life*)

EUROPEAN SUPPORTING ACTRESS OF THE YEAR
Ghita Nørby in *Freud flyttar hemifrån* (*Freud's Leaving Home*)

EUROPEAN SUPPORTING ACTOR OF THE YEAR
André Wilms in *La Vie de Bohème* (*Bohemian Life*)

EUROPEAN SCREENWRITER OF THE YEAR
István Szabó for *Edes Emma, Draga Böbe* (*Dear Emma, Sweet Böbe*)

EUROPEAN FILM COMPOSER OF THE YEAR
Vincent Van Warmerdam for *De Noorderlingen* (*The Northerners*)

EUROPEAN CINEMATOGRAPHER OF THE YEAR
Jean-Yves Escoffier for *Les Amants du Pont-Neuf* (*The Lovers on the Bridge*)

EUROPEAN EDITOR OF THE YEAR
Nelly Quettier for *Les Amants du Pont-Neuf* (*The Lovers on the Bridge*)

EUROPEAN PRODUCTION DESIGNER OF THE YEAR
Rikke Jelier for *De Noorderlingen* (*The Northerners*)

EUROPEAN DOCUMENTARY FILM OF THE YEAR
*Neregiu Zeme*, Lithuania
directed by Audrius Stonys
produced by Audrius Kuprevitchius, Studio Kinema

SPECIAL MENTION
*Dostoevsky's Travels*, UK
directed by Paul Pavlikovski
produced by BBC Television
*Les Amants d'assises* (*Lovers on Trial*), Belgium
directed by Manu Bonmariage
produced by Christine Pireaux, Wallonie Image Prod.

EUROPEAN FILM ACADEMY LIFETIME ACHIEVEMENT AWARD
Billy Wilder

EUROPEAN FILM ACADEMY AWARD OF MERIT
MOMI (Museum of the Moving Image), London

# 1991

EUROPEAN FILM OF THE YEAR
*Riff-Raff*, UK
directed by Ken Loach
produced by Sally Hibbin, Parallax for Channel Four

YOUNG EUROPEAN FILM OF THE YEAR
*Toto le Héros (Toto the Hero)*, Belgium
directed by Jaco van Dormael
produced by Pierre Drouot & Dany Geys, Iblis Films

EUROPEAN ACTOR OF THE YEAR
Michel Bouquet in *Toto le Héros (Toto the Hero)*

EUROPEAN ACTRESS OF THE YEAR
Clotilde Courau in *Le Petit Criminel (The Little Gangster)*

EUROPEAN SUPPORTING ACTOR OF THE YEAR
Ricky Memphis in *Ultrà*

EUROPEAN SUPPORTING ACTRESS OF THE YEAR
Marta Keler in *Virdzina*

EUROPEAN SCREENWRITER OF THE YEAR
Jaco Van Dormael for *Toto le Héros (Toto the Hero)*

EUROPEAN CINEMATOGRAPHER OF THE YEAR
Walther van den Ende for *Toto le Héros (Toto the Hero)*

EUROPEAN FILM COMPOSER OF THE YEAR
Hilmar Örn Hilmarsson for *Börn Natturunnar (Children of Nature)*

EUROPEAN PRODUCTION DESIGNER OF THE YEAR
Kreta Kjnakovic (sets) and Valerie Pozzo Di Borgo (costumes) for *Delicatessen*

EUROPEAN FILM EDITOR OF THE YEAR
Carla Simoncelli for *Ultrà*

EUROPEAN CINEMA SOCIETY LIFETIME ACHIEVEMENT AWARD
Alexandre Trauner, France

EUROPEAN CINEMA SOCIETY AWARD OF MERIT
La Quinzaine des Realisateurs, France

EUROPEAN DOCUMENTARY FILM OF THE YEAR
*Uslyszcie Moj Krzyk (Hear My Cry)*, Poland
directed by Maciej Janusz Drygas
produced by Film Studio Zodiak

SPECIAL MENTION
*Crimes et passions – la cicatrice*, France
directed by Mireille Dumas
produced by TF1
*The Wall*, Germany
directed by Jürgen Böttcher
produced by DEFA-Studio für Dokumentarfilme

# 1990

EUROPEAN FILM OF THE YEAR
*Porte Aperte (Open Doors)*, Italy
directed by Gianni Amelio
produced by Angelo Rizzoli

YOUNG EUROPEAN FILM OF THE YEAR
*Henry V*, UK
directed by Kenneth Branagh
produced by Bruce Sharman

EUROPEAN ACTOR OF THE YEAR
Kenneth Branagh in *Henry V*

EUROPEAN ACTRESS OF THE YEAR
Carmen Maura in *Ay, Carmela!*

EUROPEAN SUPPORTING ACTOR OF THE YEAR
Dimitrij Pevsov in *Matj (Mother)*

EUROPEAN SUPPORTING ACTRESS OF THE YEAR
Malin Ek in *Skyddsängeln (The Guardian Angel)*

EUROPEAN SCREENWRITER OF THE YEAR
Vitaly Kanevsky for *Zamri, Oumri, Voskresni! (Don't Move, Die and Rise Again!)*

EUROPEAN CINEMATOGRAPHER OF THE YEAR
Tonino Nardi for *Porte Aperte (Open Doors)*

EUROPEAN PRODUCTION DESIGNERS OF THE YEAR
Ezio Frigerio (sets) and Franca Squarciapino (costumes) for *Cyrano de Bergerac*

SPECIAL JURY AWARD
Gian Maria Volonté for *Porte Aperte* (*Open Doors*)

SPECIAL JURY AWARD II
*December Bride*, Ireland
directed by Thaddeus O'Sullivan
produced by Jonathan Cavendish

EUROPEAN DISCOVERY OF THE YEAR
Ennio Fantastichini in *Porte Aperte* (*Open Doors*)

SPECIAL MENTION
Pavel Nazarov in *Zamri, Oumri, Voskresni!* (*Don't Move, Die and Rise Again!*)

EUROPEAN DOCUMENTARY FILM OF THE YEAR
*Skersiela* (*New Times at Crossroad Street*), USSR
directed by Ivars Seletskis
produced by Riga Film Studio

SPECIAL MENTION
*Step Across the Border*, Switzerland
directed by Nicholas Humbert and Werner Penzel
produced by Cinenomades

EUROPEAN CINEMA SOCIETY LIFETIME ACHIEVEMENT AWARD
Andrzej Wajda, Poland

EUROPEAN CINEMA SOCIETY SPECIAL AWARD
Association of Film-makers of the USSR

# 1989

EUROPEAN FILM OF THE YEAR
*Topio stin Omichli* (*Landscape in the Mist*), Greece
directed by Theo Angelopoulos
produced by The Greek Film Centre

YOUNG EUROPEAN FILM OF THE YEAR
*300 Mil Do Nieba* (*300 Miles to Heaven*), Poland
directed by Maciej Dejczer
produced by Film Unit 'TOR'

EUROPEAN DIRECTOR OF THE YEAR
Geza Beremenyi for *Eldorádó* (*The Midas Touch*)

EUROPEAN ACTOR OF THE YEAR
Philippe Noiret in *La Vie et rien d'autre* (*Life and Nothing But*) and *Nuovo Cinema Paradiso* (*Cinema Paradiso*)

EUROPEAN ACTRESS OF THE YEAR
Ruth Sheen in *High Hopes*

EUROPEAN SUPPORTING PERFORMANCE OF THE YEAR
Edna Dore in *High Hopes*

EUROPEAN SCREENWRITER OF THE YEAR
Maria Khmelik for *Malenkaja Vera*

EUROPEAN CINEMATOGRAPHER OF THE YEAR
Ulf Brantas, Jörgen Persson for *Kvinnorna Pa Taket* (*The Women on the Roof*)

EUROPEAN FILM COMPOSER OF THE YEAR
Andrew Dickson for *High Hopes*

SPECIAL JURY AWARDS
Bertrand Tavernier for *La Vie et rien d'autre* (*Life and Nothing But*)
Giuseppe Tornatore for *Nuovo Cinema Paradiso* (*Cinema Paradiso*)

SPECIAL MENTION
To the creative spirit of the new films coming from Sarajevo, Yugoslavia

EUROPEAN DOCUMENTARY FILM OF THE YEAR
*RECSK 1950–1953*, Hungary
directed by Geza Böszörményi and Livia Gyarmathy
produced by István Darday

DOCUMENTARY FILM JURY SPECIAL AWARD
*Een Verhaal Van De Wind*, the Netherlands
directed by Joris Ivens & Marceline Loridan
produced by Capi Films

SPECIAL MENTION
*Obrazy Stareho Sveta* (*Pictures of the Old World*), Czechoslovakia
directed by Dušan Hanak
produced by Juraj Kral
*The Road to God Knows Where*, Ireland
directed by Alan Gilsenan
produced by Martin Mahon

LIFETIME ACHIEVEMENT AWARD
Federico Fellini, Italy

EUROPEAN CINEMA SOCIETY SPECIAL AWARD
Anatole Dauman, France

# 1988

BEST FILM
*Krótki Film o Zabijaniu* (*A Short Film About Killing*), Poland
directed by Krzysztof Kieślowski
produced by Zespoly Filmowe, Film Unit 'TOR'

BEST YOUNG FILM
*Mujeres al borde de un ataque de nervios* (*Women on the Verge of a Nervous Breakdown*), Spain
directed by Pedro Almodóvar
produced by Augustin Almodóvar

BEST DIRECTOR
Wim Wenders for *Der Himmel über Berlin* (*Wings of Desire*)

BEST ACTOR
Max von Sydow in *Pelle Erobreren* (*Pelle the Conqueror*)

BEST ACTRESS
Carmen Maura in *Mujeres al borde de un ataque de nervios* (*Women on the Verge of a Nervous Breakdown*)

BEST SUPPORTING ACTOR
Curt Bois in *Der Himmel über Berlin* (*Wings of Desire*)

BEST SUPPORTING ACTRESS
Johanna Ter Steege in *Spoorloos* (*The Vanishing*)

BEST YOUNG ACTOR
Pelle Hvenegaard for *Pelle Erobreren* (*Pelle the Conqueror*)

BEST SCRIPT
Louis Malle for *Au Revoir les Enfants* (*Goodbye Children*)

SPECIAL AWARD/BEST ART DIRECTION
G. Aleksi-Meschischiwili, N. Sandukeli, Sch. Gogolaschwili for *Ashugi Qaribi* (*The Lovelorn Minstrel*)

SPECIAL JURY AWARD
Bernardo Bertolucci for *The Last Emperor*

SPECIAL JURY AWARD
Jurij Chanin for *Dni Zatmenija* (Best Music)

LIFETIME ACHIEVEMENT AWARD
Ingmar Bergman, Sweden
Marcello Mastroianni, Italy

AWARD OF MERIT
Richard Attenborough, UK

# Appendix 2:   Founding members of the EFA

Pedro Amodóvar
Lindsay Anderson
Theo Angelopoulos
Lord Richard Attenborough
Ingmar Bergman
Bernardo Bertolucci
Henning Carlsen
Liliana Cavani
Claude Chabrol
Silvio Clementelli
Jörn Donner
Federico Fellini
Stephen Frears
Claude Goretta
Isabelle Huppert
Erland Josephson
Krzysztof Kieślowski

Sir Ben Kingsley
Peter Lilienthal
Dušan Makavejev
Louis Malle
Giuliette Masina
Marcello Mastroianni
Jiří Menzel
Nikita Mikhalkov
Sven Nykvist
Manoel de Oliveira
Carlo di Palma
Lord David Puttnam
Fernando Rey
Eric Rohmer
David Rose
Hanna Schygulla
Jorge Semprun

*Continued on next page*

Max von Sydow                      Liv Ullmann
István Szabó                       Andrzej Wajda
Paolo Taviani                      Wim Wenders
Vittorio Taviani                   Krzysztof Zanussi
Mikis Theodorakis